Solving Stonehenge

'Upon the playn of Salysbury is the stonege, whyche is certayne great stones, some standyng, and some lyenge overthawart lyeng and hangyng, that no Gemetricion can set them as they do hange.'

ANDREW BOORDE, 1555

ANTHONY JOHNSON

Solving Stonehenge

THE NEW KEY TO AN ANCIENT ENIGMA

with 150 illustrations, 45 in color

Thames & Hudson

Frontispiece *Panoramic view taken from the southwest.*

First published in 2008 in hardcover in the United States of America by Thames & Hudson Inc., 500 Fifth Avenue, New York, New York 10110

thamesandhudsonusa.com

Library of Congress Catalog Card Number 2007905837

ISBN 978-0-500-05155-9

Printed and bound in China by Midas Printing International Ltd

Contents

Acknowledgments

Writing this book has been essentially a solitary experience, running, re-running and checking computer plans of Stonehenge against the evidence from earlier documentation and excavation. Consequently there are few specific acknowledgments to make, which amplifies the debt that I owe to those who have made this book possible. Not all are archaeologists: friends and colleagues who work in other disciplines have provided me with the valuable opportunity of considering the evolution of early communities and human knowledge from the perspective of the mathematician, engineer and farmer. I am particularly grateful to Dr Russell Johnston, with whom I discussed the original concept and who recognized it as exciting and rewarding.

I would like to express my gratitude to Professor Sir Barry Cunliffe for reading and commenting on the text, to Dr Tom Higham (Radiocarbon Accelerator Unit, University of Oxford) for his contribution to my statements on radiometric dating and to Dr Stephen Johnston (Museum of the History of Science, Oxford) for information on 18th-century surveying instruments and access to the collection. Thanks are also due to Tom Bateman for his assistance with field survey experiments, to Jane Dixon and Julie Smith, of Hill End Farm, Noke for the use of their fields, and to Chris Honeywell for his aerial photography of the results. For other photographs I am indebted to Mike Pitts for providing the image from the Douai Library manuscript, to Andy Burnham for his assistance in obtaining photographs from contributors to his megalithic portal website, and also the staff of English Heritage National Monuments Record Centre in Swindon, particularly Katy Whitaker, Nigel Wilkins and Robin Steward.

I am grateful to my son Alex for the opportunity of discussing ideas and emerging trends in archaeological thought, to my son Sean for his contributions to the illustrations, and to both for their creative photographic work. I would also like to express my appreciation of the patience shown by my daughter Rachel, who had to work through her final school years and examinations in a house littered with an eclectic mix of electronics, chalk dust and string.

Finally, and most importantly, I am deeply indebted to my wife Anne, with whom I have shared a lifetime of archaeological fieldwork and research, for reading and correcting my drafts, and for tirelessly tracking down the most elusive documents and images. It is her invaluable work which has allowed me to take the ideas to publication.

Seeking Explanations

Stonehenge is a prehistoric monument without parallel. More than a phenomenal feat of engineering, it was built as an extraordinary expression of a now long-lost cosmology within a sacred site of such potency that it occupied the minds and labour of generations for over a millennium. The search for a 'solution' to the enigma of the stones has a documented history which extends back over 850 years, and no doubt the monument's mystery was a source of fascination long before the first speculative ideas were written down.

Many avenues, both rational and irrational, have been explored, inspired by contemporary perceptions of the world, its events, fashions or technological developments; some from the outset have been no more than brazen attempts to advance a particular theory or people the site with historical characters who have no connection whatsoever with the monument, resulting in a bewildering confusion of facts and fables. The single observation that the axis of Stonehenge is aligned with the solstices, first recognized by the antiquarian William Stukeley in the early 18th century, has given licence to a plethora of interpretations which rely on the supposition that prehistoric spirituality focused entirely on the theatre of the celestial dome. Such theories demand that we see the people who built and used the monument as 'observers' of external events which the stones were in some way arranged to register; no matter how astonishing or sophisticated the concept may be, it removes a vital human dimension, taking away the soul and artistry, and reducing it to no more than a very clever 1,200-ton mechanism.

But there is much more to Stonehenge than alignments. There are vital clues within the archaeological record, both from the groundplan and details

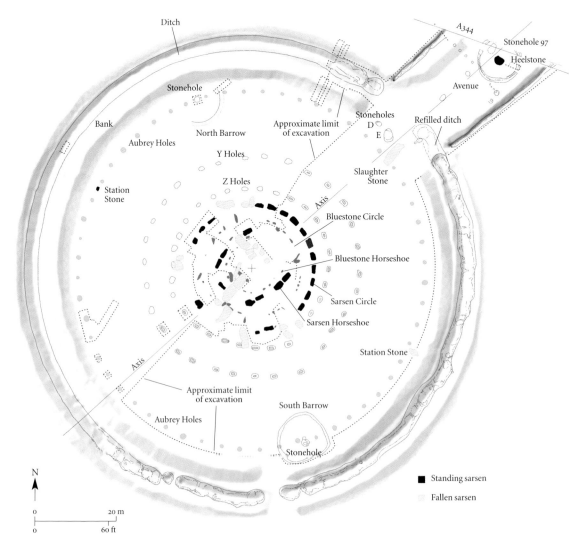

Ditch

A344

Stonehole 97

Heelstone

Stonehole

Bank

Aubrey Holes

North Barrow

Approximate limit
of excavation

Stoneholes
D
E

Avenue

Refilled ditch

Y Holes

Z Holes

Station
Stone

Slaughter
Stone

Axis

Bluestone Circle

Bluestone Horseshoe

Sarsen Circle

Sarsen Horseshoe

Station Stone

Axis

Approximate limit
of excavation

South Barrow

Aubrey Holes

Stonehole

N

0   20 m

0   60 ft

■ Standing sarsen

Fallen sarsen

1 *General plan of Stonehenge.*

of the monument's construction, to demonstrate that the minds of the
Neolithic communities who built Stonehenge were far from exclusively preoccupied with the sky, or with the landscape beyond the stones. The design is
a celebration of intellect and discovery, and the final stone construction heralded a new and enlightened age where technology and creativity flourished,
where long-established ancestral traditions were yielding to the dawn of the
inquisitive and dynamic world with which we are more familiar.

In his book *Stonehenge Decoded*, first published in 1966, the astronomer Gerald Hawkins gives an interesting concise account of early calculating devices, and of the first computer used in his work on astronomical data which he proposed had some significance to the understanding of Stonehenge. If the monument's archaeo-astronomical chronology agreed with his IBM computer results then Stonehenge itself could be described as a type of computer. They did apparently agree, leading to the conclusion that 'Stonehenge was a sophisticated and brilliantly conceived astronomical observatory', and there was no doubt that it was 'built by three separate groups of people over a 400-year period beginning in 1900 BC'.[1] Archaeology has now shown the major Stonehenge construction to be around 600 years older than the dates used in these calculations; it appears that the celestial 'goalposts' are clearly not quite so firmly rooted in the ground as the stones themselves. An implicit criticism is often directed at archaeologists for ignoring the astronomical implications of Stonehenge which 'would have been appreciated sooner had there not been an almost universal preoccupation with plans of the monument, that is, with charts in only two dimensions'.[2] This is not immediately obvious to me; I would simply say that the plan on the ground is as good a starting point as anything in the sky, and that failing to exhaust all the possibilities before looking elsewhere is the single most important mistake made by those who see the monument as entirely astronomical in its design. The crux of the Stonehenge problem is the overwhelming anxiety to explore the heavens *before* the potential implications of the recorded features on the ground have been fully considered. The often injudicious use of computers has only confounded this situation, and it is this aspect above all others that I hope to redress. My own work has been confined to the analysis of groundplans, excavation data and certain details of the elevation of the monument. I make no apology for this.

Hawkins's vision of the future application of computers was, however, prophetic. It is easy to forget just how revolutionary these machines were just a few decades ago. The $3.5 million IBM 7094, with its huge cumbersome tape spools with which Hawkins was then familiar, could achieve 250,000 additions or subtractions per second. I noticed recently that IBM announced a machine that can sustain 280 trillion calculations per second, and without the

need for the electrical equivalent of 70 horsepower that was required in the 1960s. I certainly could not have contemplated the task of examining the Stonehenge arrays without my CAD workstation, a powerful but temperamental machine assembled for this project from a wish-list of disparate components which probably had never been brought together before, and certainly ought never to be again. I suppose it is all somewhat irrelevant now, for progress is so rapid that by the time this book is published my computer will be as obsolete as the IBM 7094.

All major excavation and restoration ceased at Stonehenge in 1964. Since then a policy of preservation *in situ*, designed to protect the last of the

2 *Stonehenge at sunrise, March 2007. A panoramic view taken from an elevated camera sited approximately 20 m above the Avenue.*

surviving archaeological deposits within the monument, has naturally shifted enquiry to the surrounding landscape. But it is the elusive secret of the stones which continues to capture the popular imagination, and as Stonehenge becomes increasingly removed from the excitement of revelations made by excavation and hence the prospect of new discoveries, it is inevitable that new theories continue to emerge to fill the vacuum. This is an area where fact and speculation have become inextricably bound into what has become the Gordian knot of British archaeology. Judging by the volume of published material we might think that the purpose of Stonehenge has been identified, and that apart from refining certain ideas there is little more to say; in truth we have hardly begun to understand the significance of what we already know. The purpose of this book is to review the implications of the design of the monument. Careful computer analysis of the groundplan has been combined with an examination of the archaeological evidence compiled over the last 400 years, not least of which is a vitally important and largely overlooked 18th-century plan of the monument. The results have a significant bearing upon the way we may perceive Stonehenge, and present some insights into the vision behind its construction. I should point out that I have not focused on the engineering aspects of the transport and erection of the stones, sharing the archaeologist Robert Newall's, now 50-year-old, conclusion: 'When one remembers that far larger stones have been moved by man-power alone, it is rather the skill shown in the placing of the stones in their exact positions than the transport of them that amazes one.'[3]

It is only relatively recently that we have begun to discover the settlements of the local communities who, at the very least, were familiar with the major structures at Stonehenge, and may have been the actual designers and builders. At the beginning of the 21st century archaeologists are on the verge of a breakthrough in understanding this remarkable society. The first chapter provides a brief insight into the physical and temporal setting, and looks at recent important discoveries within the Stonehenge landscape.

Chapters 2 and 3 consider the legends, the exponents of quasi-religious themes and the activities of the early fieldworkers who merged them into the first of the theories. Few archaeologists have ever subscribed to the idea that we are looking for one, and only one, narrative which might account for the building of Stonehenge; but the idea that a single solution exists has dominated and stifled thinking for hundreds of years.

In Chapters 4 and 5 the archaeological evidence is summarized; the aim is to provide the reader with the essential evidence and 'clues' which have allowed archaeologists to piece together a structural 'history' of the site. Those who may find some of these descriptions somewhat esoteric will not be disadvantaged by focusing on the second half of the book (Chapters 6–9), which is essentially the detective story at its heart. Here I explain the puzzle of why specific numbers of timber settings and stones were set out, and how the design of the monument emerged. The simplicity and internal architectural integrity are explored, and the archaeological evidence used to present a case for the stone monument being a singular, carefully planned and quite extraordinarily executed geometric construction. I hope to involve the reader in this exploration, and to present something that breaks the confines of current theories and modern myths. New information is presented, some relating to known, but buried, features and some which has only been revealed by many months of computer analysis undertaken over a period of five years. While there are archaeological principles which need to be kept in mind, there is nothing which should prevent the interested general reader from engaging with the dynamics of the site. Perhaps the most important point is that further discoveries are waiting to be made by anyone who is prepared to look at the body of the archaeological evidence rather than select from it only the parts which sustain a particular and exclusive hypothesis.

In the final chapter I offer some alternative views which, admittedly, break certain rules by stepping into territory undefined by the boundaries of archaeological discipline. I justify this on two grounds: first, because it opens the door to the curious and novel arena where many theories are born, and secondly because it demonstrates that archaeologists may also tell stories and speculate, so long as they make clear the facts upon which their ideas are based. The reader is offered an opportunity to consider Stonehenge through the eyes of those who erected the monument, based as far as possible on facts, and unfettered by the restrictions imposed by current theories.

Science is increasingly providing new and vital clues, both to the origins of Stonehenge and the lives of the prehistoric communities of Salisbury Plain. There is no need to drag into the 21st century tools blunt with age and repetition, and theories which confound rather than aid our understanding of the monument. The title *Solving Stonehenge* focuses on the facts, rather than simply offering another grand monocausal explanation.

The ultimate secret lay within the heads of those who built Stonehenge, but by unlocking some of its design we come nearer to understanding its purpose, what the builders actually understood, and how that knowledge was

applied. This needs to be done before imagining what they were trying to achieve. Even archaeologists sometimes need to remind themselves that though we are looking back to a distant past, our 'ancient monuments' were the very substance of people's desires and aspirations, which at Stonehenge were expressed with a skill and imagination rivalling that of any age to follow. Time has long since overtaken it, but the ideas of the builders are as sharp and the concepts as fresh as when they were first enshrined in the stones.

Note on radiocarbon dating

Carbon is one of the basic biochemical elements; a very small amount, one part per trillion or less, is naturally radioactive. This isotope (known as carbon-14) is formed at altitude by cosmic bombardment of nitrogen-14. The carbon-14 produced enters the Earth's plant and animal lifeways through exchange with the ocean and photosynthesis, so that ultimately all living organisms contain radiocarbon, which is replenished through life. Once an organism dies the exchange stops, and the carbon-14 starts to decay at an exponential rate. Because the rate of decay has been

calculated (there is a loss of half the radioactive component every 5730 ± 40 years), its age can be determined.

However, the rate of carbon-14 production has not been constant over time, principally because of changes in the magnetic influence of the sun on cosmic radiation, and long-term changes in the Earth's geomagnetic field. Historic fluctuations in carbon-14 production can be measured using samples of tree rings whose age is known precisely by dendrochronological analysis. Currently, this calibration extends back over 12,000 years. Beyond this, coral, floating tree rings and lake sediment proxies extend the calibration curve to 26,000 years ago. These calibration curves allow radiocarbon dates to be converted into solar years BC/AD, with a probability attached. The precision of these calibrated (cal) dates depends greatly on the shape of the calibration curve, which at certain points comprises plateaux or 'wiggles'.

The radiocarbon determinations quoted here are conventional dates based on the original computed half life of carbon-14 (5,568 years) and calibrated in relation to radiocarbon years before present (0, i.e. zero 'BP' in radiometric dating is taken as AD 1950). For example, a radiocarbon date expressed as 3020–2910 cal BC means that statistically there is a 95% probability that the actual date lies within the quoted range.

CHAPTER 1
Landscape & Opportunity

The rolling chalk downland of Salisbury Plain is rich in prehistoric remains. An exceptional number of enclosures and burial places lie within just a few kilometres' radius of Stonehenge.[1] The earliest were the work of generations of people who lived in the Neolithic period, the 'New Stone Age' which emerged in Britain around 4000 BC, more than 1,000 years before Stonehenge was constructed. We might notice that this verdant and evocative landscape is not rich in natural resources, and, until the army found a use for vast tracts of the surrounding open downs at the end of the 19th century, much of it was neglected, the home of solitary shepherds and the domain of the recently reintroduced great bustard (the heaviest flying bird in the world, a shy creature whose security depends on camouflage ideally suited to extensive grassland plains). There is little to indicate why this region was once home to one of the most dynamic prehistoric communities in Europe.

What made the area so remarkably successful through the Neolithic period, and into the succeeding Bronze Age? The secret lies in its geographic location and geology. Three major tracts of chalkland extend from the Avon Valley. From the Stonehenge region it was possible to follow the high chalk ridges of the Upper Thames Valley northeastwards, across the Chilterns and Cambridgeshire all the way to the Norfolk coast some 250 km distant. The North Downs provided an eastward route along the edge of the Lower Thames Valley, avoiding the heavily wooded clays of the Weald, and easy access to the channel coast was afforded to the south and to the east for some 200 km via the South Downs. To the west and north the chalk is bounded by Jurassic limestone, geology equally rich in Neolithic Age monuments, extending from Lyme Bay northwards to within 40 km of the Bristol Channel, and northeastwards as far as the North Yorkshire coast.

The well-drained low hills cut by streams of crystal-clear water provided extensive areas of grazing for livestock. Evidence that land clearance had been taking place since the first hunters entered the region is provided by pollen found in ancient soils buried under the earliest Neolithic earthworks, which shows that from around the middle of the 4th millennium BC the Stonehenge region was largely clear of dense forest, the landscape comprising a 'coarse mosaic of large glades, open light woodland and shrubs in grassland'.[2] Emmer wheat, the staple cereal of prehistory, was starting to be grown, and the animal bones show a preponderance of domesticated pigs and cattle.[3] There was good hunting in the woodland, which gave cover to deer and wild pig. In the river valleys there were substantial trees for the construction of timber buildings and there was flint to be found within the matrix of the chalk and the riverbeds. These few but vital resources were not exclusive to the landscape around Stonehenge, but in combination and abundance they created extraordinary opportunities. The production of crops and the domestication of animals, which this gentle landscape encouraged, allowed prehistoric societies to organize their time more effectively, and to engage in more extensive projects that were beyond the scope of earlier communities. In Britain the first of these enterprises was the construction of distinctive earthworks in singular and characteristic forms, a tradition which was eventually to create the first simple circular bank and ditch at Stonehenge.

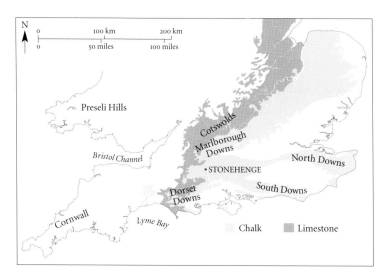

4 *Location and geological context (solid geology).*

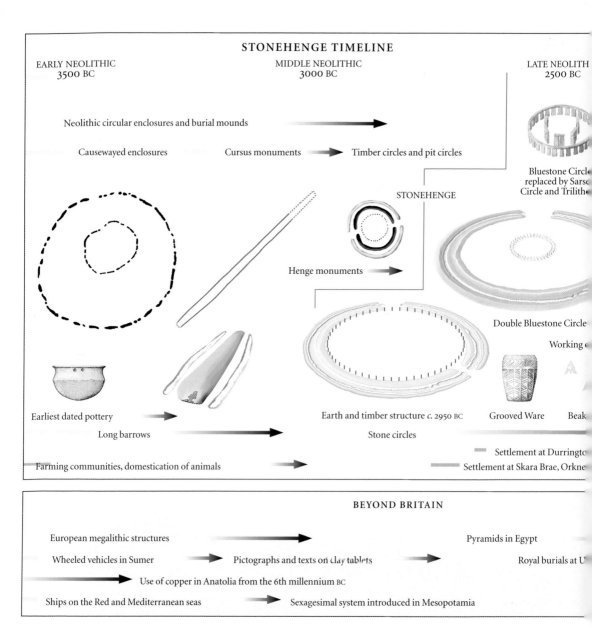

STONEHENGE TIMELINE

| EARLY NEOLITHIC 3500 BC | MIDDLE NEOLITHIC 3000 BC | LATE NEOLITH 2500 BC |

Neolithic circular enclosures and burial mounds

Causewayed enclosures → Cursus monuments → Timber circles and pit circles

Bluestone Circle replaced by Sarse Circle and Trilith

STONEHENGE

Henge monuments →

Double Bluestone Circle

Working

Earliest dated pottery → Earth and timber structure *c.* 2950 BC — Grooved Ware — Beak

Long barrows → Stone circles

Settlement at Durringto

Farming communities, domestication of animals → Settlement at Skara Brae, Orkne

BEYOND BRITAIN

European megalithic structures → Pyramids in Egypt

Wheeled vehicles in Sumer → Pictographs and texts on clay tablets → Royal burials at U

Use of copper in Anatolia from the 6th millennium BC

Ships on the Red and Mediterranean seas → Sexagesimal system introduced in Mesopotamia

Causewayed enclosures and henge monuments

Among the very earliest group of earthworks are those known as causewayed enclosures. Over 70 have been identified, almost exclusively in southern England – many more undoubtedly existed.[4] These enclosures, built in the Early Neolithic period (*c.* 3700–3000 BC), were formed by the excavation of often substantial ditches, sometimes in single circuits, in pairs, or with up to four concentric arrangements (though each circuit was not always complete), and vary in size between 1 and 28 hectares (ha); typically they are between

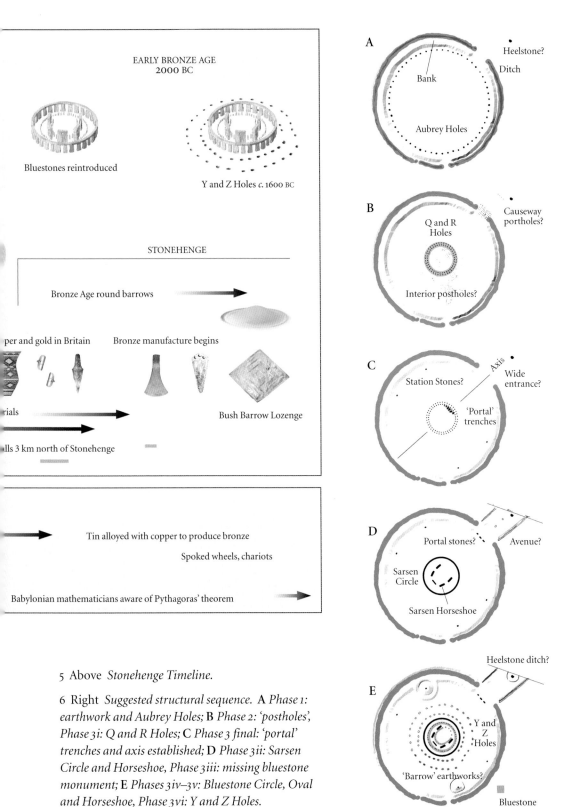

EARLY BRONZE AGE
2000 BC

Bluestones reintroduced

Y and Z Holes *c.* 1600 BC

STONEHENGE

Bronze Age round barrows

per and gold in Britain   Bronze manufacture begins

Bush Barrow Lozenge

rials

lls 3 km north of Stonehenge

Tin alloyed with copper to produce bronze

Spoked wheels, chariots

Babylonian mathematicians aware of Pythagoras' theorem

A

Heelstone?

Ditch

Bank

Aubrey Holes

B

Q and R
Holes

Causeway
portholes?

Interior postholes?

C

Station Stones?

Axis

Wide
entrance?

'Portal'
trenches

D

Portal stones?

Avenue?

Sarsen
Circle

Sarsen Horseshoe

E

Heelstone ditch?

Y and
Z
Holes

'Barrow' earthworks?

Bluestone
phases

0   50 m

0   130 ft

5 Above *Stonehenge Timeline.*

6 Right *Suggested structural sequence.* **A** *Phase 1:
earthwork and Aubrey Holes;* **B** *Phase 2: 'postholes',
Phase 3i: Q and R Holes;* **C** *Phase 3 final: 'portal'
trenches and axis established;* **D** *Phase 3ii: Sarsen
Circle and Horseshoe, Phase 3iii: missing bluestone
monument;* **E** *Phases 3iv–3v: Bluestone Circle, Oval
and Horseshoe, Phase 3vi: Y and Z Holes.*

2 and 4 ha. The upcast ditch material was used to form banks which were sometimes revetted or strengthened with timber. The banks were usually placed close to the inner edge of the ditch. The ditches were dug in a series of individual segments so that in places the bedrock remained undisturbed, forming the distinctive 'causeways' that give this very early class of earthwork its name. In recent years the function of these enclosures has become more apparent; the often archaeologically rich deposits within the ditches (which include cattle and pig bones, worked flints, pottery and other artifacts) contrast markedly with the lack of evidence for structures within the interiors, suggesting that they may have served as great open gathering places, important centres for feasting and perhaps trade or ritual practice.

Other round or oval Neolithic enclosures, usually created with a bank on the outside of the ditch and with one or two entrances (sometimes more) are termed 'henges'. These earthworks, of which well over 100 have been identified, are generally later than the causewayed enclosures, and though of similar form, they display huge variations in size, ranging from 'hengiform' which are just a few metres in diameter to extensive constructions as much as half a kilometre wide. The word 'henge' was borrowed from Stonehenge itself,[5] although its earthwork is atypical of the generic and somewhat disparate group to which the term is now applied; indeed it is not always possible to draw a hard line between the morphology of causewayed enclosures and henge monuments, and it has been suggested that the Stonehenge earthwork was influenced by the former.[6] By their nature, henge earthworks rarely display any direct physical temporal (stratigraphic) relationship with internal features. Any timber or stone settings (as at Stonehenge) cannot be assumed to have formed part of the original design, although the presence of post settings within many suggests that such structures may have been planned from the outset. There appears to be some evidence of continuity of the use of the sites; where excavation of henge enclosures has taken place 'all … seal traces of earlier, generally middle Neolithic activity below their banks'.[7] No single description adequately describes these monuments or defines their purpose. A recent work places those that might be seen as ceremonial or sacred sites at the centre of a Neolithic religious revolution, one which marks a shift from the perceived power of ancestors to that of gods and supernatural forces.[8]

7 *The setting of Stonehenge and its Avenue from the air in 1975, looking southeast, showing a number of nearby monuments including the banks of the Cursus, running obliquely from left to right across the foreground, and the line of Bronze Age round barrows which run parallel with its south side, together with further isolated barrows within the 'Stonehenge triangle'. The double-banked linear feature which runs down the left-hand side of the photograph, crossing the Avenue and cutting through a large barrow at the end of the Cursus group, is an unrelated feature, a seemingly unfinished 18th-century road.*

Enigmatic Cursus monuments and Neolithic tombs

Lying less than 1 km north of Stonehenge is an example of a curious type of Neolithic earthwork known as a 'Cursus'. These are linear works, defined by a pair of parallel banks and ditches, whose form and size are as diverse as the theories put forward to explain them. The name derives from a notion advanced in the 18th century that they were prehistoric race tracks. Since then every conceivable explanation has been explored, from the practical and the sporting to the astronomical, funerary, ceremonial and sacred; even the idea that they represent the prehistoric demarcation of the paths of tornadoes has been considered.[9] In truth, no single explanation can possibly hope to account for the variety of forms and topographic locations and distributions of these works, which vary in length from just a few hundred metres to almost 10 km. Around 150 are known. What little dating evidence there is shows that they belong to a tradition of the 4th millennium BC, but some apparently influenced the landscape and subsequent field systems for hundreds and even thousands of years.[10] Aubrey Burl, who has studied Neolithic monuments over many years, has suggested that the location for Stonehenge was chosen because it centrally overlooked the earlier (3-km long) Cursus.[11]

8 *Aerial view of the Stonehenge Cursus, looking east, with Fargo Plantation in the foreground.*

9 *Aerial view showing West Kennet Neolithic long barrow in the foreground (left) and the massive earthwork of Silbury Hill in the middle distance (right).*

The tombs of the Neolithic communities who built these early enclosures are represented by elongated, roughly rectangular or trapezoidal mounds at least twice as long as their width, formed from material excavated from the pair of flanking side ditches; some survive today to a height of several metres. Classic examples vary between 50 and 100 m in length, whilst others are smaller, sub-rectangular or oval in form. These 'long barrows' began to appear shortly after 4000 BC, and most are therefore hundreds of years earlier than the earthwork at Stonehenge. A series of new radiocarbon dates suggests that they may not be as long-lived as previously thought, and with activity focusing around the middle of the 4th millenium BC.[12] These curious structures often contained disarticulated human remains inserted at the higher, wider end of the earthwork which frequently, though not invariably, faced east. These façades may have been constructed in timber or stone (occasionally as later additions), behind which dozens of individuals have been found within sometimes quite extraordinarily elaborate mortuary structures, again constructed in either timber or stone. There is evidence from the human remains found within some of these long barrows that life was often difficult, as serious injuries, disease and cases of childhood malnutrition have been identified.[13] Stonehenge, however, was clearly not built by a group of arthritic and undernourished people; whatever the barrows may tell us about conditions that prevailed before the major phases of stone construction began, there must have been a significant improvement in the human lot by the middle of the 3rd millennium BC when, on current evidence, it appears that the first of the stones arrived.

The chalk downs of Salisbury Plain were to become the heartland of a remarkably prosperous Bronze Age community. If this needs further amplification, we have within the region the largest and grandest of all the major types of monument representing the later Neolithic and early Bronze Age period, including the huge enclosure at Avebury with its multiple stone-settings, and the astonishing man-made chalk mound at Silbury Hill. Well before 2000 BC Stonehenge was standing in the form that we recognize today. Britain was at that time undergoing a technological and social revolution, mirroring a sequence of events which had already happened further east, beyond the Mediterranean, where the exploitation of tin, copper and gold had transformed the lives of people whose wealth and status had until then been measured in livestock and arable production. Occasional discoveries of exotic material in the Stonehenge region are indicative of earlier regional trading contacts; axe heads manufactured from stone of Cornish, Welsh and Cumbrian origin, for example, were the imported products of 'factories', axe heads often derived from the mineral-rich areas of igneous geology which were soon to be explored for more valuable commodities. Yet the Stonehenge area was remote from the raw materials of the new technology. Copper and tin for bronzemaking came from localities 200–300 km to the west, while gold, which was fashioned into often quite elaborate personal ornaments or used to embellish other work, came from even further afield, including Wales and perhaps the Wicklow Mountains in Ireland.

Around the time when the massive stones were being hauled to Stonehenge, elaborate tombs were being constructed on the banks of the Euphrates, the burial places of the fabulously wealthy dynasties that ruled the southern Mesopotamian Sumerian city states in the 3rd millennium BC.[14] As with the people of Salisbury Plain, their prosperity had been founded on agriculture and cattle, and likewise the nearest sources of metal ores lay hundreds of kilometres away, largely in the mountainous regions south of the Black and Caspian seas; from here came timber, copper, tin and even meteoric iron. Gold has been found at these Sumerian sites in quite astonishing quantities, skilfully worked into most beautiful and ornate jewelry and regalia. Wheeled carts pulled by draught animals conveyed goods throughout the land, and Sumerian ships plied the rivers and coasts. In both southern England and Mesopotamia it was not the rugged outlying regions producing the raw materials that saw the greatest economic benefit; it was the people of the fertile agricultural lands who were able to command and organize extensive labour, and provide warriors who eventually controlled commerce over large areas. This is a simple model of what were complex and quite distinct societies. The object here is not to compare the two cultures but simply to illustrate that there is clearly much more to Stonehenge than ropes, rocks and muscle power. The dynamics behind the building of Stonehenge were as remarkable in their own way as events that were happening in contemporary Mesopotamia, where there is documentary evidence of royal dynasties, trading contacts and temple-building. By contrast we have no accounts of the people who constructed Stonehenge; there are no names or texts, no notion of the gods they believed in, or the cosmology that was central to their world.

An extraordinary settlement discovered close to Stonehenge

Britain's largest henge monument, a huge earthwork enclosing some 12 ha at Durrington Walls, only 3 km north of Stonehenge, has been investigated by a team led by Mike Parker Pearson.[15] The excavations have provided a rare and spectacular glimpse into the domestic life of people who would have been familiar with Stonehenge and perhaps contributed to the stone phase of its construction. Part of what must have been an extensive settlement dating to the mid-3rd millennium BC has been found; indeed this is the only Neolithic village so far discovered in southern Britain, possibly comprising 'hundreds or even thousands of small dwellings'.[16] The Durrington houses were clay-floored, square or sub-rectangular in groundplan, 2.5 to 5 m in size, each with a central hearth; many show clear evidence for timber slots which once located beds or other furniture, a pattern that echoes in wood the remarkable and perfectly preserved arrangements of Neolithic stone furniture found at sites such as Skara Brae in the Orkneys.[17] The roofs of the Durrington houses were supported by posts, with wall panels of wattle and daub (lightweight woven wooden frames plastered in clay). A small palisade timber fence or an earthwork with a fence surrounded each building. Huge quantities of pottery, animal bone (mainly pig and cattle) and flint have been found, but so far with little evidence of artifacts used in the preparation of grain, leading to the suggestion that it was perhaps a feasting place, 'a consumer site rather than a producer site'. This interpretation is further reinforced by the fact that a number of the food bones were still articulated and unfragmented, the detritus of 'wasteful consumption resulting from feasting', perhaps with an emphasis on a midwinter event; the pig teeth came from domestic animals thought to have been born in the spring, nine months before winter slaughter.[18]

Durrington also contains two substantial circular timber constructions, one within the north side of the enclosure and one to the south. Interpretations vary: some archaeologists see them as roofed buildings, others as complex timber circles.[19] Both appear to have had more than one period of use or modification: the northern ring, originally some 30 m in diameter, was later reduced to half its original size, whilst the larger southern example comprised, in its final form, a 40-m-diameter array of six concentric circles with 168 wooden posts, which was set just inside the eastern entrance of the settlement and close to the River Avon, some 100 m distant. The size of the post settings was extraordinary; some holes were 2–2.5 m in diameter, suggesting that they had been dug to house substantial uprights that may have weighed several tons. The implications of the work at Durrington Walls and its potential relationship with Stonehenge are still being explored. A recent review of the evidence from the 20th-century excavations and the radiocarbon dates shows that this site was occupied at the time that the major stone-erection phase began at Stonehenge. If the excavator's interpretation is correct, the Durrington timbers formed circles open to the sky, arranged reciprocally with respect to Stonehenge, so that the midwinter sun would *rise* between two dominant massive 'entrance posts', whereas at Stonehenge it sets between the frame of the largest pair of stones of the central array.

There may be some significance in the fact that both monuments are linked to the River Avon. It is difficult, however, to determine whether some

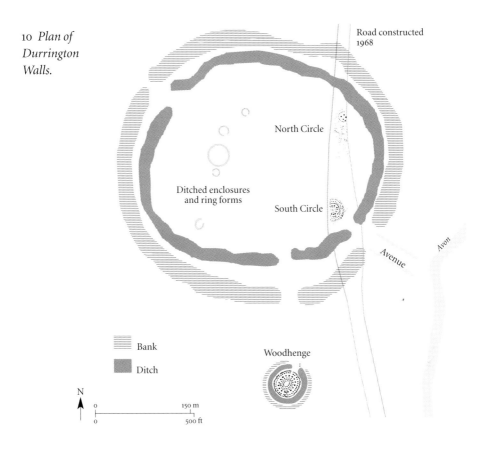

10 *Plan of Durrington Walls.*

Road constructed 1968

North Circle

Ditched enclosures and ring forms

South Circle

Avenue

Avon

Bank

Ditch

Woodhenge

N

0   150 m

0   500 ft

kind of mutual sacred relationship existed between the two sites. It would be surprising if Durrington, with its dense population, did not have convenient and direct access to the river. Its 90-m long and 20-m wide flint-cobbled roadway leading to the bank of the Avon may or may not be interpreted as having had a sacred or ritual function; in contrast, the convoluted 3-km long Stonehenge earthwork Avenue is clearly part of a grand, non-utilitarian scheme. The Durrington roadway, which is clearly defined by side gullies, though not exactly aligned on the axis of the timber circle within the entrance, does, however, have a large pit halfway along its length which 'probably held a timber post, at about the same distance to the Southern Circle as the Heelstone is to Stonehenge'.[20] Some theories see Durrington as a place of the living, its sacred structures a celebration of life, and Stonehenge as a monument to the dead, although this is certainly not a universally accepted view. Whether or not Stonehenge and the Durrington southern

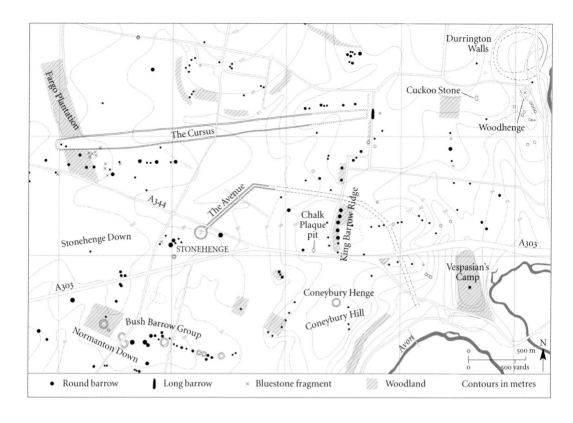

The following labels appear on the map:

Durrington Walls

Fargo Plantation

Cuckoo Stone

Woodhenge

The Cursus

A344

The Avenue

Chalk Plaque pit

King Barrow Ridge

Stonehenge Down

STONEHENGE

A303

A303

Vespasian's Camp

Coneybury Henge

Bush Barrow Group

Coneybury Hill

Normanton Down

Avon

N

0   500 m
0   500 yards

• Round barrow   ▮ Long barrow   × Bluestone fragment   ▨ Woodland   Contours in metres

11 *The Stonehenge landscape.*

timber circle formed part of a grand complementary religious complex, an emphasis on the significance of the solstice is apparent; they may have been twinned or, equally, they could have been mutually exclusive.

The Amesbury Archer and the Boscombe Bowmen

Shortly after the middle of the 3rd millennium BC, small round burial mounds containing distinctive artifacts began to appear in the Stonehenge region. The earliest British copper and gold objects have been found within these graves, frequently accompanied by ceramic beakers. These are the burials of the so-called Beaker People who were originally envisaged by archaeologists in the early 20th century as an invasive group of racially distinct peoples from Germany and Holland, a view dismissed by some archaeologists who saw in the Beaker culture no more than the adoption of new practices and materials by an indigenous population. The invasion theory was neat, and needed little elaboration. It was also very convenient – too convenient for a generation of later prehistorians who, quite rightly, questioned the validity of creating a 'people' from artifactual remains alone. The suggested physically distinctive appearance of the robust 'round-headed' Beaker People, once a key argument in the invasionist theory, began to look less secure, and certainly very unfashionable. But recent discoveries and the advent of new scientific methods in the examination of human remains have conspired to give elements of the original model a new lease of life.

In 1992, a Beaker-period burial was discovered at Amesbury, about 5 km east of Stonehenge. This is one of the richest burial sites of this period ever found. The grave contained an adult man, around 35–45 years old. Analysis of his tooth enamel (oxygen and strontium isotopes) suggests that he had been brought up in northern-central Europe, possibly Germany or Switzerland. This remarkable find has already entered into modern archaeological folk-lore as the 'Amesbury Archer'; some even muse on the idea, advanced by the media, that this man was one of the 'Kings of Stonehenge' (radiocarbon dates show that he lived somewhere between 2400 and 2200 BC, within the date range for the construction of the major stone monument, or shortly after).[21]

Typically, Beaker barrows show marked male and female divisions: male burials often contain weapons of flint, copper or bronze, daggers supplemented by stone 'battle-axes' and, commonly, the trappings of archery such as wristguards and flint arrowheads, while females are found with flint knives and occasionally bronze daggers. Both sexes wore gold or bronze jewelry, including some notably distinctive items alternatively interpreted as earrings or hair-tress loops, but only females are found with beads, usually jet or shale, whereas buttons and belt rings appear to be associated mostly with males. This division extends into the placement of individuals in the grave: the heads of men were predominantly laid to the east, and women to the west, the significance of which is obscure.

The Amesbury Archer's grave contained all the classic components of a Beaker burial, and such was his importance that ten times the usual number of finds accompanied the body. He had been in poor physical condition, having lost a kneecap in a traumatic earlier injury which had only partly healed, but this obvious disability did not detract from his social status. He had been laid on his left side, in this instance facing north. With him were buried two archer's wristguards, one of which was made from black sand-stone from the coast 50 km away, together with five beakers, three copper knives and a bone pin. Almost certainly he had been buried with a bow and a quiver containing arrows, for 17 flint arrowheads were also present. Other objects included a shale belt ring together with the tools of a flintworker and, even more importantly, what is taken to be a 'cushion stone', regarded as a piece of metalworker's equipment – a miniature anvil. Analysis of the copper from one of the knives shows it to have been made from metal obtained from Spain. The accompanying pair of sheet gold hair-tress loops (or earrings) are among the very oldest type of gold artifacts found in Britain. Buried so close to Stonehenge, and at a time broadly contemporary with the major stone building phase, this was a man who would not only have been familiar with the monument, but whose status implies that he may well have been a person of some influence – yet apparently he had not spent his whole life in Britain. This was an immensely important discovery.

One year later, in 1993, a second grave was discovered, at Boscombe Down some 6 km east of Stonehenge, containing not a single interment but the remains of seven individuals, all males: three adults, a teenager and three children. Around the older man, buried with his legs tucked up and again with the head to the north, lay the rest of the group; the youngest child had been cremated. Since the bones of the others were disarticulated and were arranged in the grave so that some lay under the burial, others above, it is probable that their bones had been first exposed elsewhere or collected from another location to be interred together, possibly as a family group (detailed examination of the skulls suggests that they were related). Included in the grave were eight beaker pots, five barbed and tanged arrowheads, a bone toggle and a boar's tusk. Radiocarbon samples returned the same date range as that of the Amesbury Archer (2400–2200 BC). Analysis of the teeth again shows that none of the group were native to the chalkland of southern England, and suggests that they may have spent their early years in west Wales or the Lake District, yet another connection that reflects the dynamic nature of these early metal-age peoples of the mid- to late 3rd millennium BC.[22]

The eclectic nature of the material from Beaker graves, the distinctive burial practices and the emerging evidence from the skeletal material itself

12 Left *Reconstruction of the Amesbury Archer.*

13 Below *Some of the items buried with him (clockwise from top left): flint arrowheads, Beaker pot (reconstructed), copper knives, gold hair-tress loops, and an archer's stone wristguards.*

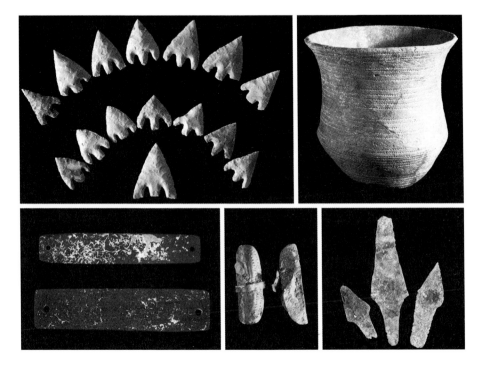

render the idea of an indigenous 'Beaker cult' untenable. These were clearly incomers, at the vanguard of the new technology and emerging trading links, who initially interacted with, and eventually assimilated into the native community.

In recent years a contemporary ring of pits about 63 m in diameter has been found on Boscombe Down, within a few hundred metres of the Amesbury Archer's grave. The pit-ring was sited on the crest of a plateau which itself had been encircled by sections of ditch and further pits. The array of 31 pits at a spacing of 3–4 m was found to contain 'a wide variety of worked flint, bone and pottery, including Late Neolithic Grooved ware'; only four of the (larger) pits appear to have housed timbers. The site was also a focus for a small 'hengiform enclosure' and an early Bronze Age barrow within which stood a timber mortuary structure which contained a primary burial, to which had been added the remains of a newborn child and perhaps two young adults. The presence of both Late Neolithic and Beaker-period pottery shows that activity on the plateau was broadly contemporary with the construction of the stone monument at Stonehenge. These finds serve further to illustrate the extensive and complex nature of the 'ritual landscape' within which Stonehenge was set, and demonstrate that before the arrival of the stones there was little to distinguish the Stonehenge site from numerous other nearby earthwork enclosures, pit groups and timber circles.[23]

Our knowledge of the transition from the Neolithic to the Bronze Age is still developing, but what is becoming increasingly clear is that extensive trading networks were being established across the whole of western Europe, and that the acquisition of wealth and status was ultimately reflected in the barrow cemeteries which appeared in the landscape over many hundreds of years following the construction of Stonehenge. As our ability to source and analyse ancient materials develops so does our understanding of the trading connections and human dynamics of the period to which Stonehenge belongs. From around 2000 BC the manufacture of bronze became increasingly important in the making of tools and weapons; this was a technological revolution requiring the alloying of copper with specific amounts of tin, a revolution in which Britain was at the forefront.[24] While copper was relatively abundant in the 'old' mining regions of Europe, tin was a scarce and highly prized commodity found in relative abundance in Cornwall and on Dartmoor. One of the earliest bronze daggers ever found in Britain was discovered in 2001 at Rameldry Farm, in Fife, Scotland, when a farmer's plough caught the capstone covering an early Bronze Age crouched inhumation; inside the stone cist lay the skeleton of an adult male aged around 40–45 years, whose bones produced a radiocarbon date of 2280–1970 BC. He had been wearing a jacket which had been fastened with six buttons, five made of Whitby jet, the sixth from a stone found only on the Lizard peninsula in Cornwall. This button bore an incised cruciform motif whose grooves carried traces of metallic tin.[25] This discovery weaves together multiple strands of the remarkable and energetic world of these early adventurers, a people whose enterprise and regional connections were opening up the British Isles to innovation, trade and emerging bronze technology, seeking and exploiting opportunities in the very furthest corners of the land, with a focus of wealth and power in the geographic centre of southern England. In the early Bronze Age, Stonehenge must have been a truly awesome sight, a powerful established landmark within the tribal heartland of a flourishing and increasingly influential community, which was to become known by archaeologists as the 'Wessex Culture'.[26] The contents of their burial mounds are remarkable, for in addition to objects of bronze they include items of gold, amber, jet and faience. The skills of the best of the metalworkers and goldsmiths were quite outstanding, rivalling those of any subsequent era.

Then, quite suddenly, or so it seems, something happened to disrupt the established order. Around 1700 BC metalwork became less common in Britain, certainly as finds accompanying burials; this period conforms roughly with the apparent abandonment of Stonehenge, or at least with any known activity or obvious structural alteration. Only in the middle to later Bronze Age, some 300 years later (*c.* 1400 BC onwards), does any quantity of metalwork find its way back into archaeological contexts, but by this time it appears that Stonehenge, already some 1,000 years old, had been abandoned.

CHAPTER 2

Myth, Legend & the Early Antiquarians

There are very few surviving early accounts before those of Julius Caesar that specifically mention the British Isles; they are little more than anecdotal, surviving only in the works of later writers, and may themselves have incorporated material which was already fable by later prehistoric times. The first written accounts of Britain (from around the early 4th century BC) are drawn from intrepid mariners and early explorers who returned to the Mediterranean from the western shores of Europe with descriptions of the lives and culture of native inhabitants. By the time Britain had been brought within the orbit of the Classical world, Stonehenge had in all probability been in a somewhat ruinous state for close to a millennium.

Diodorus Siculus, a Sicilian of Greek descent who settled in Rome around 56 BC, amassed a large amount of fabulous and largely undigested material for inclusion in his *Bibliotheca Historica*, a history of the world. One of his sources was Hecataeus of Abdera, one of a number of ancient authors who drew on the earlier writings of Pytheas of Massalia (Marseilles), an explorer and author of a fragmentary surviving account of the Atlantic fringe of Europe, 'On the Ocean' (written *c.* 320 BC).[1] Although Diodorus travelled extensively, he is not thought to have visited Britain, and he acknowledges these earlier sources in his description of an island no smaller than Sicily lying beyond the land of the Celts, taken to mean beyond the European (i.e. Gallic) mainland: 'This island … is situated in the north and is inhabited by the Hyperboreans who are so called because they live beyond the point where the north wind blows.' We are told that the inhabitants honoured Apollo more than any other deity because of a legend telling how Leto, the consort of Zeus and mother of the divine twins Artemis and Apollo, was born on this island. Where: 'a sacred enclosure is dedicated to him [Apollo] … as well as a magnificent spherical temple adorned with many rich offerings.' Some intriguing clues which could help locate this mysterious island are also given:

> They also say that the moon, as viewed from this island, appears to be but a lit-
> tle distance above the Earth and to have upon it prominences like those of the
> Earth, which are visible to the eye. The account is also given that the god vis-
> its the island every nineteen years, the period in which the return of the stars
> to the same place in the heavens is accomplished; … At the time of the appear-
> ance of the god he both plays on the cithara [lyre] and dances continuously
> the night through from the vernal equinox until the rising of the Pleiades …[2]

Is Diodorus referring to Britain, and could this be the earliest documentary reference to Stonehenge? If so, there are two reasons for thinking that the reference to the 'magnificent temple' cannot have been based on any first-hand account of Stonehenge provided by Pytheas, and must have depended on a much earlier source. First, the account suggests that the temple with its votive offerings was still in use – it is highly unlikely, from any archaeological evidence, that Stonehenge was still being used by Iron Age Britons. Secondly, by the time Pytheas visited Britain, truly phenomenal structures had been built throughout the Classical world, among them the Parthenon, which would have been standing for at least a century when Pytheas began his explorations. Though we cannot be certain that Pytheas also travelled eastward from his home in Marseilles, it would be very unlikely that such an adventurer would not have seen, or at least heard reports of, the major buildings of the Classical world. It is questionable, therefore, whether the comparatively rustic Stonehenge, or any British megalithic structure let alone one that in all probability was in a state of dereliction by this time, would have merited inclusion in a class of 'magnificent temples'. This suggests that the source of the information drawn on by Diodorus may have been significantly earlier, or even a survival of an oral tradition, perhaps originating with information gleaned from the first traders to establish links with the 'Hyperborean' peoples. This information would have been based on accounts told long before the age of the Classical Greek writers, at a time when such a temple would still have seemed impressive to ancient seafarers.

At face value Diodorus' description certainly would fit the mainland of Britain, but other possibilities have been suggested, like the Orkneys or the Hebrides – Pytheas is known to have travelled far to the north, possibly as far as Iceland.[3] The accounts are both frustrating and tantalizing. Nevertheless, the combination of elements is significant: the round or spherical form of the temple, votive offerings, the moon and astronomical observations (whatever their implication), Greek myth, festivity, dance and musical celebration. Could this relate to a British Bronze Age structure whose use was preserved in folk memory for perhaps 2,000 years before becoming woven into the fabric of Classical literature? Perhaps this is unlikely, but how dull the study of the past would be if deprived of such possibilities.

There is no further mention of anything which might be identified with Stonehenge in Classical texts, either from Julius Caesar, writing *c.* 55 BC, or from any writers during the whole of the 360 years or so that Britain was a province of Rome. Apart from what may have been a single inscribed lead tablet (see p. 46), no archaeological evidence has been found to suggest that any formal or organized religious activity took place around Stonehenge at this time; the absence of significant interest is probably in part due to its relative remoteness, as the occasional finds of pottery and coins suggest little more than the casual detritus left by passing travellers. The obvious conclusion is that the site had been deserted and its associations forgotten long before Britain became part of the Roman Empire, its outward appearance already one of abandonment and decay.

Medieval chroniclers

Writing around the year AD 1130, the English chronicler Henry of Huntingdon provides the first unambiguous reference to Stonehenge, over 1,000 years after Britain and the Atlantic fringe had been fleetingly embraced by the literacy of the Classical world, and some 2,500 years after the monument's putative abandonment. In its dilapidated condition it was ripe for medieval speculation; what ensued was a heady mixture of folklore, fragmented pseudo-history and outright fabrication, contrived and designed to capture the popular imagination of the Middle Ages.

In his *Historia Anglorum* ('The History of England'), Henry described the monument as the second (of four) Wonders of Britain:

> Stanenges, where stones of wonderful size have been erected after the manner of doorways, so that doorway appears to have been raised upon doorway; and no one can conceive how such great stones have been so raised aloft, or why they were built there.[4]

This entry is intriguing because Henry admits that he has absolutely no idea of the origin and meaning of Stonehenge; yet just six years later, Geoffrey of Monmouth (*c.* 1100–55), an altogether more ambitious British writer, confidently offered an explanation of both the origin and meaning of the monument. How could this be? Surely if Henry knew that his 'Stanenges' was one of the Wonders of Britain he would have been aware of any legend associated with the site? From his brief description we can be reasonably sure that no contemporary folklore associating Stonehenge with any historical or legendary figures can have been prevalent or considered worthy of note in the England with which Henry was familiar. Could Geoffrey really have acquired or sourced material beyond that known to Henry, or was he a charlatan who fabricated an outrageous myth?

Geoffrey of Monmouth, or Galfridus Arthurius, was a Welsh-Breton cleric and historian, who spent the years between 1129 and 1149 at the secular college of St George's in Oxford, before returning to Wales and becoming Bishop of St Asaph in 1152. Whilst at Oxford he compiled three works: *Prophetiae Merlini* ('Prophecies of Merlin') and *Historia Regium Britanniae* ('History of the Kings of Britain'), written in 1136 or shortly after, and finally a substantial narrative poem, *Vita Merlini* ('Life of Merlin'). In his *Historia* Geoffrey gives an account of the removal of a formidable stone circle from Ireland and its re-erection on the site of Stonehenge. The stones are explained by Geoffrey as a memorial to 460 British lords, treacherously massacred at Ambrius (modern-day Amesbury) by a Saxon army under the leadership of Hengist. The Saxons, we are told, had been invited to 'peace talks' by the usurper Vortigern (whose wife was the daughter of Hengist). Betraying the trust of their hosts, the Saxons, having weapons concealed in their clothes, murdered the unfortunate Britons at a pre-arranged command. Geoffrey relates how Ambrosius Aurelius returned from exile in Brittany and rallied the army of the Britons to despatch the treacherous Vortigern, and asserts that it was Ambrosius Aurelius (who he describes as a king) who built Stonehenge, to create a 'noble monument' to the murdered British. Ambrosius summoned Merlin, described by Geoffrey as 'a man of the brightest genius, either in predicting future events, or in mechanical contrivances', and was advised to:

> send for the Giant's Round [or Dance] [*Chorea Gigantu*], which is in Killaraus, a mountain in Ireland. For there is a structure of stones there, which none of this age could raise without a profound knowledge of the mechanical arts. They are stones of vast magnitude, and wonderful quality; and if they can be placed here, as they are there, quite round this spot of ground, they will stand for ever [....] Many years ago the Giants transported them from the remotest confines of Africa and set them up in Ireland, at a time when they inhabited that country. Their plan was that, whenever they felt ill, baths should be prepared at the foot of the stones; for they used to pour water over them and to run this water into baths in which their sick were cured. What is more, they mixed the water with herbal concoctions and so healed their wounds. There is not a single stone among them which hasn't some medicinal virtue.

Having arrived at Mount Killaraus, but unable to dismantle the stones, the Britons sought the help of Merlin, who:

> placed in order the engines that were necessary, [and] ... took down the stones with an incredible facility, and withal gave directions for carrying them to the ships, and placing them therein.

And, upon arrival at Stonehenge he placed the stones:

> in the same manner as they had been in the Mount of Killaraus, and thereby gave a manifest proof of the prevalence of art above strength.[5]

Geoffrey's account contains an amalgam of actual events and historical characters with a generous measure of legend and myth, shaped in no small part by his considerable imagination and a proud sense of his own British ancestry. He claimed that his account was based upon his translation of 'a book written in the British tongue, which Walter, archdeacon of Oxford, brought out of Brittany'.[6] How much of the *Historia* may have been based on this mysterious unidentified ancient book or earlier texts, if they ever existed, is entirely unknown. However, fictitious or not, the book's inclusion in the story helps to preserve both a sense of authority and mystery which was clearly Geoffrey's intention, as it conveniently allowed him to advise contemporary writers, William of Malmesbury and Henry of Huntingdon, to 'be silent concerning the Kings of the Britons, since they have not that book'.[7]

The *Historia* soon became one of the most influential works of the Middle Ages. Geoffrey purported to have traced the kings of Britain back to the legendary Brutus, and to have given British history and the British people credibility after decades of mauling at the hands of Romans, Saxons, Danes and now the Normans. According to his account, two of the key players, Ambrosius and his brother, Uther Pendragon (father of King Arthur), were buried at Stonehenge towards the end of the 5th century AD. His stories sowed the seeds for the increasingly elaborate Arthurian legends within which Stonehenge was soon to become impossibly entangled, and so remains to the present day.

Does this fabulous web of fiction preserve remarkable distant folk memory of the Stonehenge bluestones (see p. 41) being transported from a distant location? Is the story of a pre-existing stone circle having been brought by sea from 'Ireland' simply Geoffrey's invention? Although he doubted the credibility of the ancient literary sources, the archaeologist Stuart Piggott was nevertheless convinced of the potential for the survival of the story of Stonehenge in Geoffrey's *Historia* in which he considered 'we may have the only fragment left to us of a native Bronze Age literature'.[8] Such a memory would have had to bridge some 3,500 years, from the end of the Neolithic period to 12th-century England – rational thinking suggests it is almost unimaginable. However, the possibility of the transmission of some meaningful memories from the remote past must be accepted. One may consider the temporal dynamics which permit such knowledge to be transferred from generation to generation. A remarkable documented example is provided by Walter Johnson writing in 1908, who tells us that there was 'living in December 1905 a North Riding [Yorkshire] farmer, who, as a boy in 1827, had talked with a centenarian who had served under the Duke of Cumberland at Culloden in 1746'.[9] Using this model, 1,000 years of memory could theoretically be conveyed by only five or six such opportunities; even taking into account the relatively short lifespans of people of much earlier generations would not put the possibility beyond the bounds of credibility. In pre-literate societies the shaping of important facts into narrative form was a sure way of ensuring their survival in the collective consciousness of the community. I would suggest that if it is impossible for folk memory to span millennia, how do we account for the survival of pagan (pre-Christian) superstitions and traditions which are still extant in Britain today?

The potential archaeological significance of folk memory was graphically illustrated to me a number of years ago. My Irish grandmother would often say that a kettle, on taking a long time to boil, 'had stones in it'. I was six or seven years old at the time and had no idea what this meant and, more importantly, neither did she. It was almost 20 years later whilst working on an archaeological excavation, that the truth occurred to me. I was examining a collection of large scorched and fire-cracked pebbles that had been subjected to a greater episode of burning than represented by the small prehistoric hearth on which they lay. Similar stones had been found elsewhere on the site, remote from any burning – they were of course 'potboilers'. My grandmother was, unknowingly, referring to the use of stones to boil water by heating them and dropping them into earthenware pots which would have been incapable of withstanding the direct heat of a fire. This was a revelation; an ancient memory had been relayed to me from days when water was boiled not in metal pans and kettles, but in pottery vessels. I had closed the equation this time from the artifactual evidence which precisely fitted the ancient folk memory that I had received as a child. Archaeology and oral tradition are not necessarily incompatible.

Stonehenge has of course attracted a plethora of myths, legends and interpretations from the credible and potentially feasible, to the speculative and entirely implausible.[10] No archaeologist believes that the fabled Ambrosius Aurelius, Arthur or Merlin had anything whatsoever to do with the construction of Stonehenge. These stories are not simply dismissed because they are based on the dubious 'research' of a single medieval chronicler, but because we now know almost exactly when it was built; Stonehenge was at its most impressive 2,500 years before the 'Age of Arthur'. Yet it has often been suggested that the fabled 'magical skill' by which the stones were reputedly transported evoked a folk memory of a stupendous feat of engineering, and a geographical confusion between Ireland and Wales is easily forgiven given the timescale over which the story would have been related. Even the normally sceptical archaeologist Richard Atkinson, who excavated at Stonehenge in the 1950s, believed that 'the correspondence between the legend and the fact is so striking that it cannot be dismissed as mere coincidence'.[11] It took 1,000 years before a potential connection emerged between the first documented Stonehenge folklore (or utter fabrication, depending on your viewpoint) of stones brought from Ireland, related by Geoffrey of Monmouth, and a potential geological explanation when, in 1923, the geologist Herbert Thomas recognized that the Stonehenge bluestones actually came from west Wales. Routes to the solutions of archaeological problems are not always obvious. Folklore and myths can be explored, sifted and then tested for potential veracity.

Medieval illustrations of Stonehenge

Stonehenge is depicted in three medieval manuscripts. The earliest, made around 1338–40 [see ill. 14], shows Merlin lifting a lintel either onto or off a pair of uprights in an English version of Wace's 12th-century *Roman de Brut*, illustrating the legend of Merlin's transport of the stones from Ireland to Stonehenge. The image is usually taken to represent the construction of Stonehenge, although it has been recently argued that it is more likely to represent 'the deconstruction of its progenitor in Ireland' as the text surrounding the drawing relates to the first part of the story.[12] A second manuscript [15], the Corpus Christi (Cambridge) version of the *Scala Mundi* (a tabular chronicle of the world, 'world ladder'), of similar date, shows Stonehenge in a rectangular form, with lintels in place. A third illustration of the monument, in a

14 Right *One of the earliest depictions of Stonehenge from a medieval manuscript, c. 1338–40. This illustration is usually interpreted as Merlin involved in the construction of Stonehenge, although more recently it has been suggested that it may show him dismantling a pre-existing monument prior to its transport to Salisbury Plain.*

15 Below *A more formalized rectilinear Stonehenge, from a manuscript of similar (early 14th-century) date.*

16 *A sketch from a manuscript dating from c. 1440, recently discovered in the Bibliothèque de Douai, showing Stonehenge as an arrangement of four trilithons. The tenons are shown extending through the tops of the lintels; this may be an artistic device to represent the mortise and tenon construction, or perhaps the artist at ground level was unaware that the tenons did not project through the body of the lintels.*

different version of the *Scala Mundi,* that dates to around 1440–67, has recently been discovered [16]. This small sketch, which shows an arrangement of four trilithons, came to light in 2001, when it was noticed by Professor Christian Heck amongst an archive of medieval documents held at the

Bibliothèque de Douai.[13] This newly discovered drawing is interesting on two counts. First, it is the earliest known depiction showing the lintels with mortise and tenon joints; the tenons are shown apparently protruding through to the top of the stones, which is understandable if the artist had simply grasped the concept from observations of exposed tenons made from ground level. The implication is that it was either drawn by someone who had visited the site, or copied from an original whose history is quite distinct from the other medieval images, which do not appear to be based on first-hand knowledge of the stones. Secondly, but more speculatively, it may suggest that four trilithons were standing when the artist viewed the monument.

The first antiquarians

For some 400 years after Geoffrey of Monmouth wrote his *Historia,* little was contributed to the understanding of British antiquities or the structure of Stonehenge. Contemporary society and the Church in particular encouraged neither the development of new ideas about the past, nor an interest in 'pagan' stones beyond that expressed in popular and sanitized accounts. In Geoffrey's account bishops and abbots were summoned to celebrate the construction of the circle, and the view of Stonehenge as a 'memorial' to the fallen British did not break any rules. Geoffrey's story may not exactly have allowed the site to be perceived as a Christian monument but it gave Stonehenge both moral licence and credibility. This may have actually saved the stones from the paranoid attentions of the medieval Church. There are isolated instances of large stones being removed, but mainly it was gradual attrition, with occasional opportunist stone robbing of what were, in all probability, fallen stones. Other ancient monuments fared less well at this time; we know, for example, that village clergy sometimes made payments to encourage demolition at certain sites, and were responsible in no small part for toppling and smashing many of the megaliths at nearby Avebury.[14]

In 1533 Henry VIII appointed John Leland (1502–52) to 'make a search after England's Antiquities, and peruse the Libraries of all Cathedrals, Abbies, Priories, Colleges', and gave him authority to enter 'all places wherein Records, Writings and secrets of Antiquity were reposed'. Leland undertook two major journeys between the years 1533 and 1545, amassing details of the nation's antiquities from first-hand observation and from written sources. He summarized his aims in these words: 'I trust so to open this wyndow, that the lyght shal be seane, so long, that is to say, by the space of a whole thousand yeares stopped up, and the old glory of your renoumed Britaine to reflorish through the worlde.'[15] His accounts often provide the first description of many notable monuments, and proved a valuable resource for later antiquarians.

Leland is known to have visited Stonehenge only once. Being familiar with the details of the writings of Geoffrey of Monmouth and other fanciful medieval manuscripts, he was quick to dismiss the idea that the stones had been transported from Ireland: 'For everybody, however ignorant, ought to know that these enormous stones which in our own age, so short of talent, is unable to shift were brought by Merlin from some quarry near by.' He did not entirely reject other parts of the story – on the contrary, he was intrigued by the notion of Merlin's 'ingenious machines and clever inventions', for he could see no other way in which such stones could have been quarried and transported, not even, as he tells us, by the Romans. 'It would have been beyond the ability of the Romans to move things of such weight from Ireland to Amesbury, since the Avon [Bristol Avon], at its closest point, is nearly twenty miles away.' Leland's pragmatic approach and concern with the logistical problems surrounding the construction of the monument is important, as it was a novel idea to conceive the possibility of extracting further knowledge from the material evidence alone.

The interest in exploring a more 'rational' explanation of the monument is further illustrated by the thoughts of the printer and author John Rastell who, writing in 1530, considered that the stones were formed of some kind of cement and were thus not transported at all, being made of 'large Congeries of Sand, and other unctuous matter mixt together'.[16] Such a view became commonly held and often repeated, despite the protestations of the Elizabethan lawyer and antiquarian William Lambarde (1536–1601), who pointed out that 'a great Store of Stone of the same Kinde' can be found on the Marlborough Downs some miles to the north of Stonehenge, and that its arrangement is 'no more Wonder than one Post of a House hangeth above another'. Nor was moving such great stones a problem for 'by Art Thinges of greater Weight may be removed, especially if a Prince be Pay-maister'.[17]

In the late 16th century scientific study was to revolutionize the way the past and its material remains were both examined and perceived. The philosopher and essayist Francis Bacon (1561–1626) was at the forefront of this revolution. As the anthropologist Loren Eiseley notes: 'more fully than any man of his time, [Bacon] entertained the idea of the universe as a problem to be solved, examined, meditated upon, rather than as an eternally fixed stage, upon which man walked.'[18] The new 'natural philosophers' soon began breaking down the barriers that had stood in the way to understanding the significance of the nation's ancient monuments. Stonehenge and other remains were no longer to be seen simply as places of awe and wonderment, or as bland iconic illustrations to a largely invented established history, but were to be recognized as having unique stories of their own to tell.

The renowned and eminent Elizabethan historian and antiquary William Camden (1551–1623), a contemporary of Bacon, was to become one of the first and most influential of these early antiquaries. Thirty-six years after Leland's death, Camden published the results of his own extensive travels and research in his *Britannia*, first printed in Latin in 1586.[19] 'Master Camden' was known as a modest and learned man. In 1593 he became headmaster of Westminster School, and his love of his native land inspired others to take an interest in the history and topography of Britain. Camden's influence on contemporary society extended far beyond the world of antiquities;

he was tutor and mentor to Ben Jonson, the Elizabethan playwright, who was to write of him: 'Camden! most reverend head, to whom I owe all that I am in arts, all that I know.'[20]

Camden's *Britannia* is not only an outstanding work of scholarship; it is a grand Elizabethan adventure. His descriptions of the many remote and sometimes dangerous places he visited are as exciting as those of any latter-day travel writer. With a caution

17 *William Camden, 1609.*

tempered by extensive exposure to the elaborate and speculative works of medieval chroniclers, he was reluctant, in writing of Stonehenge, to be drawn into speculation about the origins of the monument and the methods of construction: 'about these points I am not curiously to argue and dispute, but rather to lament with much griefe that the Authors of so notable a monument are thus buried in oblivion.' He does, however, furnish a short description, giving dimensions of the largest stones, drawing attention to the lintels fixed by mortise and tenon, and debating whether the stones are natural or made from an ancient form of concrete.

A later antiquarian and fieldworker, William Stukeley (p. 61), writing in 1740, commented that Camden's description of Stonehenge was 'a wretched anile account';[21] true, it is certainly less than vibrant, even bordering on the despondent, which has suggested to some that his account was second-hand. Yet a frequent visitor to Stonehenge will be aware that on certain overcast days the melancholy brooding nature of the stones can be all-pervasive. Surely he must have seen Stonehenge for himself. Although its setting appears remote, it was within an hour's horse ride from Salisbury, a short distance in comparison with many of the places on Camden's itinerary that were truly difficult to reach.

From his account of Stonehenge we are left with only one new piece of information, which Camden added by way of an afterthought:

> I have heard that in the time of King Henrie the Eight, there was found neere this place a table of mettall, as it had been tinne and lead commixt, inscribed with many letters, but in so strange a Character, that neither Sir Thomas Eliot, nor master Lilye Schoole-maister of Paules, could read it, and therefore neglected it. Had it been preserved, somewhat happily might have been discovered as concerning *Stoneheng*, which now lieth obscured.[22]

This curious artifact, said to have been found 'near' Stonehenge and described as a 'table', was more probably some kind of inscribed 'tablet' (*tabella*) or plaque, and is unlikely to have been of prehistoric origin. If it was a small tablet (for we are given no indication of its size), it was just conceivably a curse or votive inscription bearing handwritten (cursive) text, not uncommon in Roman Britain. Such script, which the Roman playwright

Plautus mockingly described as appearing to have been 'scratched by a chicken',[23] would have proved quite incomprehensible to Elizabethan scholars familiar with the more formal Roman monumental inscriptions. The tablet could, of course, have been much later in date; the manufacture of the tin-lead version of pewter was an important industry in later medieval England, although had it been a relatively recent item, it would almost certainly have been recognized as such. Camden's statement clearly illustrates both that it was of sufficient interest to be sent to London for identification, and that its inscription had proved indecipherable. That he laments the loss of the potential evidence this artifact may have offered is perhaps more telling, further illustrating Camden's frustration with Stonehenge and the 'obscurity' of the origins of the monument.

By the end of the 16th century the idea that the antiquity of Stonehenge might be understood from a study of its construction and architectural form was being explored. The historian and poet Edmund Bolton (1575–1633), a friend of Camden, was familiar with Stonehenge through his friends and patrons, one of whom, the Duke of Buckingham, had himself commissioned a hole to be dug in the centre of the monument in 1620 (see p. 57). Bolton argued that Stonehenge was too crude to be Roman, and besides, the Romans 'were wont to make stones vocall by inscriptions', a statement which he qualified by saying 'unlesse the letters bee worne quite away'. He regarded the structure as a British monument to Boadicea (Boudicca), quoting the authority of the Roman historian Cassius Dio, that 'the BRITTANS enterred her pompously, or with much magnificence, cannot be better verified than by assigning these orderly irregular, and formless uniforme heapes of massiue marble, to her euerlasting remembrance'.[24]

Contemporary pictorial representations

It was not until his 1600 edition of *Britannia* (p. 60) that Camden included an engraving of the monument: 'because it could not so fitly be expressed in words, I have caused by the gravers helpe to be portraied heere underneath as it now standeth weather beaten and decaied.'[25] This engraving is a rather confused and poorly executed copy of a view of Stonehenge (since lost) which is thought to have been the work of the Flemish topographic artist Joris

Hoefnagel who was known to have been in London in the period 1568–69. There are three surviving views of Stonehenge, all executed *c.* 1575, which are so similar in their imaginary standpoint, their rare use of perspective and repetition of mistakes that they are all believed to have derived from this original.[26]

The artist, Lucas de Heere, a fellow countryman and friend of Hoefnagel, included a watercolour [18] of the monument in his manuscript book entitled *Short Description of the English Histories Compiled from the Best of Authors,* which was probably completed in 1575–76.[27] The accompanying description and history follow much the same sources as Camden and his contemporaries, but the stones themselves were said by de Heere to have been drawn first-hand 'as I myself have drawn them on the spot'. This is a bird's-eye view, looking broadly south, enabling all the principal components to be appreciated, which could never be achieved at ground level. Although a certain amount of artistic licence has been taken in the foreshortening of the ditch dimensions, nevertheless the main elements of the stone monument appear reasonably accurate: the mortises on two of the sarsen uprights are clear, the central tapering bluestone pillars distinctive. A row of lintels on the left-hand side of the painting conveys the relatively good survival of the structure on the northeast side, although the number shown is not quite correct. The three complete trilithons are shown, together with the single upright of the northern pair, albeit too close to the outer circle; the distinctive cavity in its base at the back is clearly visible. The view also shows a pair of uprights bearing a lintel on the southeast side of the Sarsen Circle which have apparently subsequently disappeared,[28] although this area is more difficult to interpret as it is clear that here the artist has made an error in assembling the various elements to produce his perspective drawing. He has mistakenly presented a mirror-image of the leaning stone of the Great Trilithon, resulting not only in its displacement outside the Sarsen Horseshoe, but also showing it leaning backwards from the centre.

A second watercolour, published by William Smith in 1588, is a crude copy of the same scene, providing no new information and exaggerating features such as de Heere's ruins on the hill, which have become a stone castle, the addition of the spire of Salisbury Cathedral in the distance, and an increase in

18 *Watercolour by Lucas de Heere, c. 1575. This is probably the earliest surviving representation of Stonehenge, using an aerial perspective to provide more information than can be conveyed from ground level. De Heere mistakenly shows the upright of the Great Trilithon leaning in the wrong direction.*

the number of barrows.[29] The third illustration [19] is an engraving entitled *Stonhing* by an unknown author (with the initials RF), dated 1575, showing obvious similarities to both watercolours, sharing the same aerial view and mistakes, but with additional stones in the outer circle. This print does, however, include an important addition: two large boulders at the entrance. A descriptive panel refers to the transport of stones from Ireland by Merlin at the behest of Ambrosius, gives the estimated height and weight of one of the trilithon uprights ('corse stones') and indicates the lintels ('coronets').[30] One of the barrows in the foreground has been populated by two men digging up a burial which is captioned: 'where great bones of men ar found'. There is a striking similarity between this engraving and that first published by Camden, which continued unchanged in the next three editions, particularly in the use of embellishments such as the annotated cartouche, the barrow diggers and the castle.

Although the RF engraving itself was not published for another 200 years (by Richard Gough in his 1789 edition of *Britannia*), it undoubtedly represents an important stage in the development of ideas regarding the origins and function of Stonehenge, marking the transition between the myths and legends of the medieval chroniclers (still repeated in its caption), and more focused curiosity which was to lead to more careful observation, measured survey and excavation (anticipated by the barrow diggers) in the following centuries.

19 'RF Print', dated 1575. Although this print may have been copied by engravers for inclusion in earlier editions of Camden's Britannia, *it was not actually published until Gough's edition of 1789.*

CHAPTER 3

Fieldwork, Excavation & Speculation

When staying with the Duke of Buckingham at Wilton House near Salisbury in 1620 the king, James I, visited Stonehenge. He was familiar with some of the folklore, and took the opportunity to test the notion that it was impossible to count the stones and return the same number twice. The king's protector, Colonel Robert Phillips, describes how the king's party 'rid the Downes, and took a view of the wonder of that country, Stoneheng, where they found that the King's Arithmaticke gave the lye to that fabulous tale that those stones cannot be told alike twice together'.[1] His curiosity with Stonehenge led James to instruct the eminent Neoclassical architect Inigo Jones (1572–1652), Surveyor General of The King's Works, to make a study of the monument and produce a detailed plan. The Stonehenge survey was to remain unfinished, and it was not until three years after Jones's death that his assistant, John Webb, working from Jones's 'few indigested notes', published his conclusions in a book entitled *The Most Notable Antiquity of Great Britain, Vulgarly Called Stone-heng, on Salisbury Plain, Restored*, a work which forced Stonehenge into a geometrically precise Classical mould. This proved far from a popular interpretation, and antiquarians and scholars of the day generally ignored it completely, or commented unfavourably.

Jones's scheme was entirely influenced by his concept of Stonehenge as Roman work. In 1624 Sir Henry Wotton had published his *Elements of Architecture* in which he translated and popularized the ideas of the Roman

architect and engineer Vitruvius. The writings of Vitruvius, consisting of ten encyclopaedic books entitled *De Architectura*, had been known to medieval builders and had inspired, among others, Michelangelo and Palladio. Vitruvius was himself influenced by Classical Greek architecture, but he did not simply present technical information – he was also concerned with the philosophy of proportion and geometry, and the origins of form and numeric sequences. It was into the Classical Vitruvian proportions that Jones attempted to fit the groundplan of Stonehenge, using as his model a drawing of a Roman theatre illustrated in a 16th-century translation of *De Architectura*

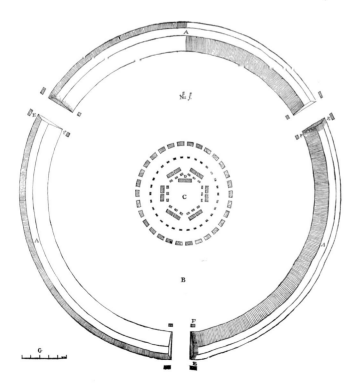

20 Above *Inigo Jones's drawing of the state of the monument in the early to mid-17th century on which his later reconstructions were based.*

21 Left *Inigo Jones's interpretation of the geometrical groundplan of the restored monument, 1655.*

22 Right *Inigo Jones's reconstruction, looking southwestwards, with his conjectured portal arrangement in the foreground.*

23 Below *Inigo Jones.*

1. *The Trench.*
2. *The Entrance thereat from the North-East.*
3. *The two Pyramids thereof, on the outside of the Trench.*
4. *The other two on the inside.*
5. *The Pylasters of the outward Circle, or Supporters of the open Gallery, as G. Cambrensis hath it.*
6. *The Architraves incumbent on them.*
7. *The Perpendicular Stones of the inner Circle.*
8. *The Pylasters of the greater Hexagon.*
9. *The Architraves that adorn them.*
10. *The Pylasters of the lesser Hexagon.*

by Daniele Barbaro. Jones must have found the final piece of information he required in a passage in which Vitruvius states that buildings of a hypaethral (open-to-the-air) style are most suited to particular gods: 'Temples are built, hypaethral and unenclosed, to Jupiter Thunderer, Coelus, the Sun and Moon; because these divinities are continually known to us by their presence night and day, and throughout all space.' Jones chose to attribute Stonehenge to Coelus, the Roman god of the sky or heavens. Apart from being open to the sky there is nothing within Jones's audacious interpretation of Vitruvius which fits Stonehenge. He interpreted the outer ditch and bank as the boundary of the sacred enclosure 'wherein the Victims for Oblation were slain and into which it was unlawful for any profane person to enter', a curious statement, as it demonstrates that he must have had only a cursory knowledge of Classical Roman temples; they were certainly not places of human sacrifice. This vision of Stonehenge includes a central 'cell' (the trilithon Horseshoe), described as the *Sanctus Sanctorum* where an altar was placed, having its 'proper position towards the east as the Romans used'.[2]

Jones's stated intention was to 'reduce into Design not only as the Ruin thereof now appears, but, as (in my Judgement) it was in its pristine Perfection'. Although his fabrication of an additional pair of trilithons and the forced symmetry of the reconstruction seriously detracts from the work, resulting in many dismissing him entirely, it must be remembered that Jones's description of the central stone arrays is the first composite account to be made of the monument, and his plan and elevation drawings represent the first field survey of this or any prehistoric monument in Britain.[3] As the king's surveyor, Jones was committed to spending a considerable amount of time at Stonehenge in measuring and recording. He did not entirely invent his raw material. Each of the elements that he used existed, but thereafter stones were mirrored, moved and multiplied into regular concentric geometric order, and pushed beyond all reasonable limits in order to fit his reconstruction.

Jones was also curious to know more about the foundations of the stones, and certain unspecified excavations were made. There is an account of his discovery of what he thought to be a pottery incense burner at a depth of about a metre below the ground within the centre of the monument, which he took to be further confirmation of his theory that the work was Roman.[4]

Other members of the royal court at this time were also fascinated with Stonehenge and the myths attached to it. The first person known to have dug there was William Harvey (1578–1657), the discoverer of the circulation of the blood, and physician to both King James and Charles I. Another royal physician, Walter Charleton (1619–1707), also took a keen interest in the monument. In his second edition of Jones's work, *Stoneheng Restored*, John Webb related that the site was also 'digged up … by Gilbert North, Esquire, brother to the Right Honourable the Lord North, and divers other persons at several other times'.[5] The Lord North to whom he refers appears to have been the 3rd Baron Dudley, who discovered the chalybeate springs at Tunbridge Wells in 1606 and popularized the salt springs at Epsom in 1618, both famed for their medicinal qualities.[6] This suggests that much of the interest may have been more than simply a preoccupation with the history of Stonehenge but perhaps, inspired by the folklore in Geoffrey of Monmouth's account which emphasized the curative properties of the stones, an attempt to find Geoffrey's fabled 'baths' or a sacred spring. That the stones may once have been perceived to be a prehistoric equivalent of Lourdes or Santiago de Compostela has recently been reconsidered.[7]

John Aubrey's Stonehenge

Forty years after Jones began his survey of the monument John Aubrey (1626–97) visited Stonehenge for the first time. Born in Wales, he spent his formative early years in Wiltshire where he was to develop a lifelong love of antiquities. The interruption to his education caused by the English Civil War meant that he was unable to finish his studies at Trinity College, Oxford; thereafter he never found a single subject to satisfy his insatiable curiosity. His character has been summarized by the novelist John Fowles as 'a genius who never completed anything' but also as 'a man who did more than anyone to point the way towards modern archaeology'.[8] Moving within the blossoming world of 17th-century scholarship, he is popularly known not for his antiquarian studies, but for his gossipy biographical work *Brief Lives* (first published in 1813). Yet he made a significant contribution to the study of antiquities in his *Monumenta Britannica, A Miscellany of British Antiquities*. Although not published in full until 1980, parts were copied and circulated and had been incorporated into Edmund Gibson's 1695 edition of Camden's *Britannia* and subsequent editions, so that even in its incomplete and chaotic form it was singularly the most influential work in the early history of British archaeology.

Aubrey's fieldwork started at Avebury in 1663 at the instigation of the king, Charles II, who had become interested in the debate raging between his physician Walter Charleton and John Webb as to the date and function of Stonehenge. (Charleton, in his *Chorea Gigantum or Stone-Heng Restored to the Danes*, published in the same year, favoured a coronation place for Danish kings rather than a Roman temple, an attribution utterly refuted by John Webb in his *Vindication of*

24 *John Aubrey.*

Stone-Heng Restored, published a year later.)[9] By 1666 Aubrey had recorded his own observations and produced a sketchplan of Stonehenge. His intention, judging from his manuscript notes, was to compare Inigo Jones's work with his own observations, 'being that which I took myself from the place, and according to the truth'; for although he had read Jones's work with 'great delight', he added 'there is a great deal of Learning in it: But having compared his Scheme with the Monument itself, I found he had not dealt fairly: but had made a Lesbians rule, which is conformed to the stone: that is, he framed the monument to his own Hypothesis, which is much differing from the Thing itself', giving Aubrey 'an edge to make more researches'.[10] John Fowles points out that Aubrey's 'delight' lay in no small part in the challenge presented by Jones's interpretation of Stonehenge as Roman work, for Aubrey was well aware that stone circles were relatively common in the remoter parts of Britain which lay beyond the major influences of Rome, including Ireland, which he had visited in 1660.

Aubrey's sketchplan, entitled *The Ichnographie of Stoneheng as it remains in the present yeare, 1666*, is shown in his manuscript at the same scale and on the opposite page to *The Ichnographie of Mr Inigo Jones*. His comments in the text are direct and unequivocal: the plan showing the restored hexagonal trilithon arrangement, which Jones had called the 'cell', was regarded by Aubrey to be 'absolutely false'. If it had been a Roman monument, 'certainly they would have made this Celle of some harmonicall figure; the Ruines of it doe cleerly enough shew … that it could neither be a Hexagon, or heptagon; nor can all the angles be forced to touch a circle', as Webb (and presumably Jones) had originally asserted. Nor did Aubrey believe in Jones's central altar stone for, referring it seems to other stone circles of which he had a particular knowledge, Aubrey states 'I find the middle of these monuments voyed'.[11]

Aubrey provided measurements of the various stone arrangements, and corrected Jones's dimensions and spacing of the stones. He sketched the trilithons in the correct horseshoe configuration, rather than a hexagonal arrangement shown by Jones. He accurately indicated those which were still standing, and marked five of the six surviving stones in the Bluestone Horseshoe, although he made no attempt to differentiate the surviving components of the Sarsen Circle. His plan and annotations contain several astute observations [25]. He recorded close to the bank circuit at least five 'little cavities in the ground' from which he supposed stones may have been removed. Excavations in the 1920s revealed that these hollows, named 'Aubrey Holes' by their excavators, were probably the result of the settlement of soft deposits in a ring of 56 former post settings. On Aubrey's plan the two surviving Station Stones are shown in more or less their correct positions, not flanking secondary entrances as depicted by Jones. He also noted the 'remains of the avenue', although its 'discovery' was credited to William Stukeley half a century later. The location of the large pit, which the Duke of Buckingham had dug in the centre of Stonehenge in 1620, was still visible over 40 years later and described by Aubrey: 'There remains a kind of pitt or cavity still; it is about the bigness of two sawe-pitts.'[12] Within the pit had been found, according to the Duke's chaplain, 'Stagges heads hornes and Bull's hornes and Charcoales'.[13]

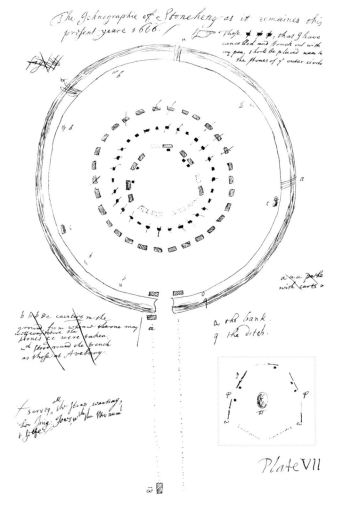

25 *Sketchplan (1666)
from John Aubrey's
Monumenta Britannica.
Inset: the location of
the Duke of Buckingham's
excavation trench in the
centre of the monument.*

Aubrey realized that stone monuments such as Stonehenge and nearby Avebury were so 'exceeding old, that no Bookes doe reach them',[14] laying wide open to questions the increasingly threadbare arguments about Merlin, Arthur and Ambrosius, the Romans, the Danes and myriad other spurious associations. Stonehenge was recognized for the first time as a truly ancient native British monument, 'a work of people settled in their country'. He identified stone circles as a distinctive class of monument that could be studied as a group; this he hoped to do 'by comparing those that I have seen one with another, and reducing them to a kind of Equation ... the Stones give Evidence for themselves'.[15]

It was whilst investigating the prehistoric works at Avebury that Aubrey made the association between megalithic monuments and the ancient 'Celtic priests', known to the Classical world as Druids. In truth it does not matter that Avebury's construction has now been shown to be over 2,000 years older than the first documentary reference to the Druids, for it was Aubrey's remarkable insight that was important. Assuming these monuments to have been ancient pagan temples, it is unsurprising that he linked them with the oldest known priestly order in Britain. A contemporary of Aubrey, the antiquarian Aylett Sammes (1636–79), who was the first to propagate the idea that Stonehenge had been built by the Phoenicians, was also responsible for the earliest iconic drawing of a Druid, firmly fixing for posterity his eccentric vision of the 'Celtic priest' which endures to the present day.

Edmund Gibson's *Britannia*

By 1695 Edmund Gibson (1669–1748), the new editor of Camden's *Britannia*, writing with the benefit of passages from John Aubrey's unpublished *Monumenta Britannica*, could say that 'the opinions about it may be reduced to seven heads', and summarized the theories then current – namely, that it was:

1 A work of the Phoenicians;
2 A temple of the Druids;
3 An old triumphal British monument erected to Anaraith, the goddess of Victory;
4 A monument raised by the Britons in memory of Queen Boadicea;

5 A temple built by the Romans;

6 The burial-place of Uther Pendragon, Constantine, Ambrosius and other Kings (and by default a memorial to the British slain by the Saxons);

7 A Danish monument, erected either for a burial-place, a trophy for some victory, or a place for the election and coronation of their kings.[16]

Gibson considered each of these proposals in turn. He asserted that it must first and foremost be seen as a British work: 'one need make no scruple to affirm, that it is a British monument, since it does not appear that any nation had so much footing in this kingdom, as to be Authors of such a rude and magnificent pile.' He was of the opinion that it was neither Phoenician, Roman nor Danish in origin, and discounted the suggestion that it was a place of burial for martyred Christian kings or warriors because ''tis strange, if so, there should be no Cross, nor any other token of the Christian Faith, upon this monument'. Nor could he reconcile the frequent discoveries of 'ashes and pieces of burnt bone here frequently found; by which it is plain, it was no Christian burial place', adding that both 'sacrifices and the custom of burning the dead grew out of use, upon the receiving of the Christian Faith'. On balance, he favoured a possible post-Roman date, the monument having been built 'in imitation of some of their structures', although he recognized that it was easier to refute the existing ideas than to 'deliver a true one'.[17] John Leland's astute eye for topography and his circumstantial use of artifactual evidence had earlier pioneered the process of archaeological enquiry. But when we look at Gibson's observations regarding the 'seven theories' we see something equally dynamic, for here is real archaeological evidence being used to construct a new perspective on Stonehenge. It is irrelevant whether the 'burnt bones' to which Gibson refers were actually human or animal: he demonstrates a rational appreciation of the potential of the previously inconsequential remains.

For his new edition of Camden's *Britannia*, Edmund Gibson had commissioned a fresh engraving of the monument by J. Kip, based not on first-hand observation but by updating the original view published in earlier editions. This resulted in the stones looking even more rustic in appearance, with the two boulders at the entrance now standing upright. By the time this

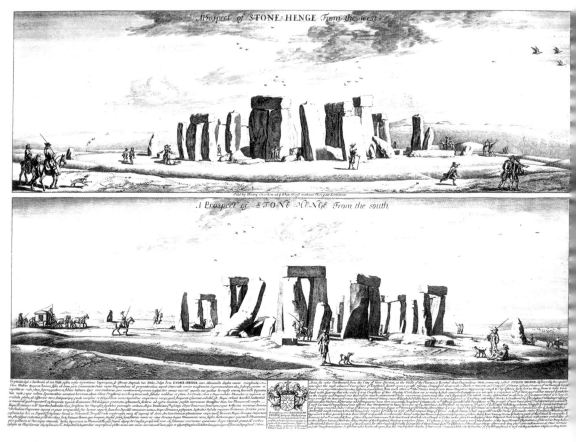

26 Opposite above *Stonehenge in Camden's* Britannia, *1600, 1607, 1610 and 1637 editions, left, and 1695 and 1722 editions, right.*

27 Opposite below *Two Prospects of Stonehenge: from the West (top) and South (bottom), engraved by David Loggan in the late 17th century.*

distorted and fanciful engraving was published, the artist and engraver David Loggan had produced two fine accurate perspective views of the monument [27]. These are the first detailed illustrations in which all the elements can be identified, including not only individual stones in the centre, but also the Station Stones and the Heelstone. Loggan was a contemporary of Aubrey. He had painted his portrait in 1686, and had been commissioned to provide further engravings of 'noble buildings and prospects' for inclusion in Aubrey's *The Natural History of Wiltshire*,[18] although none appear to have been completed before Loggan's death in about 1692. Four further prospects of the monument drawn by John Hassell at about this time provide further first-hand panoramic views, showing not only the monument but also the barrows and standing stones in the vicinity at the very beginning of the 18th century [60].[19]

The work of John Aubrey and the new antiquarians had opened the way to a past previously unknown to either oral or written tradition. Their empiricism and diligent fieldwork suggested that Stonehenge belonged to a time before Britain was a province of Rome, but how long before, and who built it, and why? If Stonehenge was pre-Roman, then it was obviously pre-Christian. The only possibility appeared to be that the 'ancient Britons' had constructed it as a temple, and that the authors of the monument were the Druids, the ancient priests of the Britons.

William Stukeley's Stonehenge

William Stukeley (1687–1765) was to bring Stonehenge from the world of antiquarian speculation firmly into the sphere of archaeological research. Whilst studying medicine at Cambridge in 1702, he had begun recording antiquities. In 1710 he undertook a series of extensive tours around England, eventually publishing his observations in his *Itinerarium Curiosum* (1725). He became the first secretary of the Society of Antiquaries in 1718; later in life he

61

28 *William Stukeley, 1727.*

was to be ordained as a clergyman. His medical train- ing and knowledge of dissection were to provide him with what was then a novel approach to under- standing aspects of the historic landscape. He noted the superimposition of ancient earthworks and the way certain ancient features had been cut through by later Roman roads, and realized that archaeological features were composite structures which displayed a temporal and contextual relation- ship, both of which could potentially reveal something about their origins and methods of construction.

Stukeley first visited Stonehenge in 1719 and was to return on numerous occasions over the next seven years. Critical of Aubrey's sketchy and inaccu- rate plans of the stones, he commenced his own measured survey [29]. He also drew reasonably accurate 'views' and 'prospects' of the monument and coined the term 'trilithon' for the stones of the Sarsen Horseshoe. It was Stukeley who first formally recorded the substantially degraded linear embanked earthwork (the 'Avenue') that approaches Stonehenge from the north east, and recognized that the axis of the monument was aligned on the summer solstice. In 1723 he discovered the parallel banks and ditches of the 'Stonehenge Cursus', the substantial nearly linear Neolithic earthwork lying just to the north (see Chapter 1).

Like many intellectuals of his day, including his friend, Sir Isaac Newton, Stukeley was convinced that the ancient world once possessed a body of knowledge which had been lost and corrupted down the ages. The key to these esoteric 'lost truths' lay largely in the deciphering of ancient texts and iconography; to these could now be added the enigmatic monuments which were beginning to be regarded as expressions of this knowledge. Stonehenge thus found itself at the forefront of this movement, as an archetype for all (then known) human history, and inextricably linked with an emerging sense of national identity. Yet scholars of the time had no other 'chronology', relative or otherwise, than those provided by the Bible and the Classical texts.

The biblical account of Creation was upheld by even the most learned men of the day. In the 1650s Archbishop James Ussher had calculated that the earth had been created in 4004 BC. So despite the new spirit of enquiry which stemmed from the growth of empirical observation, the traditional chronological framework remained essentially unchallenged.

Stukeley was now drawn into a spiral of speculation. As a doctor, antiquarian and fieldworker he was a keenly observant man, yet the more he surveyed and recorded, the more it appears that his work became encumbered with 18th-century quasi-religious and esoteric

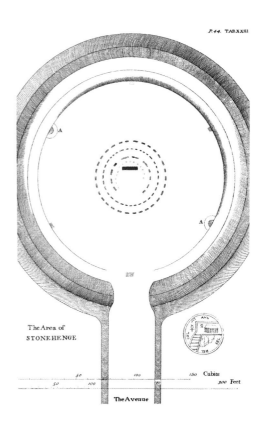

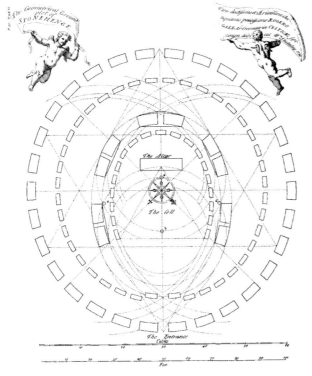

29 Above *William Stukeley's plan* The Area of Stonehenge, *1740.*

30 Left *William Stukeley's* Geometrical Groundplot of Stonehenge, *1723.*

preoccupations. If the antiquity of Stonehenge could be demonstrated, it was a very small step to bring it into line with his idea that it was a temple to the original monotheistic religion of the patriarchs. Yet to accept the cabalistic associations claimed for Stonehenge by Stukeley and others it had to be first recognized as a pre-Roman structure, and not all scholars were convinced of its ancient British origin. Stukeley had to find some other method of proving the antiquity of the monument.

One possibility was suggested by his friend Edmund Halley (1656–1742), the renowned astronomer, who visited Stonehenge in 1720, probably at Stukeley's invitation. In the same year he exhibited to the Royal Society a piece of polished sarsen from Stonehenge from which he deduced, from microscopic study of the weathering, 'that the work must be of an extraordinary antiquity, and for ought he knew, 2 or 3,000 years old'.[20]

Stukeley realized that, although the alignment of Stonehenge corresponded to the approximate midsummer sunrise, it did not 'correspond to the quantity precisely enough'. From this observation he concluded that the monument had been set up 'by the use of a magnetic compass to lay out the works, the needle varying so much, at that time, from true north'. He attempted to calculate the change in magnetic variation between the observed and theoretical (ideal) Stonehenge sunrise, which he imagined would relate to the date of construction. To achieve this it was necessary to introduce a 'calibration', which was apparently achieved, with Halley's help, by reference to 200 years of magnetic records. Halley concluded that geomagnetic variation followed a regular cycle, and that every 700 years the compass needle returned to the same point with regard to geographic north. Using this guide, three dates for the construction of Stonehenge were suggested: c. 460 BC, AD 220 or AD 920, the earlier date being the one accepted by Stukeley.[21] What they had attempted was a precursor to archaeomagnetic dating, a technique developed in the 1950s based on almost exactly the same principles of measuring temporal shift in geomagnetic declination, but applied to magnetically enhanced burnt deposits such as kilns and hearths. Stukeley and Halley's magnetic survey, and Halley's microscopic examination of the weathered sarsen, amounted to the first attempts to use scientific methods to date Stonehenge.

Inward View of Stonehenge from the high altar. Aug. 1722.

31 *William Stukeley's* Inward view of Stonehenge from the high altar, August 1722.

The potential astronomical significance of the solstice alignment had been recognized, but Stukeley needed further evidence of both the builders of Stonehenge and the method of construction. He sought the answer to the identity of those who built and used Stonehenge in the burial mounds which proliferate in the surrounding landscape. In 1722, just three years after Stukeley's first visit to Stonehenge, Lord Pembroke opened a barrow to the south, and the following year Stukeley himself opened a barrow 'close to the Cursus'. He was eventually to excavate a further 12 barrows in the parishes surrounding Stonehenge. Prior to these investigations, 'many from the great quantity of these sepulchral *tumuli* here, injudiciously conclude, that there have been great battels upon the plain, and that the slain were bury'd there'. However, their excavations showed small numbers of individuals of all ages, often accompanied by pottery, tools or weapons and ornaments, from which Stukeley concluded that 'they are really no other than family burying-places, set near this temple, for the same reason as we bury in church-yards and con-secrated ground'.[22] Clearly this was all in keeping with his view of Stonehenge serving as a 'patriarchal temple'.

There remained one further aspect that Stukeley needed to demonstrate; he was convinced that Stonehenge had been built using a biblical metrication system and therefore had to be based on 'cubits' (roughly defined as the length between the elbow to the tip of the middle finger, i.e. around 45 to 50 cm, sometimes more). Stukeley believed that 'Druids' cubits', as he chose to call them, determined the proportions of Stonehenge. The Bible gives extraordinarily detailed description of the logistics, design, construction and decoration of Solomon's Temple, accounts that provided an endless source of speculation in the 18th century, and were deemed to be steeped in hidden meanings. Isaac Newton is said to have 'spent more time on theology than he did on physics, using ancient sources in Latin, Greek and Hebrew to reconstruct the plan of Solomon's Temple'.[23]

Stukeley's increasingly alarming visions of a Druidic Stonehenge were eventually to eclipse his years of innovative field studies. His work entitled *Stonehenge, a Temple Restor'd to the British Druids,* published in 1740, was followed three years later by *Abury, A Temple of the British Druids.* By this time, 20 years after his original fieldwork, Stukeley's relatively harmless Druids had, through a convoluted process of reasoning supposedly based on Classical texts, mutated into devotees of serpent-cults, or Ophites; he saw Avebury as the principal and archetypal example, its avenues and ring forms representing what he described as his *Dracontia.*[24] His interpretation of Stonehenge undoubtedly coloured both the popular and academic view of the monument for over 200 years, and indeed, in part, persists today. The archaeological value of his earlier fieldwork is nevertheless undiminished. Richard Atkinson, the excavator of Stonehenge in the 1950s, has credited Stukeley with producing the earliest illustrated archaeological excavation report.

John Wood's survey

Amongst the increasing number of enthusiasts entering the Stonehenge arena was John Wood (1704–54), the architect who designed the Circus at Bath, a structure itself much influenced by the geometry of Stonehenge.[25] Wood's ideas about Stonehenge were truly extraordinary and unsupported by any sensible historical or archaeological evidence. Stukeley was appalled (for Wood dragged paganism into his patriarchal vision of Stonehenge), describing Wood's work as 'no more than the fermented dregs and settlement of the dullest, and most inveterate mixture of ignorance, malice, and malevolence'.[26] According to Wood, Stonehenge was modelled on the stone circles at Stanton Drew in Somerset, which he understood to have been a kind of 'Druidic university'. He elaborated on earlier antiquarian themes and asserted that, following the battle of Thermopylae and the sacking of Athens by the Persian king Xerxes I, Greek scholars had fled to Britain where they proceeded to 'instruct the Britons in the Liberal sciences'. In Wood's scheme, Stonehenge was thus clearly of Classical Greek origin, which he confidently described as a temple of the moon, and a place of human sacrifice.[27]

Because of his bizarre interpretation of the monument, Wood's considerable and historically significant contribution to Stonehenge studies has been largely overlooked. He was an extremely competent surveyor, and was wholly unimpressed by all previous attempts to produce a groundplan of Stonehenge. Inigo Jones's contrived 'Roman' reconstruction was clearly wrong, Aubrey's survey was sketchy and Stukeley's plan had been made with the assistance of 'a jobing Bricklayer and Mason of *Ambresbury*, whom he stiles an Architect'.[28]

Wood had further reason to comment adversely on previous surveys at Stonehenge, having met Gaffer Hunt, a 'venerable old man' who lived in a 'smoaky hut' close by the stones. 'In his Memory,' says Wood, 'no regular Survey had been taken of STONEHENGE; nor had any body measured it with that Accuracy which was necessary to obtain a real Plan of any part of it; though the Curiosity of many had led them to spend a great deal of Time in taking the Demensions of the Stones, and the Distances between them; for which purpose he himself always kept measuring Rods in his Cottage.'[29] Wood may have used an early theodolite, or an accurate quadrant. His detailed account of the survey shows he was certainly measuring angles to one twelfth (five minutes) of a degree, and seemingly, by interpolation, to around two minutes. Surveying instruments capable of this type of accuracy had been manufactured from at least 1725.

Wood's survey of Stonehenge is usually given as 1747, being the date of publication of his work *CHOIR GAURE Vulgarly called STONEHENGE* [32], though his plan actually records the condition of the monument in 1740, when the survey was undertaken. Wood was the first to make a truly accurate plan of Stonehenge, with hundreds of dimensions taken to a tolerance of one half, and even occasionally one quarter, of an inch. He was also the first to distinguish

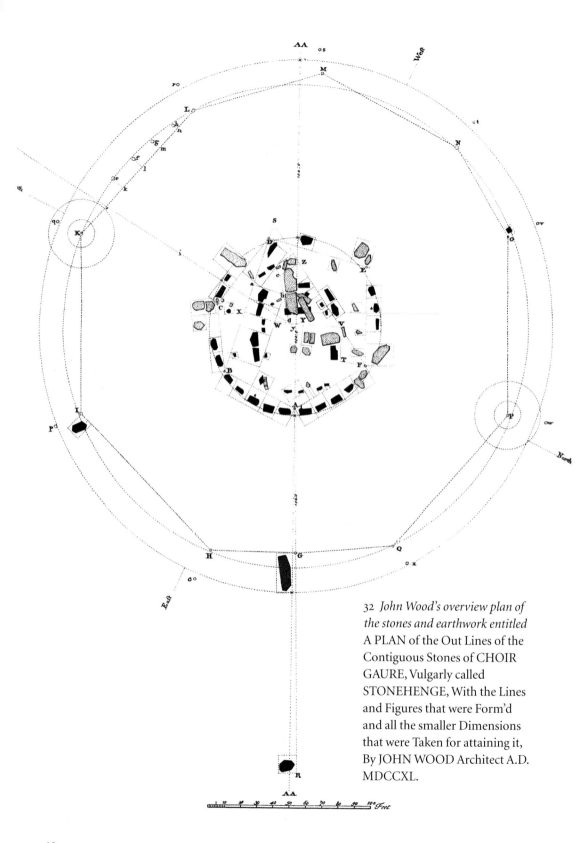

32 *John Wood's overview plan of the stones and earthwork entitled* A PLAN of the Out Lines of the Contiguous Stones of CHOIR GAURE, Vulgarly called STONEHENGE, With the Lines and Figures that were Form'd and all the smaller Dimensions that were Taken for attaining it, By JOHN WOOD Architect A.D. MDCCXL.

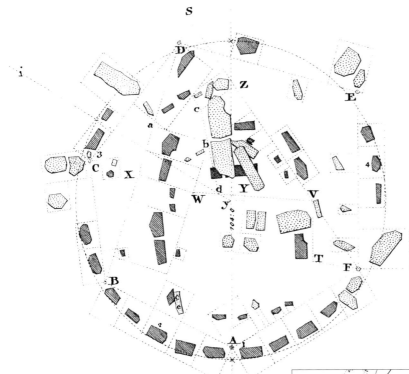

33 Left *John Wood's plan of the stone monument, as recorded in 1740. Standing stones are hatched and fallen stones stippled.*

34 Below *Detail from John Wood's survey of Stonehenge.*

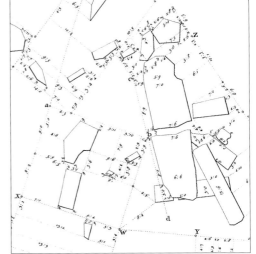

formally between 'the erect Stones in the Body of the Work, together with those in a Leaning Position, and such as are buried in the Ground from those that lye flat on the Surface of the Earth, or on the Surface of other Stones'.[30] There is no doubt that this plan is the most accurate record of the stones until Flinders Petrie's survey almost a century and a half later (see p. 80), and, importantly, Wood recorded the precise position of the western trilithon which was to collapse 57 years after his survey was completed.

Addressing his patron, Lord Oxford, Wood wrote, 'I have inserted every smaller dimension, as I took it, to convince Your Lordship of the Reality of my Survey; to shew you the possibility of measuring this Work with as much Minuteness as Monsieur *Desgodetz* measured the Remains of old *Rome*; and to present You with a Specimen of what every one ought to do that engages in taking the Plan of the Remains of a Work, the true Form and Size whereof is essential to the Knowledge of the Work itself.'[31]

Wood was familiar with the superbly detailed measured drawings of Roman monuments made by the young architectural student Antoine Desgodetz (1653–1728). A significant outcome of Desgodetz's work in Rome was to demonstrate that 'no common dimensional system prevailed and that the measurements of such renowned Renaissance authors as Serlio and Palladio were filled with inaccuracies'.[32] The same lack of uniformity at Stonehenge, in contrast to Stukeley's standardized Druidic cubits, is stressed by Wood: 'PERHAPS Your Lordship will be surprized at the great Irregularity which appears in almost all the Pillars of this Work by the Dotted Lines that I have applied to them: But You will cease to be so when You consider that in the most perfect Piece of Architecture *Rome* ever produced, the Porticoe of the Pantheon I mean, there are scarce any two Columns, or any two Intercolumnations equal and alike.'[33]

Stukeley did not appreciate the importance of Wood's survey, writing in his diary:

> 3. Aug. 1763. This day I read over Wood the architect's account of Stonehenge, written to contradict me. 'Tis such a heap, a ruin of trifling, nonsensical, impertinent and needless, mesuring of the stones, designed to be rude, as if they were the most nice and curious Grecian pillars in any of their capital temples; a tedious parade of twenty pages of feet, inches, halfs, and quarters.[34]

He failed to see the relevance of recording the exact positions of the stones. Stukeley was, however, doubtless justified in his criticism of Wood's conclusions regarding the function of the monument:

> The very best things in this book, he has pillaged from me – the design and nature of the work, the avenue, the ditch around, the 2 odd stones and cavitys thereon, even the word *trilithon*, all that is in any wise valuable, he takes from me, without the least acknowledgement; never uses my name but with a studied intent to contradict. The whole performance he stuffs with fabulous whimsys of his own crackt imaginations, wild extravagancys concerning Druids, without the least true foundation and knowledge concerning them.[35]

In the same diary entry Stukeley reveals that his antipathy towards Wood's presence at Stonehenge was so great that Wood's very 'entrance into this sacred enclosure, seems to me like Satan breaking over the hallowed mound of Paradise with no other than a murderous intent'.

The close of the 18th century

Before the end of the 18th century a very real 'lunacy' had gripped Stonehenge studies. Dr John Smith, an inoculator against smallpox, writing in 1771 in his *CHOIR GAUR; The Grand Orrery of The Ancient Druids*, thought that the Druids had erected it as a temple, 'to give a phase to the moon when she was six days old, and an egg-like form to the earth; which could not have been formed without two centres and which Dr. Stukeley seems to have had some notion of'. Smith, who has been aptly described as 'a worthy successor to Stukeley as the eccentric Medicine-Man of Stonehenge',[36] argued for 'an Astronomical Temple' and, on his own admission, commenced his alarming investigation 'without an Instrument, or any assistance whatever, but *White's Ephemeris*'.[37] He must, however, have been 'armed' not just with the almanac, but also with a copy of John Wood's plan, to which he added his own numbers and symbols. He did, nevertheless, make one or two additions, correcting a transcription mistake made by Wood in plotting broken fragments of the northernmost trilithon and revealing stones hidden by Gaffer Hunt's 'smoaky' hut, which had been removed in the intervening 30 years.[38]

As plans became circulated and more drawings and even models made, it was inevitable that Stonehenge would increasingly attract aficionados of the bizarre and irrational. Henry Wansey, writing in 1796, related a theory advanced by John Waltire, who 'endeavours to demonstrate that it [Stonehenge] has been immerged in the sea twelve miles deep; and that it was erected, judging by the precession of the equinox, at least seventeen thousand years ago'.[39]

A letter from Dr William Maton to A. B. Lambert documents a remarkable event. On 3 January 1797 'some people employed at plough, full half a mile distant from Stonehenge, suddenly felt a considerable concussion, or jarring, of the ground'. The 'concussion' was caused by the collapse of the westernmost trilithon of the Horseshoe (Stones 57, 58 and 158). The stones fell outwards in a west–northwest direction, the lintel, 'projected about two feet beyond the supporters, made an impression in the ground to the depth of seven inches, or more; it was arrested in its tendency to roll by the stone it struck whilst falling'. The stone struck by the lintel was one of the sarsens of the outer ring (Stone 21); it survived the impact, being only slightly displaced 'out of its perpendicularity'. Dr Maton suggested that:

> The immediate cause of this memorable change in the state of Stonehenge, must have been the sudden and rapid thaw that began the day before the stones fell, succeeding a very deep snow. In all probability the trilithon was *originally* perfectly upright, but it had acquired some degree of inclination long before the time of its fall. This inclination was remarked by Dr Stukeley, though it was not so considerable, I think, as is represented in his north view of Stonehenge.[40]

This sorry event brings to a close a most remarkable century, one in which the true antiquity of Stonehenge had finally been recognized, and its setting within an extensive prehistoric landscape first appreciated. Innovative methods of investigation, which were essentially archaeological in concept, had demonstrated the possibility of unlocking information from the examination of the material remains themselves. Historically, excavation had been motivated by the notion of treasure. An element of 'treasure hunting' remained, but the 18th-century barrow diggers were increasingly driven by a genuine spirit of enquiry, the relatively modest artifacts excavated often contributing to fashionable 'cabinets of curiosity', and later to the collections of local museums.

These objects were tangible links with a growing romantic vision of the past. The collection of antiquities demonstrated a level of cultural awareness which defined the intellectual and landed classes, and from which wealthy noblemen completed their education with a period of European travel. The primary destination of the 'Grand Tour' was Italy, with its ancient Roman monuments and newly discovered sites of Herculaneum and Pompeii. The tradition of the Grand Tour was to end in 1793 when France declared war on Britain, and from that time writers and artists, isolated from the continent, increasingly looked to their native landscape for inspiration. No monument in Britain inspired more awe than Stonehenge.

The work of the early 'gentleman archaeologists' was concerned largely with the investigation of the more obvious extant remains, but the Industrial Revolution had begun to have a significant impact on both the urban and rural landscape. Town development, the cutting of canals, mineral extraction pits and the building of railways were soon to reveal that the obvious upstanding monuments and visible earthworks represented only a fraction of the archaeological remains. The land surrounding Stonehenge became increasingly subject to cultivation at the expense of the traditional cattle and sheep grazing. Even in Stukeley's day some ploughing of the chalk downland had begun, and Stukeley himself was very much aware of the damage being done to the prehistoric earthworks on Salisbury Plain. It may be recalled that it was a plough team, working half a mile from Stonehenge, which heard the collapse of one of the trilithons in 1797. Some two centuries later, only the area immediately around Stonehenge remains as grassland.

Geologists too had begun to 'read' the clues which told the story of the earth's dynamic processes, including the superimposition of successive strata. James Hutton (1726–97) recognized that basalt and granite were once molten and that igneous material could thus intrude into earlier rocks, and that immensely long timescales were involved. In much the same way that Stukeley had interpreted man-made layers within barrow mounds and recognized the frequent recurrence of similar cultural artifacts, the geologist William Smith (1769–1839) identified geological strata and correlated them by comparing the fossils they contained. Hutton also confirmed in respect of natural agencies what the antiquarians and early archaeologists had acknowledged in terms of human activity for some time, when he wrote: 'the past history of our globe must be explained by what can be seen to be happening now … no powers are to be employed that are not natural to the globe, no actions to be admitted of except those of which we know the principle.'[41]

The 19th century: from excavation to astronomy

By 1800 the majority of the themes that were to preoccupy Stonehenge studies for the next 200 years had already been formulated. Medieval myth and tradition had presented a vision of Stonehenge as a monument to fabled British heroes; these ideas still found some endorsement, and even renewed support, in the 19th century.[42] The new antiquarians at first considered, then largely dismissed, Roman and post-Roman interpretations. The construction of Stonehenge they argued, and argued correctly, was ancient, and the builders were, in the absence of any real prehistory, the 'Celts' known from Classical accounts. But beyond that there was no consensus. Increasingly elaborate and fanciful explanations were explored, with biblical, pagan and Classical themes becoming entangled with ever more complex astronomical theories. Unfortunately, Aubrey's and Stukeley's Druids fitted comfortably into any scheme, for, depending on the viewpoint of the observer, they could equally be descendants of the sons of Abraham, pagan priests, Greek sages or Celtic philosopher-astronomers.

Sir Richard Colt Hoare (1758–1838) summarized the lack of progress in his *Ancient History of Wiltshire*, published in 1812: 'It is a melancholy consideration, that at a period when the sciences are progressively advancing, and when newly discovered manuscripts … throw a light on the ancient records of our country…that the history of so celebrated a monument as Stonehenge, should still remain veiled in obscurity.'[43] Colt Hoare [45] was in a better position than most to comment. In 1803 he began to sponsor a programme of fieldwork already being conducted by William Cunnington (1754–1810), a draper and wool merchant of Heytesbury, Wiltshire [45], who had taken a keen interest in geology and archaeology from an early age. Describing his first investigation at Stonehenge in 1798, Cunnington wrote in a letter to John Britton, author of *The Beauties of Wiltshire* (1801):

> I have also visited Stonehenge since I saw you, where, in digging with a large stick under those two very large stones which fell down about three years ago, I was much surprised to find several pieces of black pottery similar to those found on the above downs, among which was the bottom of a small vessel in form very like the bottom of a tumbler glass, but of the same black fine polished pottery above, which I used to think was Roman. I also found several bones of deer or sheep. From these specimens of pottery, the magnitude of this stupendous structure, and other circumstances, I am of opinion our ancestors (if I may so call them) were not so barbarous nor so ignorant of the arts as some suppose them when the Romans first invaded this isle.[44]

By 1801 Cunnington had already opened at least 24 barrows around Stonehenge, and in the following year he returned to Stonehenge to carry out excavations in front of the 'altar' stone:

> I have this summer dug in several places in the area and neighbourhood of Stonehenge, and particularly at the front of the altar, where I dug to the depth of five feet or more, and found charred wood, animal bones, and pottery; of the latter there were several pieces similar to the rude urns found in the barrows, also some pieces of Roman pottery. In several places I found stags horns ....[45]

He provided a little more detail in another letter to Britton in 1803:

> I have dug two or three times before the altar stone, once to a depth of six feet. At about three feet deep I found Roman and other pottery; at the depth of six feet some pieces of sarsen stone and three pieces of coarse half-burnt British pottery with charcoal wood ... I pledge myself to prove that the altar stone was worked with tools of some kind.[46]

There are also references to excavations 'within the area' (the earthwork enclosure) of Stonehenge at unspecified dates in which had been found 'parts of the heads and horns of Deer & other animals, & a large barbed Arrow head of Iron', the recovery of 'both Roman, British pottery, and animal bones' from the ditch[47] and the discovery of a hole beneath the Slaughter Stone.[48] Returning to Stonehenge for the last time in April 1810, Cunnington dug under the Slaughter Stone in the presence of Colt Hoare, Mr Crocker and 'an Irish gentleman', in order to confirm that this stone had originally stood upright.

By 1803 Colt Hoare had taken over not only the financing of Cunnington's fieldwork, but also the concept of publishing the results as *Ancient Wiltshire* in which, in the very opening line, he stated his intention to 'speak from facts, not theory'. There followed eight years of intensive excavation during which time they opened some 465 barrows, many in the landscape around Stonehenge. Their preferred method of excavating burial mounds was 'by sinking a shaft down to the centre, from top to bottom'. Cunnington had considered cross-sectioning (i.e. cutting across the barrows in the manner of Stukeley) but thought the shaft method better, for cosmetic rather than any archaeological reasons (though it was also usually the quickest way to access the contents). 'By the care we have always taken in refilling them, they, even now, almost bear the appearance of not having been opened.'[49] But in their efforts to identify the people who built the barrows, and by inference those who may also have been the architects of Stonehenge itself, Hoare could only admit that: 'After the result of ten years experience and constant research, we are obliged to confess our total ignorance as to the authors of these sepulchral memorials: we have evidence of the very high antiquity of our Wiltshire barrows, but none respecting the tribes to whom they appertained, that can rest on a solid foundation.'[50]

The first part of Colt Hoare's *Ancient Wiltshire* was published in May 1810; Cunnington died in December of that year. When his workmen replaced the turf on the last of their excavations, they brought to a close a remarkable phase of antiquarian activity and fieldwork that had been focused around Stonehenge and Salisbury Plain for almost 200 years. Other than a spate of further barrow digging by Dr John Thurnam, the medical superintendent of Wiltshire county asylum who opened numerous barrows between 1850 and 1873 to retrieve skeletal material,[51] very little happened within or around the stones for much of the 19th century. But there was to be a major change both in the way the past was perceived, and in the practice of field investigation. New ideas were to transform antiquarian curiosity and the collecting of artifacts into the fledgling discipline of archaeology. There was a pressing need to find a way of classifying the growing numbers of newly unearthed artifacts. Writing at the very beginning of the 19th century (before 1806), the Wiltshire antiquarian and friend of Colt Hoare, the Reverend Thomas Leman of Bath, had suggested:

> I think we distinguish three great eras by the arms of offence found in our barrows. 1st those of bone and stone, certainly belonging to the primeval inhabitants in their savage state, and which may be safely attributed to the Celts. 2nd those of brass [bronze], probably imported into this island from the more polished nations of Africa in exchange for our tin, and which may be given to the Belgae. 3rd those of iron, introduced but a little while before the invasion of the Romans.[52]

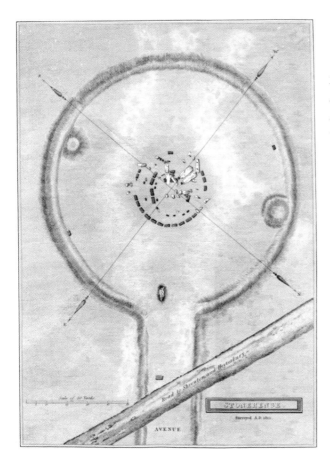

By 1818 the first curator of the Danish Natural Museum, Christian Jürgensen Thomsen, had formally proposed the adoption of the terms Stone Age, Bronze Age and Iron Age, a scheme he applied to the weapons and tools in his museum collection.[53] His assistant, and later successor as Director of the museum, Jens Jacob Worsaae, extended this Three Age System to include field monuments. His results, published in Denmark in 1843 and translated into English six years later as *The Primeval Antiquities of Denmark,* provided a firm basis for the study of prehistoric antiquities all over Europe, although the term 'prehistoric' was not coined until 1851.[54] By 1865 the Three Age System had been used by John Lubbock to suggest a relative chronology for 151 barrows in the Stonehenge landscape: only 39 contained bronze objects, and so the majority, being devoid of bronze, were therefore attributed to an earlier period.[55]

Sir Edmund Antrobus (3rd Baronet) had bought the Stonehenge estate in 1824, and until his death in 1898 further excavations at Stonehenge were routinely prohibited, and all pressure to restore any of the stones or tidy the monument strongly resisted. Societies such as the British Association and Wiltshire Archaeological and Natural History Society, and eminent archaeologists of the day such as Lord Avebury, John Evans, General Pitt-Rivers and Flinders Petrie, were all refused permission to excavate there. Rare consent seems to have been granted in about 1839 to a Captain Beamish from Devonport to dig in the centre of the monument 'in order to satisfy a society in Sweden there was no interment in the centre'. This resulted in a hole measuring 2.5 m square by 2 m deep being dug 'in front of the altar-stone, digging backward some little distance under it' which produced 'some bits of charcoal, and a considerable quantity of the bones of rabbits', probably from the relatively soft backfilling of earlier excavations.[56]

Subsequent unauthorized attempts to excavate were dealt with strictly. William Cunnington (one of William Cunnington Senior's grandsons) was to report in 1869: 'We are informed that a few months ago Captain ____ commenced digging at the foot of the largest trilithon, "for the purpose of finding how deep the stone was inserted in the ground". He was remonstrated with, but refused to desist till the police opportunely interfered and took him before a magistrate, from whom he learnt a wholesome lesson.'[57] A decade later William's brother, Henry, was to cross swords with the owner when, after reporting to the Wiltshire Archaeological and Natural History Society several episodes of his own illicit turf removal, he was forced to publish a public apology for trespass and damage in the Salisbury and Devizes newspapers.[58]

Despite the refusal to permit excavation, the fascination with the stones continued to grow. In 1867 Sir Henry James (Colonel of the Royal Engineers and Head of the Ordnance Survey) published the first photographic record of Stonehenge,[59] [36] and a decade later Charles Darwin was to conduct experiments into the dynamics and effects of earthworm activity on the settlement of three fallen sarsens.[60] The last quarter of the century saw the completion of a number of new surveys, the most notable being the work of the Egyptologist Flinders Petrie (1853–1942) in 1877, who chose Stonehenge as the first of a series of projected surveys (never completed) of megalithic monuments to determine the measurements employed by their builders, a technique (which he called 'inductive metrology') which had already proved successful in Egypt. His concern for accuracy is reflected in the fact that he

had a special surveyor's chain made for the project and claimed that the survey was measured to a fraction of an inch, with his 'plotting and copying' accurate 'to about a thousandth of an inch', although his published plan is unfortunately too small to be particularly useful. He numbered the stones (his system is still in use), distinguished between the varying outline of the stones at and above ground level, between standing and fallen stones, and sarsen and bluestone, and also added the original positions of five stones which had fallen or shifted markedly since they were recorded by Wood in 1740, for completeness. As a result of this survey, Petrie claimed to have detected not the single standard measurement ('Druids' cubit') advocated by Stukeley, but rather two distinct units: the first, associated with the earthwork, based on 'the 22.5 inch unit', to which he attributed a pre-Roman (Phoenician)

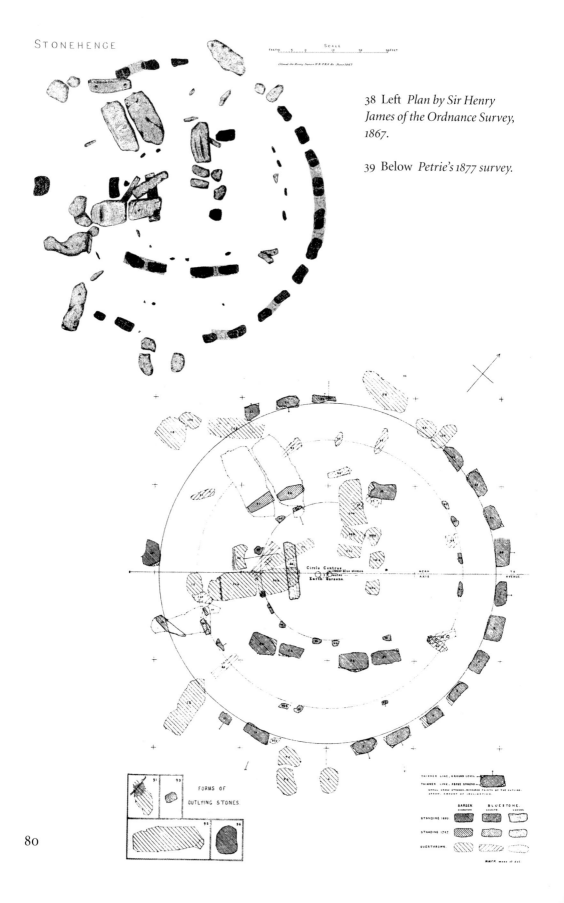

SCALE

38 Left *Plan by Sir Henry James of the Ordnance Survey, 1867.*

39 Below *Petrie's 1877 survey.*

FORMS OF OUTLYING STONES

origin, and the second, derived from the stone monument ('11.7 inch unit'), 'closely accordant with the Roman foot'. Petrie regarded Stonehenge as a skeuomorph, a massive stone version of structures normally constructed in wood which employed the carpentry methods of jointing the uprights and cross members, an idea which had been prevalent for several years.[61]

From astronomical calculations based upon the sun rising on the longest day behind the Heelstone, Petrie estimated the date of construction of Stonehenge to have been *c.* AD 730, which comfortably fitted his postulated post-Roman date for the monument, but these astronomical theories were not new. As we have seen, Stukeley and Halley had already attempted to determine the date from astronomical and magnetic declination in the 1720s. Other 19th-century calculations ranged widely.[62] Nearly 25 years later, in 1901, there was to be a renewed interest in the idea of dating Stonehenge by astronomical means when the eminent astronomer Sir Norman Lockyer, together with Francis Penrose, calculated the construction, based on a determination of the axis of the Stonehenge Avenue, to have been 1680 BC ± 200 years, later corrected to 1840 BC, remarkably close to the now accepted date.[63]

However, it is quite clear that fantasy still played no small part in the minds of many who refused, or were unable, to recognize the true antiquity of Stonehenge. A contemporary of Petrie, James Fergusson, the author of *Rude Stone Monuments* (1872), was yet again to resurrect Geoffrey of Monmouth's explanation, offered over 700 years previously, concluding that Stonehenge was indeed a cenotaph raised in memory of the British princes slain by Hengist.[64] The more imaginative proposed roofs of timber or stone; Christian Maclagan in 1875 was to interpret the whole structure as a military defensive work with a stone domed roof.[65] Amongst this confusion, however, were small but significant developments. Nevil Maskelyne, for example, pointed out that bronze tools would not work sarsen stone, and published the first petrological examination of the stones in 1878 and, although the exact provenance of the bluestones remained unknown, their igneous composition and exotic nature were formally recognized.[66] Sir Andrew Ramsay, at one time director of the British Geological Survey who had earlier been based in Tenby, Pembrokeshire, had suggested a possible Welsh origin for the 'foreign stones' (bluestones) 20 years previously.[67]

The founding of the Wiltshire Archaeological and Natural History Society in 1853 had done much to further academic interest in Stonehenge and its environs, and can also be seen as a pivotal point in engaging a wider audience in the monuments and antiquities of Salisbury Plain. Among the most significant 19th-century works published by the society is that of William Long entitled *Stonehenge and its Barrows* (1876), a major scholarly review of the monument partly based on material collected by Long's friend, the late John Thurnam.[68] Long both described the monument and summarized the theories then current regarding the date of its construction and its perceived purpose. If we add to Long's summary the ideas expressed by Edgar Barclay in 1895,[69] who considered the interplay of light and shadow within the monument, it is apparent that almost all the supposed 'new' theories advanced in the 20th century had already been proposed many years previously. In his *List of Authors on Stonehenge*, Barclay briefly reviewed the contrasting and often remarkable opinions of over 40 writers. This was followed in 1902 by a bibliography compiled by W. Jerome Harrison covering the literature of Stonehenge and Avebury, which totalled 947 publications by 732 authors.[70]

The story of the developing public interest in Stonehenge is a fascinating reflection of how the emerging idea of prehistory captured the imagination of the increasing number of day visitors, particularly after 1857 when the railway came to Salisbury. This popular interest is covered in Christopher Chippindale's classic account of the monument.[71] Letters began to appear in *The Times* noting its dilapidated state, urging greater care to be taken of the structure and that the practice of chipping off pieces as souvenirs should be discouraged. In the 1882 Ancient Monuments Protection Act, Stonehenge was entered on the first schedule. By 1899, when Stonehenge was (unsuccessfully) offered for sale, it was in a sorry state, with unsightly wooden props supporting many of the major stones and the single surviving upright of the Great Trilithon in danger of collapse. On the night of 31 December 1900 a raging gale wrenched a sarsen of the great outer ring from its socket and brought it crashing to the ground, tearing its lintel from its 4,500-year-old resting place and smashing it with such force that it broke in half, with one piece rolling a distance of almost 25 m to the west. There was now an urgent need to stop further damage; a new chapter in the monument's history was about to be opened.

The 20th century: excavation, consolidation and conservation

Engineering work to consolidate Stonehenge began in 1901 and followed a programme agreed between the new owner, another Edmund Antrobus (4th Baronet), and the Society of Antiquaries. The man appointed to oversee the project was Professor William Gowland (1842–1922), then associate of the Royal School of Mines and a Fellow of the Society of Antiquaries. Gowland was a chemist and metallurgist who had earlier worked for the Japanese government at the Imperial Mint at Osaka for many years. He was a keen amateur archaeologist in his spare time, specializing in the survey and excavation of Kofun-era tombs in Japan of the 3rd–7th centuries AD, and is today widely considered as the 'Father of Japanese Archaeology'.[72] Upon his retirement and return home, Gowland dedicated his time to archaeology and anthropology, and the metallurgical analysis of archaeological finds from the British Isles.[73] In the course of re-erecting the precariously leaning western stone of the Great Trilithon (Stone 56) [40], Gowland was to conduct the first of what was to become an extensive series of 20th-century archaeological investigations at Stonehenge.[74]

40 *Professor Gowland (centre) supervising excavations around Stone 56 prior to straightening, 1901, whilst two of his workmen are sieving the spoil.*

83

41 *One of the earliest aerial photographs of Stonehenge taken from an army balloon in 1906, shortly after the straightening of the upright of the Great Trilithon. This near-vertical photograph shows several sarsen uprights supported by wooden props, a situation which was not rectified until the early 1920s. The collapsed trilithon, which was re-erected in 1958, can be seen clearly. The fallen Slaughter Stone is seen towards the top left of the photograph. At this date the monument still provided a focus for a number of trackways.*

42, 43 Above *Photograph taken c. 1915 showing wooden props supporting many of the Sarsen Circle uprights.* Opposite *Lieutenant Colonel Hawley (front left with moustache and cap) with his workmen, 1919–20.*

Following the 1901 season nothing further was attempted until after the First World War. Stonehenge had by this time come into public ownership following its gift to the nation by Cecil Chubb, who had purchased the site at auction in 1915. The new work was carried out between 1919 and 1926 under the supervision of Lieutenant Colonel William Hawley (*c.* 1851–1941), appointed by the Society of Antiquaries [43]. He had occasional help from local archaeologist and draughtsman Robert Newall (1884–1978), but mainly he worked alone, employing a small team of local labourers. Hawley began by straightening and consolidating Stones 6 and 7 of the Sarsen Circle (although still upright and bearing a lintel, the group had moved dramatically out of position), and further stones were straightened in the following season. Eventually the focus shifted to curiosity-driven excavation. Intentions were sound, but the problems presented were too complex to be resolved by the ambitious but relatively immature discipline of early 20th-century field archaeology.[75]

Hawley identified what he described as 'The Stonehenge Layer', essentially a horizon of stone chippings lying immediately below the turf, described by

a later archaeologist, Richard Atkinson, as 'a rubbly layer composed of fragments of natural flint, chips of the Stonehenge stones, both bluestone and
sarsen, and miscellaneous rubbish representing the whole span of the site's
history'. Hawley saw this deposit as an intervening layer between the early
earthwork and the construction of the stone monument 'dividing that
period from any other which preceded it'.[76] Although rather an oversimplifi-
cation of this ubiquitous, poorly defined layer, the idea was sound since the
absence of stone chips within buried features tended to indicate, though not
necessarily prove, an early date for their filling. In 1920 Hawley and Newall
examined John Aubrey's 1666 sketchplan, noting his comments regarding
'certain depressions, or cavities', observed at intervals within the circular
earthwork (see above). Although none were visible on the ground, by using a
steel bar as a probe they located and subsequently excavated several, to which
they gave the name 'Aubrey Holes'. Hawley was later to discover two further
series of concentric holes (known as the Y and Z Holes) and to recognize the
presence of cremated human remains both within the Aubrey Holes and the
fill of the ditch. The evidence was synthesized by Robert Newall in 1929.[77]
In his penultimate interim report of 1926 Hawley had concluded by saying:
'I am sorry that the result of research should have been so unproductive of
matter having any direct bearing upon the history of the place. The more one
digs the more the mystery appears to deepen.'[78] With hindsight his investigations, which succeeded in removing a substantial part of the archaeological
deposits within the eastern half of Stonehenge, may be lamented, but they
cannot be retrospectively criticized, for he had both the approval and later the
financial support of the Society of Antiquaries. These excavations reflect no
more than a premature attempt at solving some of the outstanding questions
relating to the date and possible use of the monument. What eventually
emerged was a new model for the phasing of construction of Stonehenge, one
which is essentially correct in principle.

At the same time that Hawley was starting his work at Stonehenge,
Herbert Thomas of H.M. Geological Survey was able to confirm the source
of the bluestones from petrological examination: 'They are to be matched in
all their macroscopic and microscopic details with the dolerites that outcrop
along the Prescelly Range [West Wales], especially in the outcrops of Carn

Meini and Cerrig Marchogion.'[79] He was in no doubt that the bluestones had been brought to Stonehenge by human agency, selected for a reason other than their physical properties, possibly stones derived from a pre-existing stone circle in which the locality was particularly rich, rather than glaciation, a contention which has been subject to considerable debate ever since.[80]

The first widely available popular account of Stonehenge was written in 1916 by Frank Stevens, Curator of Salisbury Museum. For over 30 years this was the principal handbook to the monument before being replaced, in 1953, by Robert Newall's Official Guidebook, published in several editions by the Ministry of Public Building and Works. In 1924 Herbert Stone published *The Stones of Stonehenge*, which reviewed many of the important structural details, drawing on Petrie's plans and the results of the early 20th-century excavations.

Intermittently, between 1950 and 1964, Professors Richard Atkinson and Stuart Piggott (in the early years assisted by Dr John Stone and R. S. Newall) conducted further excavations (in 1950, 1952–54, 1956, 1958–59 and 1964). Their investigations were initiated by remedial work to stabilize or re-erect

44 *Stuart Piggott (left), Richard Atkinson (with cigarette holder) and John Stone (right) making a latex mould of the carvings on Stone 53, in 1956.*

87

stones, particularly the raising of the trilithon which had fallen in 1797 (Stones 57–58 and 158). In addition, some of Hawley's trenches were reopened and new areas investigated. Richard Atkinson (1920–94), former Assistant Keeper of Archaeology at the Ashmolean Museum in Oxford and latterly Professor of Archaeology at University College, Cardiff, was an innovator. He was the first in Britain to experiment with archaeological geophysical survey (the detection of subsurface features using electronic methods) and, together with his friend and colleague Stuart Piggott, explored practical aspects of excavation and field recording. In 1956 Atkinson summarized the archaeological evidence for the general reader in his book *Stonehenge* (revised in the light of later excavations in 1979).

Stuart Piggott (1910–96) held the Abercromby Chair of Archaeology at the University of Edinburgh from 1946 to 1977. In his youth he served a form of archaeological apprenticeship, working his way to the top through practical experience without taking a degree. He assisted with many excavations in the 1930s, favouring the Wessex region where he was later to direct work on several major monuments. Before the Second World War he had defined what he termed the 'Wessex Culture', characterized by the rich Bronze Age burials which lie scattered across the chalkland of southern England and notably in the vicinity of Stonehenge. Piggott had published a perceptive review of Stonehenge in 1951 which refined the two-phase model suggested in Hawley and Newall's earlier chronology.[81] His new three-phase model began with an earth-and-timber late Neolithic to early Bronze Age monument comprising the earthwork, the Aubrey Holes, and 'just possibly a central timber structure on the site of the present stone settings'. This was followed by a grand construction in stone approached by the Avenue, with a final phase occupied only by Hawley's Y and Z Holes, at that time thought to have been later prehistoric or even Roman in date. Piggott's dating was largely based on his extensive knowledge of prehistoric sites and artifacts. He also supported the idea advanced by Petrie that Stonehenge was a stone translation of a wooden structure, drawing a parallel with Buddhist shrines of the 2nd century BC known from Sanchi in India, where he had served during the war. 'A circular lintelled fence of uprights and cross-bars, approximately of the same diameter as the outer sarsen circle at Stonehenge, is rendered in very sophisticated stonework but with all the timber features (including mortice-and-tenon joints) preserved.'[82]

Piggott's sequence was essentially correct, but radiocarbon dating was about to significantly alter the chronological perspective of prehistory. Five years earlier, in 1946, Willard Libby of the University of Chicago had proposed that the then recently discovered 5,730-year half-life of a naturally occurring radioactive isotope of carbon (carbon-14) might be used to determine the age of material which had once formed part of the living biosphere.[83] In 1950 a charcoal sample from an early Stonehenge context (Aubrey Hole 32) was dated using radiocarbon methods, a momentous first step in understanding the true temporal setting of Stonehenge. The 1979 edition of Atkinson's *Stonehenge* was to provide a revision of the phases of construction, which in turn have been subject to revisions following further reappraisals of the original radiocarbon determinations.

Large areas within the centre of the monument, much of which had already been heavily disturbed by antiquarian digging and the remedial engineering work of the early part of the 20th century, were laid bare to the solid chalk by Atkinson and Piggott in the 1950s programme. Ambiguous features excavated by Hawley in the 1920s were re-examined and discovered to be placements of an early dismantled bluestone setting, and given the name Q and R Holes. In 1953, prehistoric carvings depicting daggers and axe heads were recognized on several of the sarsen uprights. The year 1964 saw the end of the extensive excavations and engineering works.

Within the next two years, Gerald Hawkins, Professor of Astronomy at Boston University, published *Stonehenge Decoded,* which further explored the potential astronomical significance of the monument. Hawkins's innovative approach used newly available, though still relatively primitive, computers to advance the idea that Stonehenge was 'a sophisticated and brilliantly conceived astronomical observatory'.[84] Earlier astronomical theories had been largely concerned with alignments; Hawkins, however, took the ideas further in suggesting that Stonehenge was itself an early computer, a notion which exceeded not only the earlier interpretations but also the limits of the archaeological evidence. This hypothesis undoubtedly caught the mood of the times and, despite proving extremely controversial and being utterly refuted by many (including Atkinson), it certainly reinforced the popular image of Stonehenge as a complex astronomical device, a concept that found favour amongst many outside the world of archaeology.

Atkinson briefly returned to Stonehenge in 1978 with Alexander Thom (1894–1985), an Oxford Professor of Engineering who had a life-long interest in megalithic structures and archaeoastronomy, and who, famously, introduced the concept of the 'megalithic yard', a revision of Stukeley's idea of an exact system of prehistoric measurement.[85] Together they investigated the stonehole of the missing Station Stone (Stone 94) which formerly stood within the 'North Barrow'. In the same year John Evans re-cut a previously investigated part of the ditch to extract environmental samples, an excavation which was by chance to expose the burial place of an adult male of early Bronze Age date cut into the upper silts of the ditch. Further small projects have been undertaken outside the monument: in 1967–68 Mrs Faith Vatcher, assisted by her husband Lance, examined areas on the opposite side of the modern road in advance of the construction of the car park and road widening, and in 1979–80 Michael Pitts, then Curator of the Alexander Keiller Museum, Avebury, excavated the route of a telephone cable which was being laid along the roadside precariously close to the Heelstone, revealing a hole immediately to the northwest which may have been the setting for a second stone.[86]

The history of Stonehenge throughout the 20th century has veered between revelation and regret, edged by no small amount of controversy. Private ownership, which ultimately allowed the monument to fall into a sorry state of decay, was replaced by state management and three phases of restorative engineering work. Two of these were followed by programmes of excavation driven largely by opportunity and curiosity; consequently the archaeological horizons which remain intact are regarded today as all but inviolable deposits. Stonehenge was granted World Heritage Site status in 1986, and in 1995 the results of a major research project by Wessex Archaeology, commissioned by English Heritage to assemble all the surviving primary records of the 20th-century work, were published, the archive being deposited at Salisbury Museum.[87] Currently a decision is awaited as to the removal of the unsightly visitor centre and the re-routing of the A303 trunk road which seriously detracts from the site's setting. A measure of the radical change in the modern conservation approach to Stonehenge and its landscape may be gauged by the contrast between recent projects to reintroduce the great bustard onto Salisbury Plain from Russia and the part played by Frank Stevens, a former curator of Salisbury Museum, who related how, in his youth (at the end of the 19th century), he dined on the last of them.[88]

Over the past 1,000 years the quest to explain when, by whom and why Stonehenge was built has ranged from medieval Arthurian legend to the investigation of the atomic structure of buried carbon. The 'when' has been largely answered by modern archaeology, using methods which would have been utterly inconceivable to the antiquarians who first challenged the accepted myths and fantasies of the Middle Ages. As to the second question, 'who' built Stonehenge, recent excavations are now beginning to illuminate the remarkable world of the Neolithic communities of Salisbury Plain. The most intriguing challenge remains: 'why' Stonehenge was built. Archaeologists have long recognized that questions of motive are the most difficult of all to answer. What was inside the minds of the people who expended such extraordinary effort? What inspired the form, and determined the exact and careful placement of each stone? Several hundred years of speculation means that it has now become all but impossible to approach Stonehenge unencumbered by ideas which presuppose the construction had a 'use' defined in terms of a calendrical and astronomical function. Such themes tend to be exclusive, offering a selective route to a hypothetical 'true' answer, but closing doors to alternative explanations; the starting point is often not the body of the archaeological evidence at all, but a theory which forms a mould into which disparate elements appear to fit.

Hopefully the reader will now be aware of the origins of both the ancient and modern myths; it is time to move on and take a closer look at the remains themselves. There is integrity to be found both within the standing monument and revealed by myriad buried features which suggests that we may be looking prematurely beyond the stones for complex answers to what may well be simple concepts. The archaeological record provides pointers to the methods, formulae and solutions used by the prehistoric surveyors which

45 Top *John Wood, c. 1735, left; William Cunnington, 1808, centre; Sir Richard Colt Hoare, 1795, right.*

46 Above *Sir John Soane's architectural students surveying at Stonehenge in the early 1800s.*

47 Opposite *Overview of fieldwork, publication and restoration 1500–1964.*

may take us a step closer to understanding the motives behind its construction. The following chapters will look at how these often small details provide vital clues to help us unravel the elusive design of Stonehenge.

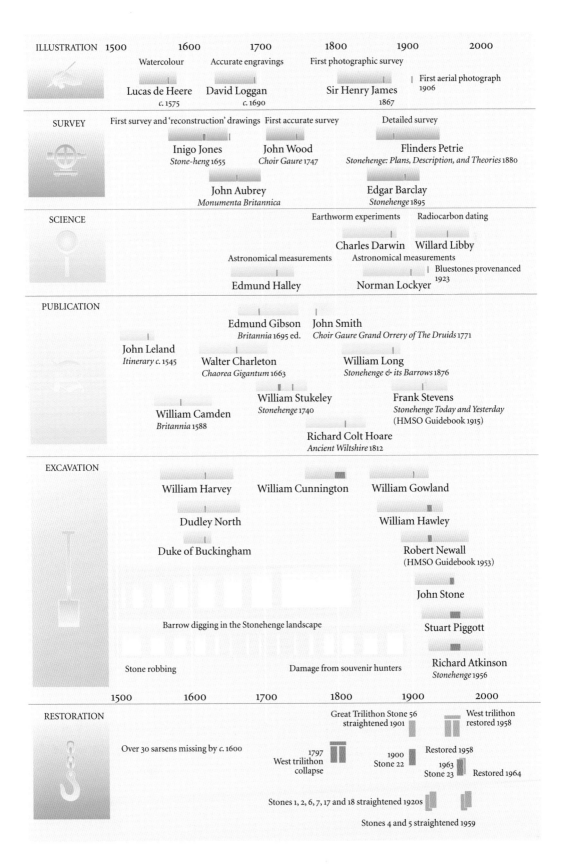

ILLUSTRATION
1500   1600   1700   1800   1900   2000

Watercolour   Accurate engravings   First photographic survey

First aerial photograph
1906

Lucas de Heere   David Loggan   Sir Henry James
c. 1575   c. 1690   1867

SURVEY

First survey and 'reconstruction' drawings   First accurate survey   Detailed survey

Inigo Jones   John Wood   Flinders Petrie
Stone-heng 1655   Choir Gaure 1747   Stonehenge: Plans, Description, and Theories 1880

John Aubrey   Edgar Barclay
Monumenta Britannica   Stonehenge 1895

SCIENCE

Earthworm experiments   Radiocarbon dating

Charles Darwin   Willard Libby

Astronomical measurements   Astronomical measurements   Bluestones provenanced
1923

Edmund Halley   Norman Lockyer

PUBLICATION

Edmund Gibson   John Smith
Britannia 1695 ed.   Choir Gaure Grand Orrery of The Druids 1771

John Leland
Itinerary c. 1545   Walter Charleton   William Long
Chaorea Gigantum 1663   Stonehenge & its Barrows 1876

William Stukeley   Frank Stevens
Stonehenge 1740   Stonehenge Today and Yesterday
(HMSO Guidebook 1915)

William Camden
Britannia 1588   Richard Colt Hoare
Ancient Wiltshire 1812

EXCAVATION

William Harvey   William Cunnington   William Gowland

Dudley North   William Hawley

Duke of Buckingham   Robert Newall
(HMSO Guidebook 1953)

John Stone

Barrow digging in the Stonehenge landscape   Stuart Piggott

Richard Atkinson
Stone robbing   Damage from souvenir hunters   Stonehenge 1956

1500   1600   1700   1800   1900   2000

RESTORATION

Great Trilithon Stone 56   West trilithon
straightened 1901   restored 1958

Over 30 sarsens missing by c. 1600   1797   1900   Restored 1958
West trilithon   Stone 22
collapse   1963   Restored 1964
Stone 23

Stones 1, 2, 6, 7, 17 and 18 straightened 1920s

Stones 4 and 5 straightened 1959

CHAPTER 4

The Early Earth &
Timber Monument

The earthwork enclosure

The first major structural event on the site of Stonehenge appears to have been the creation of a substantial chalk bank formed from material excavated from the encircling ditch. An excellent agreement between the radiocarbon dates from animal bone and antler found in the base of the ditch indicates that the earthwork was built shortly after 3000 BC.[1] The construction of this circular earthwork established the 'footprint' and geometry of the monument, and the space it defined was to become so important that it was reused, at times with great effort and much embellishment, for a further 1,500 years.

Although broadly placed within the tradition of Neolithic monuments of the 'henge' type, the Stonehenge earthwork is atypical in having its bank inside, rather than outside the ditch. Enclosing an area of only 7,000 square metres, it was certainly not among the most pre-eminent prehistoric features of the Neolithic Wessex chalkland. Morphologically amongst the closest known parallels are the circular earthworks at Flagstones House, near Dorchester in Dorset and Melbourne, Cambridgeshire.[2] A further important similarity between them is that, unlike many other contemporary constructions, all three were quite carefully and purposefully marked out on the ground [48].

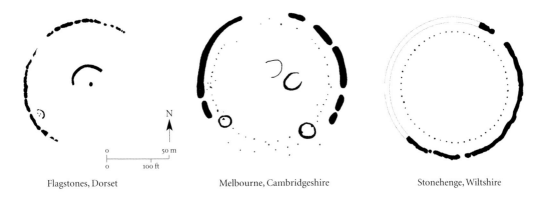

N

0   50 m

0   100 ft

Flagstones, Dorset   Melbourne, Cambridgeshire   Stonehenge, Wiltshire

48 *Two examples of contemporary sites with comparable morphology to the early Stonehenge earthwork.*

The ditch

Extensive archaeological excavation by Hawley in the early 1920s emptied just over half the ditch circuit (on the south and east sides). A complex history of silting was revealed, with periods of local and deliberate prehistoric backfilling. The ditch follows a reasonably well laid-out circle. The width varied between 2 and almost 5 m. The sides were originally steep – in places almost vertical especially towards the base – and the bottom was generally flat, varying from 1.4 m to over 2 m in depth. The ditch almost certainly began as a series of pits dug at various points around the intended circuit which were then extended laterally, leaving numerous partly excavated segments between them.

Simple but effective tools had been used: pickaxes made from the antler tines of red deer[3] and shovels improvised from the scapulae (shoulder blades) of oxen, with wicker baskets to convey the freshly broken chalk rubble from the excavation face. The probable reason why the ditch was cut laterally in this way lies in the tools used, which would have been much more effective at cutting into vertical or near vertical faces than in digging downwards, the effort of cutting sideways being aided rather than hindered by gravity. An additional, and very useful, implementation would have been the use of timber sheets in the base of the cutting, onto which the loosened material would have fallen making it easier to lift off with the shovel, the 'shovelling boards' being

progressively moved forward as the cutting face progressed. Primitive plank-
ing or even strong wicker hurdles would have sufficed, which may partly
account for the straight, facet-like sections, the generally flat appearance of
the Stonehenge and other prehistoric ditch bases, and also for what Hawley
described as 'foot-trodden chalky mud' encountered at the bottom of the
ditch, below the general level of the rubble of the primary fill;[4] this is precisely
the kind of layer which forms beneath boards used as temporary working
surfaces in the bases of modern excavations.

Most of the excavated chalk was dumped on the inside of the circuit to
form the bank, the rubble extending almost as far as the inner lip of the ditch,
without an intervening ledge (or berm). No attempt was made to disguise the
irregularity of the ditch, and remains of the upstanding 'walls' of chalk
between the various segments were left substantially untouched. This type of
segmented excavation had been typical of Neolithic ditches for hundreds of
years before the Stonehenge earthwork, and indeed was characteristic of
causewayed camps such as Windmill Hill, some 35 km north of Stonehenge.

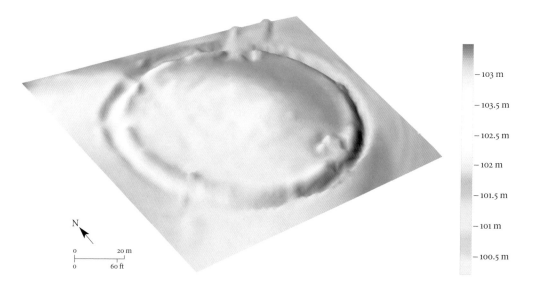

— 103 m

— 103.5 m

— 102.5 m

— 102 m

— 101.5 m

— 101 m

— 100.5 m

N

0   20 m

0   60 ft

49 *Computer model of the Stonehenge topography looking northeast (with vertical
exaggeration). The section of ditch excavated by Hawley in the 1920s on the east side of the
circuit, which was only partly backfilled, contrasts markedly with the unexcavated section
to the west. The ground rises c. 3 m from east to west.*

50 *Hawley's cutting across the ditch on the east side of the circuit, looking southeast (1922).*

Here, three massive concentric interrupted ditch circuits, over 2 km in total length, had been cut around the top of a low chalk hill.[5] The Stonehenge and Windmill Hill ditches are not greatly dissimilar in width and depth, although it should be stressed that the diversity and nature of the 'cultural material' found within the ditches of causewayed enclosures, usually interpreted as gathering places, are markedly different from that found at Stonehenge. Compared with many other early engineering achievements the Stonehenge ditch, with a total length of around 345 m from which an estimated 3,000–3,500 tons of chalk was removed, was a relatively small undertaking; the total ditch circuits at Windmill Hill measured over 2 km, whilst at neighbouring Avebury the Neolithic monument is surrounded by over 1 km of ditch (12–15 m wide and over 6 m deep), from which an estimated 167,500 tonnes of chalk had been extracted using similar implements to those found in the Stonehenge ditch.[6]

On the southeast side of the circuit, at the base of the ditch and below a layer of clean white chalk, Hawley found a cremation burial. It lay 'within a bowl-shaped cavity in the solid chalk', implying that it had been deposited whilst the ditch was relatively fresh, which seemingly provides evidence for

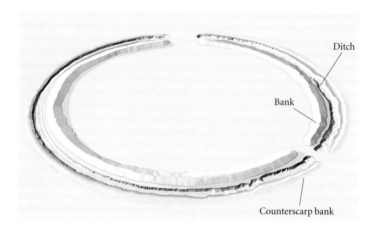

Ditch

Bank

Counterscarp bank

51 Model showing the freshly dug earthwork as it would have appeared c. 2950 BC, looking northeast.

very early deposition of human remains at Stonehenge. Although he found several other cremations in the ditch, this burial is particularly unusual as most were clearly later, having been somewhat haphazardly inserted into the ditch as it silted.[7] From the scarcity of wood ash in the ditch cremations, compared with those discovered in other parts of the site, he inferred that these bones 'had been carefully taken out of the mass of the fire',[8] implying a tradition either temporally or culturally distinct. The ditch also contained flint tools, struck flint, food bones and several deliberately placed ox bones (at least two skulls and two lower jaws). The jaw bones had been placed in the ends of the ditch on either side of the southern entrance, whilst one large broken ox skull had apparently been introduced into a cavity cut into the silt at the bottom of the ditch. A radiocarbon date obtained from this skull (estimated to be between 3510 and 2920 BC) indicates that the animal had died before the earthwork had been constructed. The generally accepted explanation is that this was a significant 'curated' item of symbolic value, already of some antiquity when it was deliberately buried in the base of the newly cut ditch; the second ox skull was found just west of what may have been a third small entrance in the southwest ditch sector.

Very little pottery was found in the primary ditchfill, reinforcing the nature of the site as a non-secular earthwork, making it more difficult than usual to obtain dated sequences of activity, in contrast to domestic occupation sites. Only three pottery sherds of distinctive Neolithic Grooved Ware were recorded by Hawley from two locations.[9] A curious feature was found in the very bottom of the ditch west of the southern causeway: 'a small long hole 2 in. to 3 in. [5–7.5 cm] in diameter, apparently the core of a long stick which had decayed' in the compacted chalk.[10] This horizontal void, at least 1.4 m long, may represent an abandoned Neolithic survey pole or marker.

During its early use the ditch was occasionally locally cleaned, whilst at other times there were periods of deliberate backfilling, often with clean chalk, perhaps derived from excavating further features within the enclosure. Natural weathering and erosion gradually caused the ditch substantially to silt up [52]. Occasionally human and animal bone fragments, as well as human cremations, wood ash and charcoal, were deposited in this 'secondary' fill. The ditchfills were further confused by subsequent turbation caused by burrowing animals.[11] Almost all the archaeological arguments focusing on the deposits in the ditchfills and their relationships with the history of the construction of the monument remain unresolved as few

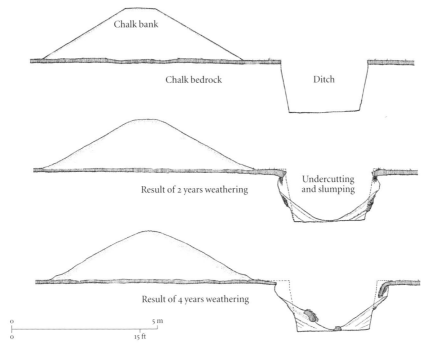

52 *The effects of weathering of a bank and rapid silting of a ditch over a four-year period, based on the results of the experimental chalk earthwork at Overton Down, Wiltshire.*

significant relationships were determined by the 1920s excavations. There is, however, clear archaeological evidence that the ditch was almost full by the time the major stonework was complete, not least because an early Bronze Age burial was cut into its upper fill.[12]

The bank

The bank stands on a base 6 m wide and has a diameter (from crest to crest) of almost 100 m. It is now extremely denuded and nowhere survives more than around 40 to 50 cm high. The best-preserved section lies in the south-west quadrant – in other places it has almost entirely disappeared, although the original height is estimated to have approached 2 m.[13] When newly constructed the enclosure must have been an impressive sight, the bank being given the appearance of increased elevation by the dazzling clean face of freshly exposed chalk on the ditch sides. Richard Atkinson suggested that this internal bank formed a barrier between 'the sacred and the secular, or the initiated and the profane', an opinion largely influenced by the casual and erratic nature of the ditch cut compared with the perceived order and symmetry of the bank, the ditch 'having no meaning, in itself, as a structural or symbolic feature' being merely a 'quarry for material to build the bank'.[14] However, examination of what survives of the bank shows it to have been no more accurately laid out than the ditch, the segments echoing the slightly irregular geometry of the faceted ditch cuts.

There has been hardly any archaeological investigation of the bank and very few contemporary artifacts have been found incorporated into the surviving rubble core (Hawley recorded two sherds of what he thought to be Bronze Age pottery together with a few fragments of sarsen stone). Cremation burials had been cut into the eroded bank at several locations, which is further evidence of the relatively rapid demise of the earthwork.

An investigation by Atkinson in 1954 revealed three holes, approximately 20 cm in diameter and spaced 50 cm apart, running along the spine of the bank in the southeast quadrant, about 30 m from the minor southern causeway. The evidence is ambiguous. The discovery of quantities of bluestone fragments within the bank rubble in the vicinity of these holes may indicate a disturbed later context, possibly the remains of a timber palisade or barrier

53 *Postholes running along the crest of the bank, just east of the southern entrance, excavated by Atkinson in 1954. The Heelstone and markers for Hawley's excavated Aubrey Holes are visible in the top left corner of the photograph.*

contemporary with the stone monument, the posts having been set into sockets dug through the bank long after it had been eroded by weathering, thereby re-establishing a perimeter to the monument at a much later date.[15] However, as the holes have more of a resemblance to 'post-pipes' (i.e. the voids left where a post has rotted *in situ*) than to postholes (i.e. cuts to insert timbers) it is quite possible that the timbers had been erected at regular intervals along the centreline of the footprint of the bank before or during its construction. What is certain is that they cannot have been inserted soon after the bank was built, as it would have been too high (2 m) for a post setting to have been cut through.

A small amount of the chalk rubble dug from the ditch was placed around its outer lip, forming what is often called a 'counterscarp bank', a term borrowed from earthwork fortifications, where an outer low bank was set on the down-slope of a ditch. This outer work may have originally been several metres wide, indeed geophysical survey suggests it to have been almost as wide as the main bank,[16] although it was probably quite a low construction, perhaps not much more than 75 cm high. John Wood noticed it in 1740 when he described Stonehenge as being 'almost surrounded with a double bank of

Earth separated by a ditch'.[17] Although almost imperceptible now, this bank, like its counterpart on the inside, is important to the archaeology of Stonehenge, because it preserves beneath it a buried prehistoric land surface.

The entrances

There are two, possibly three, entrances into the enclosure where sections of the ditch have been interrupted to create causeways. The principal entrance lies on the northeast, originally perhaps 12 m wide, and there is a smaller entrance on the south side; a third may have existed to the southwest. Although almost half the ditch remains unexcavated, geophysical survey has indicated no further major breaks in the circuit.[18]

On either side of the entrance causeways the ditch terminates in wide, deep, and well-defined pits. These are somewhat more pronounced and formalized versions of those present elsewhere within the segments of the ditch. Hawley recorded that two 'craters' at the principal entrance were the only places where fires of any consequence had been lit in the bottom of the ditch.

The principal entrance and causeway

In 1923 Hawley discovered a pattern, almost a 'grid', of 53 postholes on the causeway between the ditch terminals; it is possible that others have been destroyed by wheel ruts (cart tracks that have cumulatively etched into the chalk cross the eastern side of the entrance). Most were related by size, geometric arrangement and by their clean chalk rubble fill, although within the group are several larger anomalous holes which lie on a different trend and are entirely unrelated. It can also be clearly seen from his excavation photograph [54] that two postholes were exposed in the very end of the eastern terminal of the ditch, giving the impression that they were asymmetrically displaced eastwards across the causeway. It is inconceivable that substantial timber uprights could originally have been erected on the very lip of the open ditch, so the conclusion must be that the posts had stood there *before* the ditch was dug, or were partly cut into the backfill of re-deposited chalk when the entrance was subsequently widened.

Hawley's method of excavating the ditch was by 'sinking a transverse trench of 3 ft and afterwards advancing by vertical sections of a foot'.[19]

His workmen were already at the bottom of the ditch and working north-westwards when they were 'stopped by a nearly perpendicular wall of solid chalk, 4 ft 9 in [1.5 m] high, evidently a causeway across the ditch'.[20] Not only was the ditchfill being quarried against a vertical face, but the turf had not even been removed, for it was only after his unexpected encounter with the 'chalk wall' that the surface of the undisturbed chalk, into which the ditch had been cut, was exposed. It is more than likely therefore that the workmen had mistakenly cut a little beyond the actual end of the ditch, slicing through the postholes on the edge of the causeway. Somewhere in this mêlée the relation-ship between the causeway postholes and the ditch terminal was lost, together with precise dimensions of the original entrance with which an early align-ment might have been associated.

Several other features seem to have been cut by the ditch, or by where the workmen deemed the sides of the ditch to be. The majority of these lay in the final 15 m stretch approaching the eastern terminal of the main causeway from the south. The most enigmatic is a substantial stonehole which Hawley

54 *Hawley's excavation of the entrance causeway, looking northwest, showing the eastern ditch terminal and two rows of postholes running across the causeway; these are the more substantial of a series of six concentric settings discovered at this location in 1922. A second line of 4 major post settings is aligned at 45 degrees.*

described as having 'a portion of it being exposed in the side'. This hole measured 1.06 m by 0.9 m and extended 0.9 m into the chalk bedrock. Its fill was
'chalky rubble' and within it were found the 'bones of a young person about
the age of eight or nine, consisting of fragments of ribs and femurs and bones
of the lower extremities', together with four pieces of clean white sarsen stone.[21]

Hawley's work was to reveal that early in the history of the monument, and
before any depth of silt had accumulated in the base of the ditch, the principal entrance of the early earthwork was enlarged to the east by backfilling a
10 m stretch of the ditch with chalk. It is interesting to note that amongst the
earliest photographs of Stonehenge, taken from an army observation balloon
in 1906 (before any sections of the ditch were excavated), is one which clearly
shows the original ditch circuit continuing half way across the Avenue as a
darker band in the turf. Hawley was clearly unaware of this early narrow
entrance, for, having anticipated finding a terminal close to its junction
with the Avenue on the east side, he found that the ditch 'continued on an
unaltered course independently of the proximity of the Avenue', and that
from this point onwards the profile and nature of the ditchfill changed significantly. Archaeologist Maud Cunnington, who must have visited Hawley's
ongoing excavation, was convinced that the absence of silts in the early ditch
terminal meant that it must have been infilled almost immediately after it
was cut.[22]

The southern causeway

At the southern extremity of the ditch circuit a second section of chalk was
left intact. This provided an entrance which may originally have been c. 3.5 m
wide. That this was intended to be a formal, though seemingly minor,
approach to the interior of the earthwork is reinforced by the discovery of
deliberately placed cattle jaw-bones in the ditch terminals on either side.
Atkinson, however, was for some reason doubtful that it was an entrance,
believing that 'probably the only intentional gap in the circular earthwork is
the entrance causeway on the northeast side'.[23] There is certainly a corresponding break in the bank on the south side, but then there were several gaps
elsewhere in the circuit, some having been enlarged and distorted by tracks
which were still in use until relatively recently, though none, to judge from the

English Heritage geophysical survey, relates to reciprocal unambiguous discontinuities in the ditch. The idea of a small formal southern entrance to the monument is also supported by the discovery by Hawley of a series of postholes within the enclosure approximately aligned on this causeway, which are often, though somewhat optimistically, described as a 'passageway'. A narrow third entrance, perhaps partially blocked by the digging of a pit, may be represented by a 1-m wide block of undisturbed chalk in the ditch circuit, located 22 m to the west of the southern entrance. This interpretation is supported by the discovery by Hawley of a domestic cattle skull in the base of the ditch terminal immediately to the west, which is taken to have the same 'structural' or ritual implication as the cattle skulls deposited in the termini on either side of the southern entrance; radiocarbon dating showed the bones to be of a similar age.[24]

The Interior

The centre

There is anecdotal evidence to suggest that 'bulls' heads' (i.e. the skulls of oxen) have been found in the centre of Stonehenge on more than one occasion; this is sometimes taken to imply that it was not only within the ditchfill that deliberate deposits of animal bones were placed. However, no 20th-century excavations were able to substantiate this, and we can only conclude that the interior has been too badly disturbed by antiquarian activity to know exactly what originally lay within the centre of the monument. Moreover, John Webb's statements in 1655, relating the discovery of animal skulls at locations both within and near the monument, is clearly not an exclusive reference to a single votive deposit in the centre.[25]

The positions of previous holes and trenches dug within the stone circle were revealed in the dry summer of 1994, showing as bleached parchmarks in marked contrast to the green turf over apparently undisturbed zones. One such mark, for which no excavation record is known, may be the large hole dug by the Duke of Buckingham in the 1620s (and still partly open 40 years later, see Chapter 3), although other antiquarians were also known to have dug here. Hand augering by Wessex Archaeology on the edge of this area confirmed the presence of 'loose soil' (backfill), rather than solid chalk beneath the turf.[26]

The Aubrey Holes

Sometime during the early use of the enclosure – perhaps from its inception – a ring of 56 pits was cut in a near perfect circle running just inside the tail of the chalk bank and some 5 m from its median line. It is not entirely clear whether the hollows noted by John Aubrey in 1666 (see Chapter 3) represent the tops of these pits, but his notes certainly led to their discovery by Hawley, who explained how they were found: 'Aubrey mentions and marks on his plan certain depressions, or cavities, at intervals within the circular earthwork. None of them were visible to us, but with a steel bar we searched for and found one, and subsequently more, all apparently at regular intervals round the earthwork.'[27]

Importantly, the Aubrey Holes are the first early accurate manifestation of the circular internal geometry which was later to be reflected in the precision of the major stone construction phase. They display no 'alignment' whatsoever, nor do they even acknowledge the existence of the narrow early entrance causeway; the widest gap in the circuit, between Holes 53 and 54, lies over 12 degrees west of any axis which might be inferred from a line projected between the ditch terminals. If any directional emphasis was given to the array it is not apparent from the excavated plan, and could only have existed within the vertical component of the structure.

Thirty-four of the holes have been excavated, 32 in the 1920s by Hawley and Newall (mainly by the latter), and two by Atkinson in 1950. One of the holes (Hole 46) appears to have been cut into by Cunnington and Colt Hoare in the 19th century when they investigated the low chalk mound known as the 'North Barrow'. Three more were revealed by Hawley beneath the 'South Barrow'; these appeared to have been disturbed and one of them, closest to the modern track edge, contained brick. There are very few stratigraphic or intercutting relationships recorded between the Aubrey Holes and other Stonehenge features beyond the fact that they clearly pre-date these two enigmatic 'Barrow' earthworks. The chalk rubble deposits in the bottom of the holes contained none of the bluestone fragments which have found their way into the bases of many other intrusions within the earthwork, and it appears that they were dug, and received their first deposits, before the stones were brought to the site, or at least before any substantial working of stone took

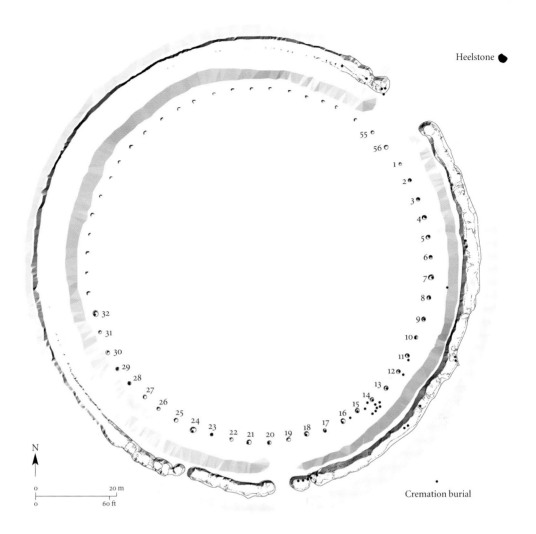

Heelstone

55 ○
56 ○
1 ○
2 ○
3 ○
4 ○
5 ○
6 ○
7 ○
8 ○
9 ○
10 ○
11 ○
12 ○
13 ○
14 ○
15 ○
16 ○
17 ○
18 ○
19 ○
20 ○
21 ○
22 ○
23 ●
24 ○
25 ○
26 ○
27 ○
28
29 ●
30 ○
31 ○
32 ○

N

0   20 m
0   60 ft

Cremation burial

55 *The Aubrey Holes (only the excavated holes are numbered) and the subsequent distribution of cremation burials in both the holes and the earthwork (cremations are shown as black dots).*

place. Considerable care had been taken in both establishing the circuit and in fixing the spacing between the centres of the pits. If they date from the same period of activity which saw the construction of the enclosure earthwork, or shortly afterwards, then their position provides the best indication of where the exact centre of the first phase of the monument lay.

Hawley interpreted patches of clean chalk found at several locations in the ditch, which were interleaved with the silt, as material derived from the original digging of the Aubrey Holes. If this interpretation is correct, both the evidence of the partly silted ditch and the fact that the intervening bank would have been substantially eroded (and no longer a major barrier) imply that an interval of some time would have elapsed before the holes were dug. However, as no direct link can be made between the chalk horizons in the silt and the digging of the Aubrey Holes, Hawley's interpretation must remain speculative.

Archaeological excavation has shown the holes to be roughly circular, varying in diameter between 0.74 m and 1.82 m, and in depth between 0.56 m and 1.14 m. All were cut directly into clean undisturbed chalk, and have been described as either 'pits or postholes'.[28] The greater part of the filling of all the holes was 'earthy chalk rubble', interpreted as the remains of packing around timbers, while five holes (AH 9, 16, 18, 28 and 29) had 'brown earth' or 'humus', which may represent infilling where timbers or broken stumps of posts had been left to rot *in situ*. Another four holes (AH 6, 8, 21 and 25) had humic fill just in their centres, again implying that posts were formerly present, although here they may have been deliberately removed before they decayed, allowing soil to enter the voids.

The current interpretation is thus that the Aubrey Holes originally contained substantial posts of around 40 or 50 cm, perhaps up to 60 cm in diameter, requiring the digging of large deep holes to secure them. An explanation for the varying depths may be provided by the topography of the site. Today, the ground within the Stonehenge enclosure is about 1.5 m higher on the west side. Had it been the intention to set a ring of similar-sized posts with their tops more or less level, a considerable adjustment would have been needed to accommodate such a slope. There are only two ways this could have been achieved: either the down-slope posts needed to be taller, or the up-slope posts had to be set in deeper postholes. The three deepest holes so far excavated (AH 28, 29, and 32) are all situated on the highest part of the site, suggesting that allowances were indeed made to allow for the rising ground.

The posts were eventually removed, and it appears to have been at this stage in their history, or shortly afterwards, that cremated bone and artifacts found their way into the majority of the holes. This is unlikely to have been a single event. It may be that the posts were pulled out over a period of time, or some had already substantially decayed at the base and were thus incapable of being removed intact, the soft sunken deposits providing an opportunity to place cremated remains within what was still a sacred enclosure. Whatever happened, most of the original post sockets were not left vacant, for there is little indication of silting, only deliberate infilling, although the occurrence of burning within some pits suggests that they had been open at some time. Hole 10, for example, showed *in situ* burning which had scorched the sides; others appear to have had fires in their bases which had not apparently extended as far as the pit sides.

Eventually almost all the Aubrey Holes were to contain cremation burials or cremated bone fragments, sometimes randomly dispersed with the fills (though some of this is undoubtedly the result of post-depositional turbation which has caused Roman pottery and even modern bottle glass to find its way into the matrix of material in some of the holes). These cremations are consistent with the disparate and dispersed nature of the cremations found within various stages of the ditchfilling, implying an extended period with sporadic activity, although Hawley was careful to differentiate between them. Unburnt bone skewer pins (which may have fastened bags containing the cremated remains) were found in five of the Aubrey Holes, but only two were found in the ditch. It may be significant that cremations were conspicuously absent from the three Aubrey Holes fronting the widened principal entrance (see below).[29]

Other finds from the Aubrey Holes include worked flint, which being the most obdurate of materials finds its way into many contexts. Few of these pieces were actually tools of any kind, although in Hole 22 a large collection of worked flint was unearthed, several of whose pieces could be joined back together, implying that they had been worked on the site from a single flint core. Further stone fragments, both bluestone and sarsen, were ubiquitous, and sarsen stone mauls were also recovered, although all the stone came from the secondary deposits or from within the fills of later intrusions. Antler and animal bone was also relatively common.

The accuracy with which the Aubrey Holes were set out shows they were created at the same time for a common purpose (see Chapter 8). On present evidence they are most likely to have been post settings which, having served their purpose, became the focus for a variety of subsequent activities. The difference in depth of the up-slope holes hints at a concern for some structural consideration. The idea that these pits had been created primarily to receive cremations is untenable as cremated bone is absent from the lower fills – or at least none has been securely identified as belonging to a primary context. Perhaps the soft sunken deposits of earlier post settings were seen as both 'sacred', by association with the former structure, and opportunist in respect of their being reasonably visible for a long period and easy to re-cut. The building of timber circles within earthworks is generally in keeping with later Neolithic tradition, although if the Stonehenge earthwork and the Aubrey Holes are contemporary, as they appear to be, they would represent one of the earliest known examples in Britain.[30]

It was noted above that the community using the Aubrey Holes for cremation burials does not appear to have placed them in the three holes which spanned the wide entrance. This may be significant, but cannot be taken as conclusive evidence that the cremations were deposited after the modification of the entrance, or that they necessarily belong to the period when a new alignment, and perhaps the first stones were introduced, for at least three of the other excavated holes also lacked cremations; but it is suggestive.

Post settings in the interior

A large number and variety of holes have been dug within the interior of the monument. Excluding the principal stone settings and Aubrey Holes, over 200 such holes are currently known, some of which belong to clearly related groups, whilst others are isolated or so badly damaged that any potential relationships have been destroyed by later activity; all are enigmatic. The centre has been particularly heavily cratered by successive phases of construction and later disturbance, including diggings by numerous antiquarians. This activity, together with the considerable natural erosion of the chalk bedrock, has truncated and entirely removed the ground surfaces which would have been contemporary with any timber arrangements standing within the enclosure.

A popular Stonehenge myth has arisen in recent years suggesting that some sense can be made of these holes.[31] It should be recognized that nothing exists within the pattern of putative postholes that can confidently be identified as forming a structure to which any purpose or function can be applied.

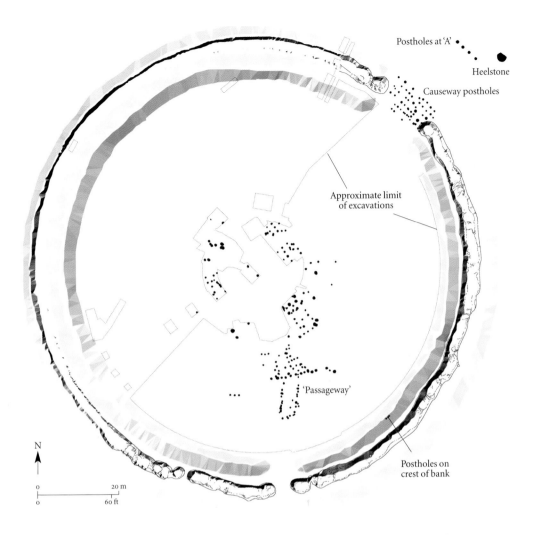

Postholes at 'A'

Heelstone

Causeway postholes

Approximate limit
of excavations

'Passageway'

N

0   20 m
0   60 ft

Postholes on
crest of bank

56 *The distribution of postholes. There is generally insufficient evidence to assign a date to the disparate groups or ascribe any function to their pattern. The causeway group is shown in more detail on p. 173.*

What survives is a complex of disparate, badly recorded post settings and pit-like intrusions from which imaginary constructions have been created by 'joining-the-dots'. Most significantly, there is no evidence from either the nature of the holes, their contents, or their geometry to support the idea that Stonehenge ever contained a central 'roundhouse' or funerary structure.

There are, however, some postholes which, by comparing size, depth, distribution and fills, may be considered as forming potential groups. The most convincing pattern of structural post-settings are 20 or so holes which align approximately on the southern causeway and lie some 19 m north of the southern entrance. Here, two rows spaced 3.7 m apart form what Hawley described as a 'corridor'-like arrangement just over 7 m in length (i.e. a configuration roughly twice as long as its width). Both sets of posts were associated with what were described as broad 'furrows'; the west furrow being the most pronounced at 50 cm deep, the east 30 cm. The eastern row forms an almost straight line, whilst the west is somewhat irregular. The overall form of the arrangement, indicated by the two northernmost posts on each side, and the southeast post, fix three corners of an accurate rectangle. From the southeast corner of this rectangle a line of three posts extends 3 m to the southwest. The description of the timber settings as a 'passageway' is based essentially on the observation that its long axis points approximately towards the causeway of the southern entrance, and because Hawley thought them too shallow to represent postholes of a more substantial structure; but when he was writing in the 1920s the fact that substantial chalk erosion had removed a considerable amount of the prehistoric ground surface was not appreciated. This 'passageway' shows no relationship with the geometry or symmetry of the enclosure; it does not lie on a radial from the middle of the

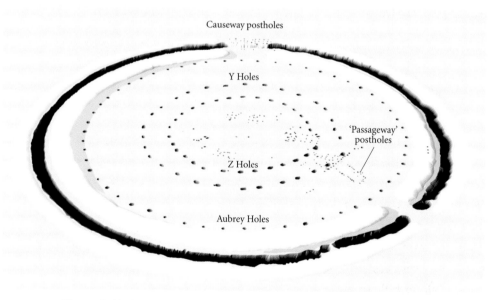

Causeway postholes

Y Holes

'Passageway' postholes

Z Holes

Aubrey Holes

57 All recorded holes in the interior, excluding stone foundations.

monument but deflects 14 degrees to the northeast. It has been forced to take on a meaning which it may or may not warrant. No stratigraphic or artifactual link exists between these posts and any of the Stonehenge phases of construction or use.

There is even less coherence to be found amongst the remainder of the postholes; some form tenuous groups and alignments, and fleeting elements of both linear and curvilinear arrangements appear to be present. Others may have played a temporary role in the constructional activity associated with the major stone phases, a few may even be related to much more modern activities such as stalls erected at the annual fairs held here from the end of the 17th century. Firm conclusions cannot be drawn from the perceived groupings, and there is certainly insufficient evidence to write any kind of 'early history' of Stonehenge from such poorly understood features.

Postholes outside the earthwork

In the 1920s several pits and postholes were discovered beyond the northeast causeway, between the banks of the Avenue. These intrusions, cut into previously undisturbed chalk, included an alignment of four regularly spaced postholes, 1.8 m apart, running on a northwest–southeast alignment, at a distance of 20 m from the centre of the entrance causeway. Known by archaeologists as the 'Postholes at A' [58], they are interpreted as the sockets for timbers between 50 and 70 cm in diameter.

Hawley described them as resembling those found on the causeway and considered them to be early in the Stonehenge phasing as 'the Avenue bank passed over the first and partly over the second'.[32] The most southerly of these postholes is cut into an infilled trench which perhaps served as a construction ramp for either the Heelstone or its neighbour. As a group they lie some 74 m distant from the centre of Stonehenge. Inevitably these undated post settings have been incorporated into various and often complex alignment and sightline theories. Importantly, there are other post settings which lie at a similar distance from the centre of the monument. Two were found on the eastern side of the Avenue, spaced 80 cm apart. Excavations by Mike Pitts in 1979–80 found another hole on the verge of the road northwest of the main group, which could equally be part of this series. No other posts were found in the

16-m wide space between the outer circuit of the causeway postholes and these outlying timbers; a case therefore exists for considering them as a group, and perhaps the radius of *c.* 74 m as a significant dimension within the scheme of the early earth and timber monument (see Chapter 8).

In the 1960s three large postholes and part of a substantial northeast–southwest 'palisade' were found during the construction of a car park and visitor facilities to the northwest of the monument. The three postholes, which were determined to have contained substantial pine timbers up to 70 cm in diameter, were spaced *c.* 10–12 m apart on an east–west alignment; the posts appear to have rotted *in situ*. The settings were initially thought to have been late Neolithic in date. Their discovery was greeted with some excitement by some archaeoastronomers, who found little difficulty in fitting them into a complex pattern of Stonehenge solar and lunar 'sightlines' that embodied 'a remarkable combination of astronomical alignments, right-angle triangles, and measurements based on a standard unit of length'.[33] However, radiocarbon dating has subsequently demonstrated that the posts were much earlier than first thought, and are actually of Mesolithic date (8500–7650 BC); that these posts were pine is also in keeping with the nature of the 'open mixed pine and hazel woodland' of the early Mesolithic period. A 4,000–5,000-year gap in the archaeological record is more than sufficient grounds to argue against any idea of continuity of 'sacred' function.

The palisade running on a southwest–northeast trend was discovered about 75 m to the northwest of the Stonehenge earthwork. The palisade posts, originally a series of abutting timbers each 25–35 cm in diameter, were set in a 'V' profile trench some 2 m wide by 1.4 m deep. A stretch nearly 11 m long was revealed, which included one side of a break or 'entrance', the width of which is unknown. Relatively clear traces of the former posts were still visible, suggesting that the timbers had been left to decay in the ground, although there was also evidence for some later re-cutting of the ditch itself. A late Bronze Age burial had been inserted into the terminal showing that the ditch had been almost completely filled in by the middle of the 1st millennium BC, although a sinkage hollow must still have been evident, providing a focus for the burial. The palisade ditch has been traced from aerial photographs and geophysical survey for several hundred metres north of Stonehenge on a

58 *Hawley's 1923 excavation across the Avenue, looking east along the line of the A344.*
The cutting revealed the Avenue earthworks, the so-called 'Postholes at A' (in the foreground),
and the Heelstone ditch. The large depression visible in the centre contained Hawley's putative
Stonehole B and the beginning of a large area of disturbance descending towards the Heelstone,
variously interpreted as a construction ramp or possibly the original hollow from which the
Heelstone was extracted. A large bowl barrow is visible in the middle distance to the right of
the Heelstone.

roughly southwest–northeast alignment. What might have been a continua-
tion had been excavated some years previously (in 1953) by Richard Atkinson
at a location close to the 'elbow' of the Stonehenge Avenue.[34] The ditch was re-
examined in 1978, in this vicinity, but here no traces of the palisade timbers
were found.[35] There is currently no firm date for its construction and no relationship has been established with any of the Stonehenge phases, although it
is thought to be late Neolithic.

Palisades were constructed for a variety of purposes including security
and the management of livestock, and there is no reason to favour any one in
particular in respect of the Stonehenge example. The fact that it displays a
break, presumably a causeway, immediately opposite the Stonehenge earthwork may be significant, although there is no known approach through the

Stonehenge bank and ditch circuit on this northwest side. The most important detail is that the palisade ditch appears to acknowledge the turn of the Stonehenge Avenue. As both seem to be of different dates, this implies that both converged on a feature or landmark which is no longer extant. William Stukeley had sketched a divergence, a bifurcation, of the Avenue here, although it is uncertain as to how much his interpretation had been influenced by the line of an old trackway to Durrington. Geophysical survey has confirmed the course of the palisade ditch curving northwards on the west side of, and running broadly parallel with, the former track at this point.

The Heelstone

Standing some 25 m beyond the median line of the Stonehenge causeway, within the Avenue, is a massive, seemingly unworked and southward-leaning sarsen, known as the Heelstone (Stone 96), 4.87 m high, measuring at least 2.4 m thick at its base, and tapering unevenly to a bluntly rounded top roughly equal to half its width. Excavation by Atkinson in 1953 showed that it

59 Left *The Heelstone, looking northeast.*

60 Opposite *Hassell & Kirkall engraving, 1725, looking southeast. Two outlying standing stones are visible in the middle distance on the left-hand side of the print.*

stands in a hole dug at least 1.2 m into the chalk.[36] This weatherworn stone presents the more rounded face of its deeply pocked and fissure-scarred surface to the centre of the monument. Many explanations have been offered to explain the epithet, some suggesting that it simply reflects the fact that it leans or 'heels'. It is not a unique name – there was another in Dorset, also leaning, which may suggest that this is, or was, a relatively local generic rather than specific term.[37] More imaginative accounts tell the story of how the impression of a 'friar's heel' came to be made on one of the Stonehenge stones, a piece of folklore which later became associated with the Heelstone.

The position of the Heelstone in the sequence of construction is uncertain, although its rough irregular form is entirely out of keeping with the carefully engineered and dressed stonework of the sarsen phase (with which it is so often structurally associated). Sarsen monoliths are not unique in the Stonehenge landscape. John Aubrey, writing in the middle of the 17th century, reported the removal of standing stones from the vicinity of the Kings [King Barrow Ridge] Graves: 'At the end of these graves were stones, which the people of late yeares, sc. since 1640, have fetcht away; for in these parts, stones (except flint stones) are very scarce,' and William Stukeley, writing 80 years later, also recorded stones from this location being 'lately carried away'. An engraving of the *North Prospect of Stonehenge*, published in 1725 [60], shows two standing stones in the background at the end of the barrow ridge, probably on the western slope of Coneybury Hill. These may have been the last survivors, removed shortly afterwards by the landowner, the Marquess of

61 *The Cuckoo Stone in Durrington Fields in the late 19th century.*

Queensbury, probably to provide roadstone.[38] Other isolated sarsen stones were still standing into the beginning of the 18th century within a few kilometres of Stonehenge. The 'Cuckoo' or 'Cuckold' Stone [61], an irregular block now lying flat in Durrington Fields, 2 km to the northeast, adjacent to the Neolithic henge monument at Woodhenge, which was described by William Stukeley 'as big as any at Stonehenge', may be the standing stone visible in David Loggan's late 17th-century *Prospect of Stonehenge from the South*, behind the Heelstone; it had apparently fallen by 1810.[39] The 1887 OS map shows a second stone nearby. Stukeley listed further examples, some still standing and others reused, at Milford, Fighelden, in the river at Bulford, and 'on the London Road, east of Amesbury'.[40]

A stonehole was discovered almost immediately to the north of the Heelstone by Mike Pitts in 1979.[41] This hole (Stonehole 97) proved substantial, 1.75 m across and 1 m deep; its length is unknown, as it continued under the roadside fence, although Pitts estimated that it may have been as large as one of the stoneholes (Stonehole E) at the entrance, next to the Slaughter Stone. In the wide flat base of Stonehole 97 was a 'bowl-shaped hollow', interpreted as the base of a former standing stone. The upper levels of the pit were filled with chalk and earth, some of the chalky deposit 'clearly the packing around that side of the stone'. The hole seems to have encroached as close as 1.5–2 m to the Heelstone. One detail connects this stonehole with Stonehole E, excavated by Hawley on the inner causeway: in its base were preserved the casts of decayed wooden rods, laid flat, exactly as described by Hawley in his excavation diary.[42] If the Heelstone was one of a pair, they would have straddled the axis and formed a 'gunsight'-like arrangement which might have framed the rising sun at the midsummer solstice.[43]

The Heelstone is surrounded by an irregular ring ditch, some 10 m in diameter, with steep sides 1.2 m deep and a narrow flat base 1.1 m wide. Apart from a fragment of 'freshly fractured bluestone' found by Atkinson in the lower ditch fill, all the stone recovered was either sarsen or flint, mostly from the upper levels. Hawley also recorded a 'decayed horn pick and some flint chips' in the base. Atkinson believed that it had been 'infilled with chalk rubble very shortly after it was dug'. However, work by Mike Pitts showed that the upper part of the ditch cuts through cryoturbated (i.e. frosted and frost-churned) chalk, which would have accelerated weathering and the deposits may be the result of this rather than deliberate infilling. This factor alters the interpretation offered by Atkinson who suggested that it formed 'a symbolic

62 *Detail from David Loggan's engraving* Prospect of Stonehenge from the South *(late 17th century) showing in the distance, to the right of the Heelstone, what may be a standing stone at Durrington (circled).*

rather than a physical barrier', which it may of course have done, but not necessarily one which had been dug and then immediately backfilled.

The Heelstone ditch is often linked to the similar but slightly smaller ring ditches cut around the North and South Barrows within the Stonehenge earthwork (see p. 149). The symbolic nature of these small ditches is evident, but it is not clear why only these three features were singled out in this way. The date of these ditches is uncertain, although as the one centred on the Heelstone extends across the area which would have been occupied by its twin (cutting through the packing of Stonehole 97) it is probable that the neighbouring stone had been removed before the ditch was dug. It has also been suggested that the Heelstone ditch (and by implication the Barrow ditches) predated the Avenue bank, and were therefore dug before the main sarsen phase. However, the bank material is wide and dispersed at this point, the chalk rubble seemingly spread from the bank's destruction. This relationship cannot therefore be used to conclusively demonstrate a relative sequence of construction, and the Heelstone ditch could have been dug significantly later in the monument's history.

Recent geophysical survey and excavation in the vicinity of a fallen sarsen monolith (known as the Torstone) near Bulford, some 5.5 km east of Stonehenge, has shown that it too had been encircled, at an unknown date, by a ring ditch with an internal bank (although a much larger area, c. 25 m in diameter, was enclosed than around the Heelstone). Less than 3 m away from the stone socket a shallow pit filled with 'broken flint nodules and sarsen flakes', similar in shape to the sarsen itself, probably marks the position in which it had originally lain before it was erected, the base of the hollow and one side worn smooth as a result of dragging the stone out of the ground. This important discovery implies either that naturally occurring sarsen boulders were stood on end and 'sanctified' within precincts subsequently demarcated by ring ditches, or that ring ditches were cut around stones that were already perceived to be significant.[44] The antiquity of this standing stone is unknown, although at some stage in its history, around the beginning of the 2nd millennium BC, it provided a focus for early Bronze Age cremation burials.

Knowledge of the area around the Heelstone is incomplete. Hawley did not remove the turf when digging the surrounding ditch, and he 'avoided going nearer to it [the Heelstone] than 10 ft [3 m]… fearing to disturb its stability'. It is not impossible that, like the Bulford Torstone, the Heelstone was set up close to the position in which it originally lay, perhaps long before any other stones were brought to Stonehenge. In 1922 Hawley found a 'crater-shaped' hole measuring 1.5 m in diameter and 1.37 m deep approximately 7 m south of the Heelstone, which he thought may once have held a 'large natural stone'.[45] Hawley concluded that the Heelstone was 'probably one of two rough stones standing in rather shallow craters to the south and southwest of its present site' and that 'a wide groove which passed through the circular trench in the direction of its [the Heelstone's] present site' marked the route along which one of the stones had been moved.[46] The relatively shallow nature of other often irregular holes within the Avenue is quite in keeping with the former occurrence of natural boulders which often lie in insubstantial hollows.

One final point which must be stressed is that the bulky and rounded form of the Heelstone is entirely unmanageable in comparison with the other Stonehenge sarsens, lacking the flat tabular surfaces that would have allowed the stone to have been readily conveyed on rollers. Thus moving it any great distance would have required a huge effort. It is more likely that the Heelstone may simply have been a venerable and revered survivor considered too sacred to remove or replace, and it may never have been necessary to do so, as the later sarsen monument appears to focus in the opposite direction.

Towards the middle of the 3rd millennium BC we enter the period of transition between the late Neolithic and the early Bronze Age. There is no comfortable and well-defined chronology – there appears to be an overlap rather than any abrupt break in traditions. However, by around 2500 BC, the emergence of a new order is reflected in the dynamics of the nearby settlement at Durrington Walls. The earlier emphasis on communal and 'ancestral' tombs was to be replaced by individual burials normally beneath round barrows, and accompanied by trappings reflecting a variety of often exotic material implying wealth and status and the advent of a social hierarchy. The introduction of metal technology shows that extensive trading networks had become established within the region. This was the emerging world of the people who were about to embark on the first phase of stone construction within the now 500-year-old earthwork.

CHAPTER 5

The Stone Monument

What the visitor to Stonehenge sees today is grand and ruinous, the 4,500-year-old skeletal remains of the final monumental structure set within its even more ancient, and now barely perceptible, earthwork. Very little survives of the various phases of re-modelling which took place before the final design materialized. Beneath the turf, and etched deep into the chalk bedrock, the archaeological evidence for the sequence of structural events within the interior is intriguing and problematic, a fact reflected in the terminology used in the archaeological literature which is suggestive of code-like enigmas: such as the 'Q' and associated 'R', and the equally cryptic 'Y' and 'Z' Holes. It is not insignificant that archaeologists elected to use and have adhered to these esoteric terms, for they hint at the truly perplexing nature of the buried features which occupy the centre of the site. In this brief overview it is impossible to present all the evidence and the often complex arguments which attempt to explain every aspect of the monument. Our current understanding of the sequence of even some of the major constructional phases is flimsy and often hangs on the interpretation of a single vital inter-cutting relationship, although sometimes the smallest detail is sufficient to show the order of events, akin to finding a footprint on sand freshly exposed by the tide.

Recent reappraisals of the evidence agree on two major points: that there is a general dearth of coherent associations within the disparate groups of stones and their settings, and that there is often only a cursory record of those which have been noted. To gain some understanding of events we need to look beyond the grand and spectacular and consider the lesser but potentially equally informative aspects; here there are clues not only to its construction and design but also, perhaps, something of the rationale behind the monument which may point to the methods and aspirations of its builders. Importantly, there is still information to be gained from both 20th-century records and the field notes of the early antiquarians.

The archaeology of the stone monument is complex because over a period of more than 1,000 years of prehistory a huge amount of activity was focused on an area of chalk just 30 m in diameter, not just the major structural events but also minor and sometimes transitory alterations. These are described in the archaeological literature as belonging to Stonehenge Phase 3, 'the stone monument', within which several periods of building and refurbishment have been identified. These do not necessarily reflect events which were widely separated in time; some of the activity may well be broadly contemporaneous or even currently misunderstood. The terminology used by archaeologists for the sub-phases of the stone monument uses a combination of numbers and letters (i–vi and a–c); those used here are based on the 1995 revision of Atkinson's earlier proposals.[1] Anyone familiar with Stonehenge can easily forget how arcane these terms appear to the general reader; they are used here sparingly.

Before looking at the details, it would be useful to underline a very important point. In archaeological literature the dynamics of stratification of buried deposits (the elucidation of the sequence of superimposed buried strata) are necessarily emphasized, but at Stonehenge there is another dimension, for the relationships extend above ground into the fabric of the engineered stonework. It is within the construction both above and below ground level that the skill and knowledge of the prehistoric designers and builders are locked.

In 1877 Flinders Petrie allocated a numbering sequence to each of the stones which continues to be used today, the numbers following in clockwise rotation, beginning at the axis. Those for the Sarsen Circle are numbered 1–30, with the lintels numbered '100 more than their highest numbered supporter' e.g. the lintel which spans Stones 1 and 2 becomes 'Stone 102'. This rotational system of numbering was also applied to the other concentric arrays of extant stones: encompassing the Bluestone Circle (Stones 31–49),

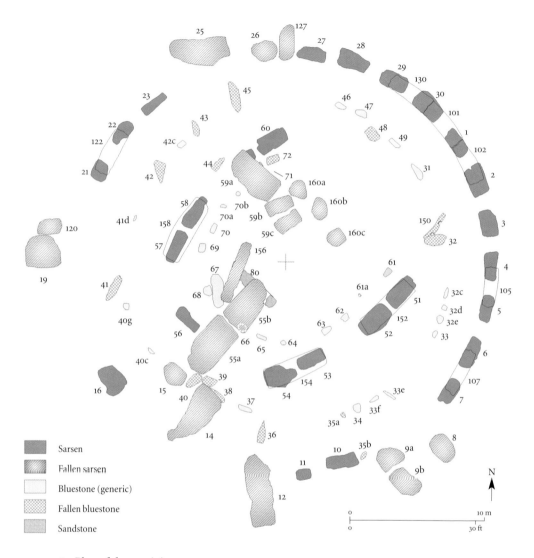

63 *Plan of the surviving stones.*

the trilithons of the Sarsen Horseshoe (Stones 51–60) and the Bluestone
Horseshoe (Stones 61–72). The Altar Stone is Stone 80, the Station Stones
91 and 92, the Slaughter Stone 95 and the Heelstone, Stone 96, the sequence
finishing with its putative twin (Stonehole) 97.

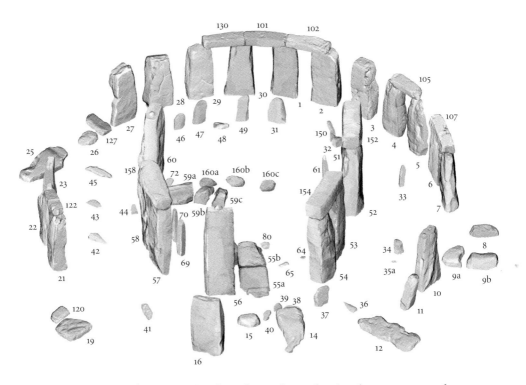

64 *Computer-generated isometric view from the southwest showing the present state of the stone monument.*

The origin of the stones

A number of types of stone were used in the construction, many markedly different in their region of origin and petrology. The two main groups are commonly referred to as 'sarsens' and 'bluestones', a term which has traditionally included, amongst others, micaceous sandstone and limestone, and a few other rock types not found in the close vicinity of Stonehenge.

The earliest to arrive within the centre of the earthwork were the relatively small igneous rocks of the generic bluestone group; how many were brought is not exactly known, although the spacing between the known stoneholes would allow for a double circle each with perhaps 40 pairs of uprights. The name 'bluestone' was given to these stones in the 19th century; although outwardly grey, they are often described as displaying a somewhat bluish colour when freshly broken (in contrast to the slightly lighter-coloured sedimentary rocks of Stonehenge). They had long been recognized by antiquarians as a distinctive group ('Foreign Stones'), exotic to Salisbury Plain, before being finally provenanced in 1923 to an outcrop some 250 km to the west of Stonehenge, in the eastern part of the Preseli Hills in Pembrokeshire, West Wales. Richard Atkinson's observations in the mid-1950s narrowed down their origin: 'on the southern crest of Carn Meini [Menyn], are great bare jagged outcrops of spotted dolerite from which the winter frosts are still detaching columnar and slab-like boulders' which 'match very closely, in size, shape, and surface appearance, almost any of the intact stones in the blue-stone circle at Stonehenge.' More recent fieldwork in the Preseli region by Timothy Darvill and Geoffrey Wainwright suggests that the great majority probably derived from a single source within a radius of not more than 1.5 km, whilst geochemical analysis has pinpointed a particular outcrop.[2] Darvill has drawn attention to a specific site known as Bedd Arthur, over-looking Carn Menyn, where 'an oval setting of bluestones of such similar shape, size and orientation to the Bluestone Oval at Stonehenge' has been identified, arguing that 'the two must be closely connected, if not the work of the same people'.[3] As yet no cultural material has been found to confirm the antiquity of the Carn Menyn quarries; as stone has been extracted from them in recent centuries the question of prehistoric usage remains open.

The undisputed Welsh origin of the Stonehenge bluestones has caused controversy: either they were glacial in origin, deposited on Salisbury Plain by the last or some remote ice age, or they had been moved a considerable dis-tance over land and water by human agency. Significant in this respect is the supposed recovery by William Cunnington, in 1801, of a bluestone amongst a large number of sarsen boulders from a (Neolithic) long barrow, known as Boles Barrow, on Heytesbury Downs, approximately 18.5 km northwest of Stonehenge. This barrow is thought to have been constructed centuries before the first Stonehenge bluestones were set up, implying that these Pembrokeshire stones were present elsewhere on Salisbury Plain long before any were used at Stonehenge. This find is considered by some as evidence for the presence of glacial erratics and has been hailed as 'the most compelling evidence for glacial transport of the bluestones',[4] although neither the identi-fication nor exact provenance of the Boles Barrow stone has been securely established (see below p. 164). However, as there appear to be so relatively few

bluestone finds outside Stonehenge and its immediate environs, with no
extensive distribution across the Plain or its river valleys, a glacial derivation
is considered unlikely.[5] The glaciation theory has to address why the people
building the earliest stone monument at Stonehenge appear to have selected
only exotic stones; if Salisbury Plain had been littered with a variety of rocks,
including local sarsen, was the intention to gather material suitable to build
the first stone circle, or primarily an exercise in prehistoric field geology? It is
far easier to envisage the bluestones collected at the *source* (i.e. where they
outcrop), than to see them as having been selectively chosen from the surrounding landscape. There is also another important point to consider here:
whilst a variety of large exotic stones and even hammer-stones and mauls was
used in the packing of the sarsen uprights, implying that stone for this
purpose was in short supply (p. 146), none was bluestone; had it been generally present within a local glacial assemblage it would undoubtedly have been
collected and utilized.

Another distinctive group of stones is represented by a small number of
limestone blocks and slabs that were seemingly used only for a very specific
purpose, to pack and support several of the larger sarsen uprights, which were
identified by Hawley as Chilmark limestone (in one instance as 'Chilmark and
Hurdcot ragstone').[6] The Chilmark quarries, which provided much of the
stone to build Salisbury Cathedral, lie some 20 km west of Stonehenge, and
Hurdcot 6 km south-southeast. In some instances the limestone mass was so
completely solid that Hawley suspected that it was deliberate 'cement'. A sample sent by him for analysis confirmed a natural origin, the limestone having
fused over the millennia with calcite from the chalk bedrock; the tendency for
groups of buried stones to naturally concrete had been noted earlier by
Professor Gowland, and was seen by him as an indicator of ancient contexts.
The tabular nature of the limestone would have made it ideal for packing, and
in some cases it was clearly arranged to brace upright stones, though it is
unlikely that the relatively small amounts so far recorded would have war-
ranted its being sourced simply for this function, and its presence therefore
suggests that it was originally brought into the area for another purpose.

In both stature and numbers the sarsens form the largest surviving group
of stones, of which just over 50 of perhaps an original group of at least 80

massive blocks are still extant. The sarsens are hard silicified sandstone belonging to the Lower Tertiary geology of southern England and are naturally found resting on, or just below the surface of, the chalk downland. Those used in the construction of Stonehenge have long been thought to be derived from the Marlborough Downs some 30 km to the north, although little petrological analysis has actually been undertaken, and much more local sources have been proposed.[7] Traditionally (and until relatively recently), sarsens were quarried and prized for their exceptional durability as road kerbs and steps, which is why blocks the same size as the Stonehenge examples are no longer common in the landscape. They are so notoriously difficult to work that the art of tempering and sharpening the metal tools with which the modern industry cut these stones was kept a closely guarded trade secret. Historically, the stones were broken using fire-and-water techniques.[8]

The so-called 'Altar Stone' is formed from an exotic slab of sandstone derived from the Senni beds of Old Red Sandstone of central south Wales.[9] There is good reason to believe that it was selected for its visual appearance, as its micaceous inclusions, more apparent on fracture, are reflective and

65 *Sketch by William Stukeley, dated 20 May 1724, showing the breaking up of large sarsens at Avebury using fire-and-water techniques.*

display a distinctive sparkling effect. This is the only example of this particular stone known at Stonehenge. Other fragments of sandstone are known from the Bluestone Circle (Stone 40g and Stump 40c), from the ditch, from a general scatter across the site, and within the wider landscape north of Stonehenge.[10]

In 1901 Gowland described a single occurrence of a further unique type of stone: 'a hard compact rock which cannot, as yet, be referred to any of the existing stones', which was used as packing for Stone 54.[11] No further mention of this unidentified rock appears to have been made in subsequent 20th-century excavations.

Evidence for the first stone structure: the Q and R Holes

Just inside the later Sarsen Circle, beneath the turf, lies a double arc of buried stoneholes, the only surviving evidence of the first stone circle erected within the centre of Stonehenge and currently regarded as initiating the period known as Stonehenge Phase 3i (2550–2200 BC). Although first encountered by Hawley, it was Atkinson in 1954 who formally identified and named these irregular settings: 'In choosing this designation [Q Holes], I had in mind John Aubrey's frequent use, as a marginal note … of the phrase "quaere quo" – "enquire how many" – which seemed appropriate to the occasion.'[12] Their place at the beginning of the stone monument phase has been recognized from their stratigraphic relationships: in places they were cut through by the settings of the later, and still partly surviving, Bluestone Circle and also by a stonehole dug for one of the uprights of the Sarsen Circle.[13]

The diameter of the outer (Q) circuit is c. 26.2 m and that of the inner (R) circuit 22.5 m, with an average spacing between the paired stone settings of 1.5 m. These curious holes are roughly 2 m long and 1 m wide, set radially and slightly enlarged at each end to provide paired sockets for stones set to a depth of around 60 cm, the strip between the sockets generally re-filled with chalk rubble. Atkinson described them as being 'dumb-bell' shaped, although not all were of this form. The bases of some sockets bore 'impressions … of heavy stones', some with 'minute chips of dolerite [i.e. bluestone] embedded',[14] and clearly once contained a double concentric array of paired bluestones. It is not immediately evident why trenches were cut only to be backfilled in the

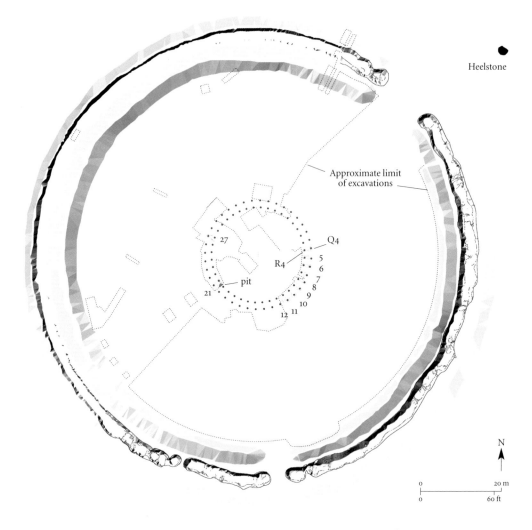

Heelstone

Approximate limit
of excavations

Q4

R4

27

5
6
7
8
9
10
11
12

21

pit

N

0   20 m
0   60 ft

66 *The Q and R Holes, a double ring of stoneholes at a spacing which suggests an original
setting of 40 pairs of stones (only the excavated holes are numbered). If complete the group
would have displayed no axial symmetry. However, the arrangement is poorly known and
has been heavily disturbed by later intrusions.*

centre. One possible explanation is that for some reason there was a
requirement to make adjustments in the radial spacing of the stones before
the actual position of each could be fixed, and that it was simply easier to
dig a short trench rather than a pair of closely spaced holes. The arc of stoneholes extends over the better part of the eastern half of a possible circle, where
11 settings were excavated, but only three settings are known from
the western half, where there has been less excavation and generally more

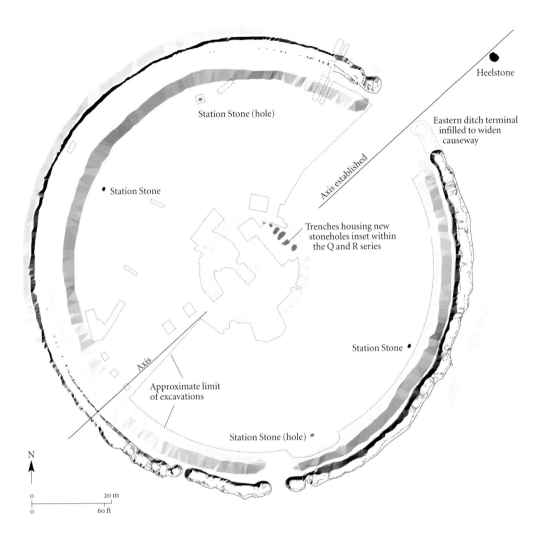

Heelstone

Station Stone (hole)

Eastern ditch terminal
infilled to widen
causeway

Axis established

Station Stone

Trenches housing new
stoneholes inset within
the Q and R series

Station Stone

Axis

Approximate limit
of excavations

Station Stone (hole)

N

0   20 m
0   60 ft

67 *Trenches housing additional stoneholes were inset within the inner ring of R Holes on the northeast side. The structure may have been abandoned before completion. The new work has a spacing indicative of 30 (rather than the 40 of the Q and R Holes), and creates a 'portal' group which provides the earliest evidence for the establishment of an axis. The four Station Stones were erected and the entrance widened to match the symmetry of the emerging design.*

disturbance. Atkinson was careful not to describe them as necessarily forming a circle, but did consider it a possibility. Computer modelling using the
spacing of all the excavated Q and R settings (the angle between each pair
being nine degrees) suggests that if the circuits were complete, they would
have consisted of a double circle of 40 settings. Importantly, the axis used by
the later arrays is not reflected within the symmetry of this circuit.

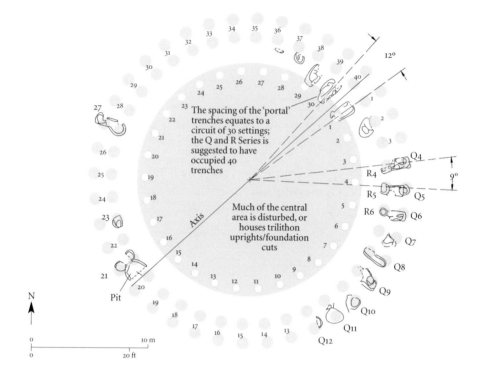

The spacing of the 'portal' trenches equates to a circuit of 30 settings; the Q and R Series is suggested to have occupied 40 trenches

Much of the central area is disturbed, or houses trilithon uprights/foundation cuts

68 *A computer-generated model showing the differences between the spacing of the Q and R Holes (40 pairs, nine degrees apart) and the later inset 'portal' trenches whose 12-degree splay indicates a potential setting of 30. Note also that excavated Q and R Holes do not fall symmetrically about the accepted Stonehenge axis, in contrast to the 'portal' trenches.*

Some reconstruction drawings suggest that each pair of uprights was topped with a radial lintel.[15] Two bluestones standing as pillars in the later Bluestone Circle are sometimes thought to have originally derived from this phase of construction, as both are former lintels and are clearly re-used (Stones 36 and 150), but it seems unlikely that these lintels could be survivors of such an arrangement as their mortise holes are too close together to have spanned any of the excavated stone settings. It is equally possible that these two stones may never have formed part of the early bluestone monument, and that they are derived from a completely different structure, erected either at Stonehenge or elsewhere.

An additional pair of trenches, radially inset by approximately 1 m from the R Holes on the northeast side, both housed three rather than two regularly spaced stone settings [67]. On either side of them, and inset no more than perhaps 50 cm, lie another two holes, each apparently containing a single socket, although Atkinson believed that 'neither hole had been finished, and no stone had ever stood in them'.[16] It is presumed that these two groupings were additional to the outer arc of Q and R Holes, as they are markedly different in character, their wider spacing (with a radial angle of 12 degrees) implying 30 rather than 40 settings, anticipating the later sarsen monument both in the number of settings, and by flanking, thereby providing the earliest evidence for the employment of the midsummer sunrise–midwinter sunset axis at Stonehenge [68]. It is unclear whether the circuit was ever completed, as most of the ground in which the remainder of the array would be anticipated is either extremely disturbed by later trilithon construction, or largely unexcavated. The position of a very badly disturbed grave, containing Beaker fragments but also more recent objects, discovered by Hawley cutting almost perpendicularly across the axis and some 2 m southwest of the innermost of its flanking 'portal' trenches, may be significant, possibly representing a ritual interment to sanctify the monument. A close parallel may be seen in the grave of a child which had been sited perpendicularly across the solsticial axis at Woodhenge, the Neolithic earthwork northeast of Stonehenge that also displays multiple concentric arrays of post settings.[17] Situated diametrically opposite the 'portal' trenches, between the Q and R circuits, lies a large pit at least 2 m in diameter which is attributed to the same phase. Its base was intact, revealing what may be a socket for a stone precisely on the axis of the Q and R monument; it has been suggested that a prominent upright stone once stood here, possibly the so-called 'Altar Stone'.[18]

How long the bluestones remained in these settings is not known, but they must have been dismantled and the site cleared to enable the marking out and manoeuvring of the massive sarsens. Their removal appears to have been done with care, with apparently no wholesale breaking up of the stones, as during this phase the site does not seem to have been littered with bluestone fragments; certainly Hawley recorded hardly any bluestone chippings in the lower filling of the nearby sarsen stoneholes.[19] Perhaps the Q and R ring was never completed; Atkinson believed it to be unfinished. Whatever the truth, the occurrence of early Beaker pottery in the 'earth and chalk fill' of Q5[20]

69 *The 1958 excavation of the trenches which held 'portal' stone settings immediately inside the R Holes (on either side of the ranging pole). Looking directly northeast, the photograph also shows Stones 49 (left) and 31 (right) of the later Bluestone Circle, which were to stand in similar positions on either side of the axis.*

indicates that this structure had a relatively short life, its demolition belonging to the period of transition between the Neolithic and Bronze Age, perhaps not long after 2500 BC, around the same time as, or within a few decades of, the currently accepted radiocarbon dates for the construction of the sarsen monument.

The Altar Stone

Lying trapped and broken beneath the fallen sarsen upright of the Great Trilithon and its displaced lintel is a fine tabular sandstone block (Stone 80), the largest of the non-sarsen stones, originating from central south Wales, measuring 4.4 m by 0.9 m by some 0.5 m thick and weighing an estimated 6 to 6.5 tons.[21] Inigo Jones first described this stone, and indeed it was probably he who originally called it the Altar Stone, which he depicted flat and lying perpendicular to the centreline of his *Stonehenge Restored*. Richard Atkinson stressed that the name 'should not be taken to imply any knowledge of the real purpose of the stone, which is entirely unknown'. But undoubtedly both its position and the distinctive petrology of the slab indicate that its role within the grand design was truly important. Its function is a matter of contention: it may have stood alone, marking a focal or geometrically significant location, or alternatively it may have been one of a pair which stood on either side of the axis. If a matching sandstone (twin) pillar ever existed, unprotected by fallen sarsen, it would almost certainly have been robbed in antiquity.

Excavations around the stone by Atkinson and Piggott in 1958 showed that it had originally been 'carefully dressed to shape', and confirmed that it had once stood upright; the northwest end, although damaged by souvenir hunters, nevertheless showed clear evidence that it had once been squared-off, whilst the opposite end revealed an 'obliquely pointed base'.[22] Its stonehole remains unidentified. A large adjacent hole excavated in 1958, beneath Stone 55b, was considered by Atkinson too shallow to have supported such a large stone; he later thought that a pair of bluestones reused in the later Bluestone Horseshoe, one with a tongue down one side and the other with a groove, may originally have been united in this hole to 'form a large single block which would have more nearly matched the size of the Altar Stone'.[23] It has been suggested that it may originally stood in the large disturbed pit[24] situated close to the axis on the southwest side of the Q and R Series, approximately 8.5 m southwest of its current position (described above), although it is equally possible that the stonehole remains buried beneath either the fallen Altar Stone itself or one of the jumble of other large fallen stones in the vicinity. The hole may, of course, have been destroyed by antiquarian digging.

Trilithons of the Sarsen Horseshoe and the Sarsen Circle

These Stonehenge megaliths are the foremost icons of British prehistory. Illuminated in sunlight the stones defy their mass; they are welcoming and betray no sense of the grey brooding and melancholy nature they assume on days when the Wiltshire Downs are shrouded in mist or lashed with rain. One may reflect that the descendants of the prehistoric communities who built the monument would have felt no less a sense of awe in respect of this grand sarsen structure, the earlier works in earth and timber and stone erased and long forgotten.

The 'best estimate' of the date of construction of the Sarsen Horseshoe and Circle, based upon a single radiocarbon determination from each, lies within the range 2600–2400 BC,[25] within Phase 3ii. There is no direct evidence to demonstrate the order in which the sarsen arrays were built or even to show whether the central trilithon Horseshoe and Sarsen Circle were contemporary, although logically the trilithons must have been erected before the Circle was completed. The similarity of the methods used in building the two structures argues strongly that they were designed and constructed by the same people over a relatively short period of time. At this period a well-defined geometric mirrored symmetry became the paramount feature of Stonehenge, its axis aligned along that of the solstice, a theme already apparent in the now dismantled early bluestone array and also the four Station Stones (see p. 148) on the periphery of the monument, which although currently undated, seem likely to have been set up before the central structures.

The mean weight of the sarsen uprights is estimated to be in the region of 25 tons, with each lintel weighing around a further 5 to 6 tons, thus the complete circle would have used some 900 tons of stone. If we add to this the five massive trilithons, around 1,200 tons of sarsen stone was used within the centre of Stonehenge – not a huge amount in comparison with, for example the 70,000 tons of limestone employed at Salisbury Cathedral, but it is the sheer size of the Stonehenge blocks and the fact they were set up with such extraordinary accuracy by their prehistoric builders which are so astonishing.

The Sarsen Horseshoe

The largest and most impressive stones on the site are those which form the central Sarsen Horseshoe (Stones 51–60). Each of the five pairs of uprights carried cross-members or 'lintels', sometimes referred to as 'transoms', a design which had inspired William Stukeley to call them 'trilithons' (from the Greek, meaning 'three-stones'). These are the largest stones at Stonehenge. The fallen southeast stone of the tallest, the Great Trilithon, now broken in two, was almost 8 m long; its partner, straightened in 1901, which is even longer (some 9 m), had been set into a hole about 2.5 m deep. The uprights average around 2.5 m in width and 1–1.6 m in thickness, the greatest of the stones weighing in excess of a staggering 40 tons each. The lintels are also substantial: each is almost 5 m long, around 1.2 m wide and just over 1 m thick, weighing approximately 15–16 tons. The lintel which topped the Great

Trilithon was shallower, some 25–30 cm thinner than its neighbours. Opposing pairs of stones flanking the axis were arranged so that the lintel tops were of corresponding height, stepping up from the more northerly pairs at 6 m to an intermediate 6.25 m, and rising to the top of the Great Trilithon lintel which would have stood some 7.5 m high. These dimensions are based on the best estimates provided by Petrie's careful 1877 survey (recorded prior to 20th-century engineering works), the Chief Architect's Report of 1919, measurements made by Atkinson in the 1950s, and subsequent laser scans of the restored stones although, in truth, there is no exact agreement between the published dimensions.

Each of the trilithon uprights was carefully worked with considerable effort expended to make one face (the innermost, except for the Great Trilithon) as smooth as possible, although the outsides were left relatively rough. They were dressed to taper upwards, the average reduction from the base to top of the stones being around 15 cm on each side. It is often suggested that this taper was used to increase the illusion of height, a remarkable innovation for a community which had no known tradition of building such substantial stone structures, although no doubt the effect had been noticed when tall naturally tapering posts were set in the ground. The top of each upright was worked to produce a single substantial 'tenon' onto which a mortise, a deep hollow on the underside of the lintel, was designed to fit. The oval tenon on the upright of the Great Trilithon (Stone 56) projects 28 cm. The lintels were shaped so they were wider at the top than the bottom by some 15 cm, another architectural subtlety to make them appear square and imposing when viewed from ground level. The curvature of the 'horseshoe plan' on which the ten uprights stood was emphasized by dressing the lintels to reflect the sweep of an arc approximating to the diameter of the encircling sarsen ring; the effect is particularly noticeable on the outer sides of the lintels. Two lintels bear traces of shallow mortises on their upper surfaces, implying that some re-thinking had been needed in the course of construction.[26]

Only the more easterly of the five trilithons (Stones 51, 52 and 152) has not been subject to modern engineering work. Its neighbour to the southwest (Stones 53, 54 and 154) was straightened in 1964. Before its restoration by William Gowland in 1901 the western upright of the Great Trilithon (Stone 56)

70 Above left *The two trilithons on the eastern and southern sides of the Sarsen Horseshoe (Stones 51, 52 and 152 and 53, 54 and 154) with pillars of the Bluestone Horseshoe (Stones 61–63) in front.*

71 Above right *The underside of the fallen lintel of the Great Trilithon (Stone 156) showing its mortise holes, with its surviving supporter (the straightened Stone 56) in the background. Three pillars of the Bluestone Horseshoe are also visible.*

was leaning considerably inwards, and early photographs show it apparently resting against one of the larger bluestones (although in 1876 the vicar of Amesbury had been assured 'that a handkerchief edgewise had often been passed between the two stones, and, therefore, what appears to be their point of union is only an accumulation of some foreign substance').[27] Its fallen neighbour (Stone 55) broke in two as it crashed forward onto standing bluestones, its base displaced outwards by 2.5 m, presumably partly by the lateral pressure exerted by the force of the huge lintel as it shifted beyond the point of stability. This stone was 1 m shorter than its partner, so a large unworked 'foot' was left on the base, which would have weighted and anchored it more securely beneath the ground. Gowland could find no substantial hole for this stone which, in order to match its partner's height, must have been 1.55 m deep below the present ground level. A recent reappraisal has suggested that a hole, similar in nature to Stonehole 56, which Gowland recorded a little further forward in the interior, may have been its stonehole, although he had deemed it unlikely as in this position the stone would not have aligned with its neighbour; as this stone was undoubtedly replaced too far to the southwest (see p. 241 below), this may after all be the correct interpretation.[28] The tenon on top of Stone 56 has suffered little from weathering, suggesting that the fall of its partner and their lintel may be counted in centuries rather than millennia. John Aubrey attributed the partial collapse to the Duke of Buckingham digging too close in 1620, but de Heere's watercolour shows it ruined nearly

72 The ruined Great Trilithon (centre right). Stone 56 was straightened in 1901, its partner (Stone 55) to the right lies fallen and broken in half; the large unworked foot left on its base to aid stability is clearly visible, with the fallen lintel to the left and the grooved pillar of the Bluestone Horseshoe (Stone 68) in front of it. Note that Stone 56 is unique in having its smoother, flatter face on the outside of the monument in contrast to its neighbours (Stones 57, 58 and 158 on the left and 53, 54 and 154 to the right), which have flat inner faces and rounded, largely unworked, outer faces.

50 years earlier, and there is a good reason for thinking that it had probably fallen before the Middle Ages, as pinned beneath it lies the carefully worked Altar Stone which, had it been readily accessible, would doubtless have been prized by stone robbers or road builders. The western trilithon (Stones 57, 58, and 158) fell in 1797, the lintel slightly displacing one of the stones of the outer circle as it fell and rolled outwards. It was restored in 1958. Only one upright (Stone 60) of the fifth trilithon is still standing. During excavation prior to straightening this stone in 1959, Atkinson noted that a large piece had broken off the base during construction, making it too short to match its neighbour, so that 'the builders adopted the bold expedient of supporting the stone upon a foundation of piled sarsen boulders'.[29] Its partner (Stone 59) has fallen inwards, and broken into three pieces (Stones 59a, b and c), the base displaced slightly outwards. The lintel, also broken in three (Stones 160a, b and c), lies almost parallel to the fallen upright, across the centre of the Horseshoe.

73 *Engineering work in 1958 to re-erect the northwest trilithon (Stones 57, 58 and 158), which fell in 1797.*

74 *An early photograph of Stonehenge, showing the two eastern trilithons. Although the figure stands almost 20 m away from the photographer, the carvings on Stone 53 (to his left) are visible.*

75 Right *Detail of carvings on Stone 53 showing dagger and axe carvings beneath a 17th-century graffito.*

76 Far right *Sketch of the purported 'Stonehenge Goddess' carving on Stone 57 (measuring almost 1 m square).*

In 1953 carvings, presumed to be of Bronze Age date, were discovered on the inner face of Stone 53; Atkinson describes 'a hilted dagger, point downwards, and four axe-heads, cutting-edge upwards' together with 'several vaguer markings'.[30] Further carvings were later recognized on this and other stones: Stone 57 has an enigmatic quadrilateral (nearly 1 m high) on the inner face representing, according to some commentators, 'a highly convention-alised figure of a god or goddess' which 'bears some resemblance to the series of *idoles* of the first passage-graves ... of the late fifth millennium BC in north-west France', a description and parallel which truly stretches the imagination; Atkinson described it looking more like 'an old fashioned tea-cosy, not everyone's idea of a goddess'.[31] Although only formally recorded from 1953 onwards, it is quite clear from the earliest photographs of Stonehenge that the more graphic of the carvings were always clearly visible, albeit unnoticed.

The Sarsen Circle

This impressive array originally consisted of a carefully laid-out ring of 30 uprights (Stones 1–30) topped by an interlocking ring of substantial lintels. Today only 17 uprights and 6 lintels are still in position. Two uprights have been re-erected (Stone 22 in 1958, after falling on 31 December 1900, and Stone 23 having fallen in a storm as recently as March 1963, restored in the following year), and all but four of the surviving stones (Stones 3, 10, 11 and 16) have been straightened and set in concrete. The remainder have either fallen and lie more or less intact, have broken into fragments or, in the case of five stones, disappeared completely, as have 22 lintels. Sarsens were still being broken up into relatively modern times, as shown by the abortive attempt to cleave the Slaughter Stone, evidenced by a neat row of hand-drilled holes across its base, indicative of the use of the 'wedge and feather' technique employed by quarrymen and masons until recently. The best-

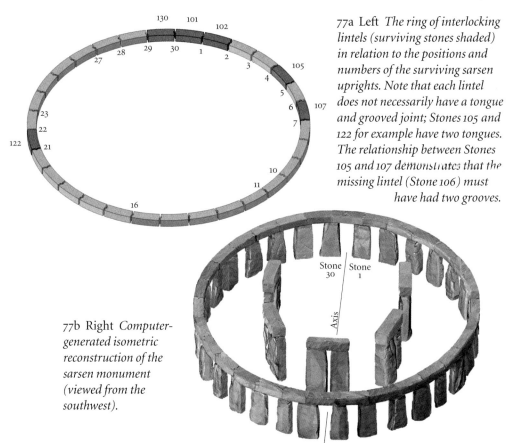

77a Left *The ring of interlocking lintels (surviving stones shaded) in relation to the positions and numbers of the surviving sarsen uprights. Note that each lintel does not necessarily have a tongue and grooved joint; Stones 105 and 122 for example have two tongues. The relationship between Stones 105 and 107 demonstrates that the missing lintel (Stone 106) must have had two grooves.*

77b Right *Computer-generated isometric reconstruction of the sarsen monument (viewed from the southwest).*

78 *The Sarsen Circle (looking southeast) showing the curvature of the lintels.*

preserved section of the Sarsen Circle lies in the northeast quadrant, and there may be some significance in the fact that the most ruined, and missing, stones are essentially those originally standing on the 'weather side', i.e. those exposed to the prevailing southwesterly winds and rain.

The uprights, which average just over 4.1 m high (to lintel base), are roughly rectangular in cross-section and have been slightly tapered so that the uppermost part of each vertical face has been reduced by several centimetres; some taper quite significantly (Stone 30, for example, is 2.5 m wide at the base but only *c.* 1.25 m at the top), others hardly at all. Nor is the reduction of the sides always equal, sometimes being evident on one side only, seemingly due to the natural form of the stones rather than any deliberate shaping. It is also clear that stones were chosen to match their reciprocal

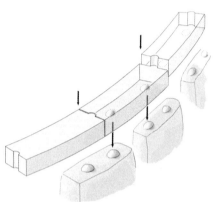

79 Left *Tenons visible on the top of an upright of the Sarsen Circle (Stone 23) during reconstruction work in 1964.*

80 Below *The remarkable interlocking joints, mortises and tenons, which secured the ring of lintels to the top of the uprights of the Sarsen Circle.*

partners, mirroring each other in form, stature and even texture, at least on the northeast, on either side of the axis, where sufficient stones survive to permit such comparisons. The smoother faces of the uprights look inwards to the centre of the monument and are set on a true circle of just under 30 m in diameter. The average width of the stones is 2.1 m. They vary in thickness between 0.9 and 1.2 m, the gap between them being about half a stone's width. On the top of each supporting upright are two tenons, designed, as with the trilithons, precisely to locate recessed sockets (mortises) at each end of the underside of the lintel [79, 80]. Atkinson described the tops of the uprights as having been slightly 'dished' to prevent movement of the lintels (he also noted this effect on the trilithon tops); this may not have been part of the original design, but may simply be the product of four millennia of weathering and minute movement bedding the two surfaces together.

The sarsen lintels have a rectangular cross-section some 1–1.2 m wide and 0.75 m deep. Five of the six examples still *in situ* are closely comparable in length, averaging 3.4 m (showing a Standard Deviation of only 6 cm); the sixth and smallest, spanning Stones 4 and 5 (Stone 105), is only 2.9 m long.

Each stone had been painstakingly dressed on both the inner and outer faces to follow the curvature of the circle of the stone uprights supporting them. Each lintel was tongue-and-groove jointed to its neighbours.[32] There appears to have been no fixed scheme to these joints: some have both a tongue and groove, others a pair of tongues, and the surviving arrangement indicates that some of the missing lintels must have had two grooves. The lintel tops stand about 4.9 m above ground level. In placing the lintels, great care was taken to ensure that the tops were set as level as possible; graphic evidence of this is seen on the underside of the deeper-than-average 'entrance' lintel (Stone 101), which was rebated at one end to allow it to sit a fraction lower on its supporting upright. The only reason to do this would have been to ensure that the upper surface exactly matched that of its immediate neighbour. In 1877 Flinders Petrie measured the heights of the stones to a common datum (an Ordnance Survey benchmark established on the Heelstone). The results of his measurements show the accuracy with which the stones had been set: even after some 4,500 years of settlement and lateral movement, the tops of the surviving Sarsen Circle were found to be still almost level.[33]

To achieve a consistent height for the uprights, the prehistoric engineers compensated for variations in the stone lengths by sinking the foundation holes to different depths [82]. Excavation has shown that the depths of these pits varied between 1 and 1.5 m and that they were often, though not invariably, cut so that the outermost sides (i.e. furthest from the centre of the monument) formed a 'ramp' down which the stones could be slid prior to erection; for an unknown reason, Stone 21 appears to have been put up from inside the Circle, also the hole for Stone 27 appears somewhat larger on the inside, suggesting that it may also have been put up from this side. One stonehole on the south side of the monument had been dug to receive a stone (Stone 13, now missing) which proved to be too short. Perhaps this was only discovered when it arrived on site, or it had broken as it was being manoeuvred. Consequently the base of the newly excavated stonehole had to be refilled with chalk and flint to a depth of 30 cm; Hawley believed that the 34 sarsen packing blocks he found in this hole may have been fragments broken off the stone.[34]

There is evidence to show that posts were placed against the innermost face of the stoneholes to act as a friction-reducing device when lowering the foot of the upright into the hole. Large numbers of packing stones were used to secure the uprights; they were mostly sarsens, including both complete and broken mauls, together with limestone slabs and other locally sourced flint blocks and glauconite (a mineral from the chalk/greensand geology) which seem to have been used because there was simply insufficient other packing stone available.[37] As noted previously, it is curious that no large broken fragments of bluestone from the earlier monument were found to have been deliberately used for packing the later sarsen uprights, the implication being that the bluestones which formerly stood in the Q and R Holes had been carefully removed and not broken, and were presumably not 'available' to provide a ready source of stone for this purpose. The stoneholes also yielded items of flint, bone and antler, including antler picks. Pottery was absent from all but two of the holes: a single decorated Beaker-period potsherd came from Stonehole 3, and a piece of Roman pottery was found at 'a considerable depth' in Stonehole 2 within a deposit of 'brown earth',[36] suggesting that it had been introduced by rabbits.

One of the uprights (Stone 11) is of much smaller proportions than the rest, measuring only 1.2 m wide by 0.8 m thick. Despite its narrow size, the centre face of the stone is placed precisely with regard to the original setting-out survey points (see Chapter 9). Although today it only survives as a broken stump some 2.75 m high, this stone shows no signs of having been dressed to a taper. Its relatively narrow width has given rise to a number of modern myths: that the Sarsen Circle was never completed, that this stone required a timber support for its lintel, or that it marks an entrance or some other structural device. If we look carefully at the evidence it need imply nothing of the kind. Stone 11 is simply a slightly smaller and now damaged upright in the circuit, no less capable than its neighbours of supporting a lintel. Looking at the groundplan, it is clear that the 1.25 m gap between this stone and its neighbour to the east (Stone 10) is not significantly different from those between the other stones (and actually narrower than the gap between Stones 5 and 6 for example). Importantly, both Stones 10 and 12 have *pairs* of tenons on top, clearly showing that originally Stone 11 must have supported lintels carried across from each of its neighbours. The most important pointer is that the absence of a taper gives Stone 11 no less of an upper (lintel-bearing) surface than several

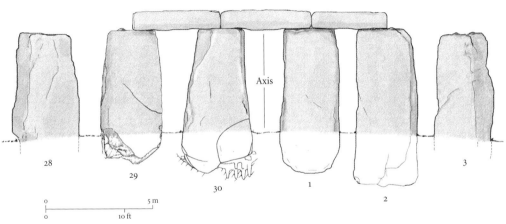

81 Top *Looking northeast along the axis through the Bluestone and Sarsen Circles towards the Heelstone. The photograph graphically illustrates the way in which the sarsen stones on either side of the axis were selected for their similarity of form.*

82 Above *Details of the foundations. (Stones 28 and 3 have been included to show the builders' continued concern for mirrored symmetry and proportion by matching the physical appearance of the stones.)*

other stones in the circuit; even one of the portal stones (Stone 30), which tapers dramatically on the west side, offers a surface of only 1.5 m to support its lintels (only 0.25 m more than was potentially available on Stone 11). Lintels of normal proportions would therefore have lain easily between 10 and 11 and 12.

We may wonder why such a narrow stone was used. Its selection may simply reflect a shortage of stones of the stature used on the northeast side of the circle, something which the adjustments to the foundations of Stone 13 also imply, but it does not mean that the integrity of the Sarsen Circle and its lintels was compromised or that it was incomplete. As seen with the trilithons, it appears that adjustments to the lintels of the Sarsen Circle were sometimes necessary. Stone 122 had two sets of mortises on its under-surface, showing that the sockets had been pre-cut but sometimes needed to be corrected on-site, in this case probably because the top of one of its supporting stones (Stone 21) had broken; the mortise holes on the prepared lintel then being too close together, modifications were needed. The resultant bearing surface left on top of Stone 21 was only half that of the narrow Stone 11 and yet it successfully supported its lintels. The need to adjust the stone height in this way provides further confirmation that lintels were still being continued around this part of the circuit.

Five of the uprights retain evidence of carvings of bronze axe heads, iconic symbols of the wealth of the region in the early Bronze Age: Stone 3 has three, their blades uppermost, on the lower outer face; Stone 4 has at least 26, again on the outer face, one of which is quite large (36 × 28 cm), all with their blades uppermost, and Stone 5 has a single axe. Stone 25 is reported to bear a 'small knife' on the inner face, and there is a supposed 'torso' (41 cm high) on the inside of Stone 29.[37]

The Station Stones and 'Barrows'

Situated close to the bank are two superficially worked sarsen stones, the survivors of an original group of four stones placed diametrically opposite each other. As lines drawn between each pair across the monument cross at 45 degrees and pass within a few centimetres of the centre of the Sarsen Circle, they are assumed to represent the survivors of key survey stations used in the setting-out of the stone monument, and are therefore generally known as the 'Station Stones'.[38] The geometry of these stones is considered further later on (Chapter 8). They are currently regarded as belonging to Phase 3b, although the sequence of events to which they belong is uncertain.

Of the two surviving stones, one (the better-dressed stone on the north-west side of the circuit) is still in position (Stone 93). It stands 1.2 m high and measures 1 m wide by 0.75 m thick, the wide axis facing the centre of the mon-ument; its stonehole has apparently never been investigated. The other, on the southeast side (Stone 91), was leaning in the 1720s when drawn by William Stukeley and had fallen by 1740. Hawley found its stonehole in 1923 (its long axis also on the circumference). The stone itself, a rough boulder-like form 3 m long, now partly buried and inclining at an angle of 30 degrees, is similar in width and thickness to Stone 93.

The two missing Station Stones are known to have stood 33–34 m clock-wise from each of their surviving neighbours. Both lost stones were enclosed within low chalk mounds which were originally mistaken for burial mounds and named as such ('North and South Barrows') by Stukeley in his 18th-century accounts of Stonehenge. Although the 'Barrow' stones had disap-peared before the end of the 17th century, when the artist and engraver David Loggan visited the site, both stoneholes were still sufficiently visible in 1740 for John Wood to use them as reference points in his survey of the 'general form' of Stonehenge: 'Two Stone Pillars appear at the Foot of the inner Bank next the Area in which the Building stands; and these are answered by two Spherical Pits at the foot of the same Bank; one with a single Bank of Earth about it; and the other with a double Bank separated by a Ditch.'[39] Neither excavations by Hawley (South Barrow) nor Atkinson (North Barrow) were able to demonstrate any direct stratigraphic relationship between the former stone settings and the mounds themselves.

The South Barrow is a very low and eroded chalk mound surrounded by a shallow V-shaped ditch, 12 m in diameter, which cuts though the filling of an Aubrey Hole. The mound itself covers another three infilled Aubrey Holes, its chalky rubble infilling a shallow depression above one of the holes demon-strating that although the hole had been largely filled there was still a sinkage hollow at the time the mound was constructed. In the centre Hawley found a large hole for the missing Station Stone, 1.2 m deep and some 1 m by 0.5 m across with the long axis set slightly askew to the Station Stone circumference. On its north side was evidence for a ramp down which the stone would have been slid into its socket. Over 100 bluestone fragments were found in the mound, together with 12 pieces of sarsen and the usual mixed assemblage of Stonehenge material: flints, pottery (a single Bronze Age and several Romano-British sherds), and a piece of finely polished stone axe. The inter-cutting relationships show the barrow to have been later than both the Stonehenge bank and the Aubrey Hole sequence. As the barrow ditch sliced through one infilled Aubrey Hole there cannot have been any uprights (either stone or timber) in them when the mound was constructed.

The North Barrow is defined by a 30-cm high bank some 18 m in diameter surrounded by a roughly circular V-shaped ditch. Examination of the former stone setting by Atkinson and Alexander Thom revealed a socket measuring not less than 1.25 m by 0.9 m, again with the wide axis facing inwards; the pres-ence of a deposit described as 'soil' within it suggests that the stone had survived until relatively modern times.[40]

Although Atkinson considered that they fulfilled a role in establishing the centre of the monument, he thought the Station Stones themselves 'too large and imprecise' to have been 'surveyor's reference-posts', rather they provided 'permanent and symbolic memorials of an operation of field geometry which, if it were to be repeated today, would tax the skill of many a profes-sional surveyor'.[41] Such stones could have been marked with some more exact point from which precise measurements could have been made, although a cord looped around diagonally opposed stones and stretched taut would effectively 'self centre'; the error where they crossed in the centre would have been marginal (see Chapter 8).

The position of the Station Stones within the structural sequence never-theless remains problematic. As Atkinson has pointed out, apart from some 'small patches of tooling' they are 'much more like the Heel Stone, in that they are substantially natural boulders'.[42] The fact that two had ditches dug around them similar to that around the Heelstone, and were thus seemingly singled out as notable stones worthy of special demarcation, provides an important link between them, although why only two of the Station Stones were marked out in this way is not apparent. Until some real idea of their date can be estab-lished, the suggestion that they are axial reference points, either for the bluestone monument that stood in the Q and R Holes or for the later sarsens, is a reasonable assumption.

The Slaughter Stone

A substantial weather-beaten, but obviously worked, sarsen slab lies face-down on the principal entrance causeway; the stone has fallen inwards and lies parallel with the axis of the monument, its base in line with the centreline of the bank. This stone is known today as the 'Slaughter Stone' (Stone 95), a gruesome epithet only acquired after Stonehenge had become entangled in the Druidic fantasies of late 18th-century antiquarians. Weighing an esti-mated 28 tons, it measures 6.5 m long, 2.2 m wide and 0.83 m thick, and must once have stood at least 5 m above the ground, approximately the same height as the top of the lintels of the Sarsen Circle. The stone's position today corre-sponds with the eastern ditch terminal of the early narrow entrance, but this is an entirely false impression as it was originally associated with the widened entrance, sited at least 7.5 m from the later ditch terminal. This visual confu-sion has been created because the early ditch excavated by Hawley was not

83 *Looking towards the Heelstone from the Slaughter Stone, the origin of whose name is apparent from the blood-like iron stain on its weather-beaten surface.*

completely backfilled and the spoil never removed; now grassed over, the surplus appears as a low bank extending up to, although bearing no relationship with, the stone.[43]

The Slaughter Stone lies partially buried, the uneven ground surrounding it bearing testament to past attempts to dig both around and under the stone. William Cunnington examined it on two occasions in the early 19th century, seeking to prove that it had originally stood upright. He observed that one end (on the northeast side) was pointed and rough, implying that it had been buried, in contrast to the tooling on the rest of the stone where it had originally been visible above ground level. He also dug underneath and appears to have found a stonehole.[44] When Hawley came to examine the stone in 1920 he described 'a cavity for about 3 ft or 4 ft around the stone' which he attributed to Cunnington's excavations; a void underneath was filled with rubble and rubbish within which he 'found a bottle of port wine left under the stone, presumably by him [Cunnington] out of consideration for future excavators'.[45] Hawley found that both ends of the stone were supported on sloping chalk, whilst the area around and underneath had been disturbed, and interpreted this as evidence that it had been rejected as unsuitable by the prehistoric builders and that a pit dug to bury it proved too short for the purpose. It seems more likely that the stone was left well supported at each end on the chalk bedrock by Cunnington and his predecessors when burrowing underneath. It is uncertain whether Hawley actually dug beneath the stone itself, but as he indicated that the disturbance around, and presumably beneath, had evidently extended to a depth of at least 1.22 m it is quite possible that most if not all of the stonehole had already been obliterated by Cunnington's excavations.

Hawley discovered two further stoneholes, spaced 4 m apart, on the entrance causeway immediately northwest of the Slaughter Stone, in line with the crest of the bank; in the Stonehenge literature these holes are named Stoneholes 'D' and 'E', the latter being the pit nearest the Slaughter Stone. It has not yet proved possible to establish any relationship between the three. Stonehole E comprised a very substantial pit, 3 m wide and 2 m deep, in the base of which were found 'two deer horn picks … resting against the curved side' and a slab of 'very soft Sarsen that crumbled if pinched between thumb and finger'. Hawley had no doubt that this pit had once held a large stone, speculating that an imprint in the bottom bore 'rather a resemblance to an impression of the base of the Slaughter Stone, but I cannot state definitely if this is so …'. The hole appeared to have been enlarged as a result of extracting the stone.[46] Radiocarbon determination of the deer horn picks returned date ranges of 2490–2200 and 2860–2350 BC.[47] Casts of 'wooden rods, laid flat' within the chalk at the base of this stonehole may provide a link with similar rods found within a stonehole in the Avenue, a putative twin to the Heelstone (Stonehole 97; see Chapter 4). Hole D also retained 'a very good impression of the stone on the soft chalky matter which had been packed between the stone and the side of hole on the west side'.[48] Measuring some 1.5 by 1.44 m and just over 1 m in depth, it was considerably smaller in size than E, and would not have been large enough to have accommodated a stone as large as the Slaughter Stone.

Atkinson believed the Slaughter Stone to have been the survivor of 'a pair of upright pillars which formed the gateway to the monument', lying symmetrically on either side of the axis of Stonehenge, its twin standing in the large Stonehole E; Atkinson envisaged pillars rather than a trilithon, because no traces of tenons have been found to suggest that the Slaughter Stone ever bore a lintel.[49] Hawley's final interpretation saw three stones ranged across the entranceway 'in the circumferential line of the crest of the rampart', one in Stonehole D, the Slaughter Stone inexplicably placed in the central (Stonehole E) socket, and a putative third stone standing on the present site of the fallen Slaughter Stone. Had all three stones stood as a contemporary group the gaps between them would have been little more than 1.5 m and the total array would have spanned 10 m across the entrance. The most recent analysis also favours three uprights across the entrance, with stones in Holes D and E and the Slaughter Stone in its own hole, the stone settings probably replacing a timber phase.[50]

The Slaughter Stone was lying flat when Stukeley first arrived at Stonehenge in 1719. There has been considerable debate as to whether this stone and possibly three partners could have been standing at the entrance a century earlier, due partly to a rather ambiguous description and plan of the monument published posthumously from Inigo Jones's notes by his assistant John Webb in 1655, whose stated intention was to show the monument not as it appeared as a ruin but how it would have been in its final form (see Chapter 3). The reconstructed plan shows three equally spaced entrances each flanked by four stones: two on the inside 'four foot broad, and three foot thick; but they lie so broken, and ruined by time, that their proportion in height cannot be distinguisht, much lesse exactly measured', and two much larger stones on the outside: 'seven foot broad, three foot thick, and twenty foot high'.[51] William Stukeley was in no doubt that Webb had conflated the large stone (not called the Slaughter Stone until much later) with the two Station Stones in the interior to produce three sets of entrance stones in order to support his geometrical reconstruction: 'Mr Webb ... pretends to give us the measure of it, confounding it with the other two before-mention'd to be within the *vallum* [Station Stones], to which they have no relation, no similarity in proportion.'[52] It is also clear that the relatively narrow main entrance shown by Webb, his 'portal' stones placed in line with the ends of the bank and ditch on either side of the causeway, bears little relation to reality, as the entrance of the monument defined by the Avenue ditches (the only entrance known until Hawley's excavations in the 1920s) was significantly wider.

John Aubrey had visited the site in 1666 with the express intention of comparing Webb's plan with the real thing. Amongst his manuscript notes survives an annotated sketchplan showing a single entrance flanked by a pair of stones on the inside, and a single stone outside (on the east side). If the evidence of the Webb and Aubrey plans is taken at face value, at least one massive entrance portal stone had disappeared, its neighbour had been pulled down and partially buried, and two smaller stones removed from the principal entrance in the intervening 40-year period, together with eight stones from the two other entrances. However, there is no need to place undue reliance on Aubrey's sketch, as it is derived from manuscript notes and never intended for publication in that form. It is essentially Jones's plan taken into the field and annotated with some changes in measurements and additional observations; Aubrey did not re-survey the monument himself. Looking more closely at his written account it becomes clear that what Aubrey actually saw in 1666 is precisely what survives today – the fallen Slaughter Stone with the Heelstone beyond. A reference to one of the stones retaining a mark to 'show how deep it should be in the earth', precisely the same observation made by Cunnington at the beginning of the 19th century, is extremely significant, as it clearly demonstrates that the Slaughter Stone was no longer standing in his day. Although he searched for Jones's pairs of 'portal stones' 300 years later, Hawley could find no trace of them, concluding that 'had they existed as ancient stones the holes would certainly have been found'.[53]

Further evidence cited to suggest that the Slaughter Stone and possibly its twin were still standing has been argued from a close examination of late 16th- and 17th-century illustrations.[54] The engraving commissioned for the 1695 edition of Camden's *Britannia* clearly shows two standing stones at the entrance. However, tracing the origin of this print in earlier editions of this work, it becomes clear that this is merely a rather flamboyant interpretation by the engraver of its predecessor in which the edges of two large stones (probably the Slaughter Stone and Heelstone) are shown in a foreshortened view of the monument, seemingly included within the ditch circuit for artistic 'completeness' rather than being fully to scale with the stones in the centre. The earlier illustration shows the pair as either large boulders or possibly leaning stones, but certainly not tall uprights (see p. 60, [26]).

On present evidence the fact that the upper surface of the Slaughter Stone is so weathered, its tooling only revealed in low sunlight, notably late on a summer evening, and even then best seen on its sides and inner end rather than the upper side,[55] suggests that it has lain in the same position for a considerable period of time. Neither it nor its possible partner have been standing in the past 400 years; indeed the missing stone may have been removed in antiquity, as the hole from which it was taken contained no bluestone or modern material which would undoubtedly have found its way into the void had it been open in relatively modern times.

Possible stone at the southwest end of the axis

William Stukeley reported that 'there seems to have been another stone lying upon the ground, by the *vallum* of the court, directly opposite to the entrance of the avenue', depicted with a broken line on his groundplan close to the bank at the southwest end of the axis,[56] which Atkinson judged to be in the vicinity of Aubrey Hole 28. Towards the end of the 19th century, the Stonehenge guide and photographer, William Judd, claimed to have found the stone: 'I find the base is still in the earth, about a foot under the surface, and is situated about 51 degrees west of south', although it could not be located when probed for 'by means of a sword and an auger' in 1901, and no obvious anomaly was recorded by recent geophysical survey.[57]

The Bluestone Monument

Two groups of bluestone uprights, the Bluestone Circle and Bluestone Horseshoe, were placed within the Sarsen Circle and Horseshoe, mirroring their design. These bluestones, some of which are quite substantial blocks weighing several tons, are dwarfed by their sarsen neighbours. Many of these stones are still standing, although they have suffered considerably through the ravages of time, the activity of stone-robbers and at the hands of 19th-century Stonehenge visitors armed with hammers and chisels.[58]

The Stonehenge literature is riddled with descriptions of bluestone curvilinear geometric forms: ovals, circles, semi-circles, arcs, some real, and some

84 Opposite *The Sarsen and Bluestone Circles looking southeast.*

85 Left *Excavations in 1958 prior to re-erection of the fallen trilithon revealed the astonishing pockmarked surface of the chalk left by the removal of various bluestone and sarsen settings within the centre of the monument. The photograph, looking northeast, shows the excavators Richard Atkinson (left) and Stuart Piggott (right). Two stones of the Sarsen Circle are visible directly behind the excavation area (on the right-hand side): Stone 21 to the left and Stone 22 on the right (encased in timber), their lintel having been removed during this phase of the restoration work.*

imaginary, which may represent intermediate bluestone settings. However, the maze of holes, hollows, abandoned settings and residual stone fragments in the centre of the monument has left the underlying chalk resembling a very badly mauled Swiss cheese which, compounded by extensive disturbance from rabbit burrows, has made the disentangling of the various periods of activity almost impossible, leading Hawley to conclude: 'I frankly confess that I have no explanation to offer in elucidation of this tangle, and I doubt if anybody will ever be able to explain it satisfactorily.'[59] No amount of retrospective examination of earlier excavation reports and photographs can hope to make any real 'sense' of the record, and what these remains represent, or rather represented, will inevitably continue to be the subject of speculation.

The Bluestone Circle

Between the Sarsen Circle and Horseshoe stands the remains of a Bluestone Circle (Stones 31–49) which was constructed after the sarsen monument, and conventionally (together with the Bluestone Horseshoe, below) assigned to Phase 3iv; two radiocarbon dates from animal bone and antler, both from the same context, provide an estimate of 2280–2030 BC. The slightly irregular circle has a diameter of some 23–24 m. As it would have been impossible for the surveyors to strike a circle from the centre (the area being occupied by the sarsen trilithons), the bluestones could only have been sited by measuring from the inner face of the uprights of the Sarsen Circle. The Bluestone Circle is so dilapidated, with stones broken, surviving as stumps or removed altogether, and with large areas of the circuit unexcavated or disturbed, that there is no way of determining the original number of stones. Taking the spacing of the closest surviving stumps in the southeast quadrant (Stones 34 and 35) which lie 1.16 m apart (centre-to-centre), there would probably have been room for 60–62 uprights in the circuit, but if the spacings on the north side are used, for example between Stones 46 and 47 (which lie 1.65 m apart centre-to-centre), there would be room for only 44.

Atkinson observed that, apart from two stones, both reused lintels (Stones 150 and 36) 'all bluestones of the circle are in their natural state and none show any sign of deliberate tooling or dressing'.[60] He attributed the rounded and smooth forms of some of them to their natural qualities and weathering (looking not dissimilar to the way they occur in their natural outcrops in Pembrokeshire). The stones vary in shape: some are tabular in cross-section, others taper. Only six survive more-or-less intact (and standing upright), five are leaning, eight have fallen, and ten are barely visible as stumps protruding through the turf. The largest in the circle are a pair of tabular stones flanking the axis on the northeast side (Stones 49 and 31) which stand some 1.9 m above the ground, their centre-to-centre spacing of 2.7 m, wider than average for the circuit, giving a 'portal' width of 1.5 m. The sarsen work placed emphasis on mirrored symmetry in which reciprocal stones on either side of the axis were carefully matched in plan and, as far as possible, in form. That the reused bluestones break this rule is hardly surprising, as here we find, especially in the circle, stones of all shapes and sizes used in a seemingly random way, almost a 'garden ornament' phase, which must be considered in an entirely different light from the carefully planned sarsen monument. The idea that something meaningful or precise can be read from the plan of this disparate collection of reused stones is untenable.

The two lintels reused as pillars were recycled from an earlier and more refined structure, to which the bluestones in the Bluestone Horseshoe also seem to have been related. On the south side of the circuit, fallen and largely buried, lies Stone 36, which was lifted and recorded, then reburied in 1954. It proved to be beautifully worked, 1.9 m long and c. 0.7 m deep, displaying a subtle and elegant curvature on both axes of its long outer faces [87]. It had been dressed and smoothed to taper upwards from its base to the top, which is around two thirds of its maximum thickness. On the base are two mortise holes spaced almost 90 cm apart, which confirm that it was once a lintel. There is no doubt that it had been used in a trilithon configuration as the mortise holes are set too near the centre of the stone to have been part of an interlocking continuous array, and the ends are simply squared,

86 *The shattered stumps of uprights from the Bluestone Circle revealed by excavation in 1954, on the east side of the monument; only one pillar remains standing (Stone 33) at the far end of the excavation trench.*

87 *A superbly shaped bluestone lintel (Stone 36) which had been reused as a pillar in the Bluestone Circle, buried in the ground to the depth of one of its mortise holes. The stone was excavated and photographed in 1954 and subsequently reburied as it was found.*

displaying no working to accommodate an abutting stone. The second lintel (Stone 150) now lies prostrate in the northeast quadrant, its two mortise holes (1.02 m apart) uppermost. Atkinson could not identify any stoneholes, at any period, which could have held bluestone trilithons with these dimensions.[61] However, the survival of these lintels provides a vital clue to the potential sequence of events both at Stonehenge and in respect of pieces of bluestone found in the wider Stonehenge landscape (considered on p. 235).

The Bluestone Horseshoe

Standing inside and up to 1.8 m from the Sarsen Horseshoe is a group of highly distinctive tall and beautifully worked bluestone pillars (Stones 61–70) [88]. They appear to be contemporary with the Bluestone Circle, and both incorporate elements of a more elaborate setting. There is only one radiocarbon determination, from a piece of antler found in Stonehole 63a, which returned an estimated date of 2270–1930 BC, although this is a far from secure context as the stone was missing and the hole somewhat disturbed.[62] The relationship of one of the pillars (Stone 68) whose stonehole was cut into a disturbed area which was thought by Gowland to be the ramp for the remaining upright of the Great Trilithon (Stone 56), apparently confirmed the sequence, although the length of time between the two events is unknown. Gowland, in the course of restoration work in 1901, was convinced of the stratigraphic security of a 'thin stain of copper carbonate' observed on a sarsen fragment found beneath the base of Stone 68, at a depth of at least 1.8 m.[63] If the stain had been produced by a contemporary copper object this would be the only evidence for metal ever found associated with the building of any phase of Stonehenge. The occurrence of copper in the foundation cut for a standing bluestone need not be surprising as we currently have no real idea of the date at which these stones were set up; the single radiocarbon date noted above allows its construction to be bracketed within a period when copper and even bronze was in use. However, the problems of later disturbance exacerbated by the presence of rabbit burrows require this stain to be regarded as insecure evidence for the presence of metal during the construction of the Bluestone Horseshoe.

It has been proposed that the surviving horseshoe arrangement was preceded by an oval array from whose 'northern arc' perhaps six stones had been removed to mimic the geometry of the sarsen trilithons,[64] which in its final form contained 19 stones of which six impressive carefully worked smooth pillars survive. Square or sub-rectangular in cross-section (at ground level measuring typically 60–80 cm by up to 60 cm), set 1.7 m apart and up to 2.6 m in height, they stood in holes up to 1.5 m deep. It has also been suggested that, like the sarsen trilithons, these stones were graded in height, although as so few survive to anything like their original height this is uncertain.[65] The majority of the stones, all dolerite, were worked to a taper, which prompted Inigo Jones in the mid-17th century to describe them as the 'Pyramidal Stones'. Stone 70, for example, loses exactly half its width and thickness over its 2.5 m height. This stone also bears evidence of a tenon, as does Stone 67, although both projections have been largely removed and flattened. A third stone (Stone 69) also shows signs of having been worked at the top to fix a lintel,[66] although from their stature it is unlikely that any of these stones would have fitted either of the surviving bluestone lintels, as their tapering uprights would have stood too close together at the base.

A highly distinctive pair of stones within this group lacks the classic tapering form; they were set in prominent positions, spaced 3.5 m apart on either side of the axis in front of the Great Trilithon. The stone on the west side

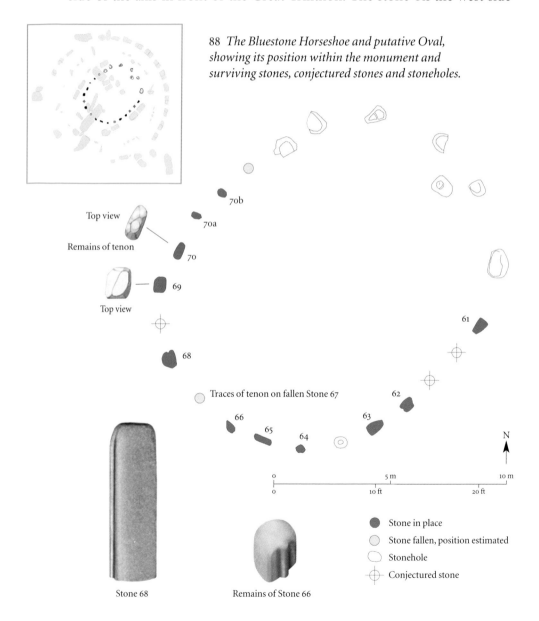

88 *The Bluestone Horseshoe and putative Oval, showing its position within the monument and surviving stones, conjectured stones and stoneholes.*

Top view

Remains of tenon

70b

70a

70

69

Top view

68

61

Traces of tenon on fallen Stone 67

62

66

63

65

64

N

0   5 m   10 m

0   10 ft   20 ft

● Stone in place

○ Stone fallen, position estimated

⬭ Stonehole

⊕ Conjectured stone

Stone 68

Remains of Stone 66

(Stone 68), a tabular block with a slightly rounded top still standing 2.5 m high, carries a continuous vertical groove along its northwest face; its partner (Stone 66), now a broken stump which lies buried beneath the fallen trilithon (under the southeast corner of Stone 55b), has a tongue along its east side.[67] This stone must have been broken long before the collapse of the Great Trilithon, the top of the stump having been rounded by weathering.

Bluestones at Stonehenge and in the wider landscape

The Bluestone Horseshoe and Circle were set up after the massive sarsen monument. But, how long after and where did the dressed bluestone trilithons and pillars stand before they were placed in their current positions? If Atkinson's interpretation of the wear pattern on the underside of one of the reused lintels (Stone 36) is correct, then it must have stood in a trilithon con-figuration for a significant period of time before finding itself incorporated into the poorly designed and eclectic assemblage which does little more than mimic the sarsen monument. Accepting present evidence that the earliest bluestone monument, set in the Q and R Holes, was relatively short-lived and may even have been unfinished, this lintel is unlikely to have been part of this setting; it cannot have developed such a deeply etched weathering scar from attrition with one of its supporting stones in this relatively short time, nor does the dimension between the mortise holes of either of the two surviving reused lintels correspond with the spacing of uprights suggested by these stoneholes.

Excavations in front of the fallen western trilithon (Stones 57, 58 and 158) in 1956 demonstrated at least two abandoned arrangements of stone uprights predating the current Bluestone Horseshoe.[68] Other than the stratigraphic relationship which shows these elements to have been earlier than the Horseshoe, these holes cannot be interpreted; they simply demonstrate that there is at least one 'missing element in the development of the monument' which, although not defined, has merited a sub-phase in the Stonehenge chronology (Phase 3iii).[69] Atkinson thought that this phase may have accom-modated the elaborately dressed bluestones and their lintels, although again the time span of activity required to produce the weathering on the underside of the reused lintel appears too short. If these bluestone lintels did not form part of one of these earlier settings, where did they come from? Is it possible that they never stood as trilithons at Stonehenge at all? Could they have been standing elsewhere for a considerable period of time and been brought to the site at a much later date, only to be arranged in a poor and quite feeble echo not only of the grand sarsen monument, but of the former elegant bluestone structure to which some, if not all, of the stones quite clearly once belonged? Could the original batch of bluestones from Wales have been destined for more than one location, some to the Q and R Holes at Stonehenge, and some elsewhere for a completely different monument? Could more than one consignment of bluestones have been brought onto Salisbury Plain in the late Neolithic-Bronze Age? Could they have even derived from a dismantled Welsh lintelled bluestone circle? Is there evidence for the presence of bluestones in the wider landscape which may give a clue to where they might have stood in the interim?

William Cunnington reported the discovery of a bluestone from a Neolithic long barrow at Heytesbury (Boles Barrow) (see p. 126 above), 18.5 km from Stonehenge which, if correctly identified and attributable to a primary context, would confirm the presence of bluestones on Salisbury Plain long before they were ever used at Stonehenge. Cunnington's find was documented in a letter, but not published in Colt Hoare's *Ancient Wiltshire*, an omission which seems strange as one might imagine that the two men would have broadcast the fact more widely, as it would have had both a direct bearing upon the relative chronology of the monuments and provided a link between their builders.[70] Regrettably, as Cunnington's collection has long since been dispersed it is impossible in retrospect, more than 200 years after the event, even to identify the stone in question to permit modern identification and analysis; it may or may not be the stone donated by the writer Siegfried Sassoon to Salisbury Museum in 1934.[71] Assuming that Cunnington was correct, and that the bluestone was found in a Neolithic barrow, it was undoubtedly a rarity, for despite two re-excavations of the same barrow, by John Thurnam in 1864, and by William and Henry Cunnington in 1885–86, no further bluestones were recorded[72] (importantly, it should be noted that William was a geologist). Therefore, the significance or otherwise of the Boles Barrow bluestone to Stonehenge studies must remain unresolved.

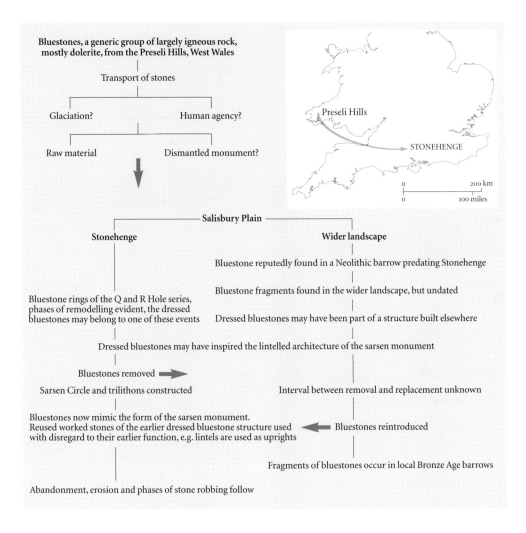

Bluestones, a generic group of largely igneous rock, mostly dolerite, from the Preseli Hills, West Wales

Transport of stones

Glaciation?   Human agency?

Raw material   Dismantled monument?

Preseli Hills

STONEHENGE

0   200 km

0   100 miles

Salisbury Plain

Stonehenge   Wider landscape

Bluestone reputedly found in a Neolithic barrow predating Stonehenge

Bluestone fragments found in the wider landscape, but undated

Bluestone rings of the Q and R Hole series, phases of remodelling evident, the dressed bluestones may belong to one of these events   Dressed bluestones may have been part of a structure built elsewhere

Dressed bluestones may have inspired the lintelled architecture of the sarsen monument

Bluestones removed ➤

Sarsen Circle and trilithons constructed   Interval between removal and replacement unknown

Bluestones now mimic the form of the sarsen monument. Reused worked stones of the earlier dressed bluestone structure used ◄ Bluestones reintroduced with disregard to their earlier function, e.g. lintels are used as uprights

Fragments of bluestones occur in local Bronze Age barrows

Abandonment, erosion and phases of stone robbing follow

89 *The bluestone conundrum: the unresolved issues surrounding the origin and use of bluestones at Stonehenge and its environs.*

Unsurprisingly, other bluestone fragments are known from the immediate vicinity of Stonehenge. Cunnington's find, in 1807, of bluestone in a round barrow in which Stukeley had also earlier found 'chippings of blue marble' came from one of the group of barrows lying less than 300 m west of Stonehenge.[73] Cunnington also recalled a similar find in another (unspecified) barrow in the vicinity. These barrows were, of course, constructed several hundred years after the first stones were brought to Stonehenge, so the

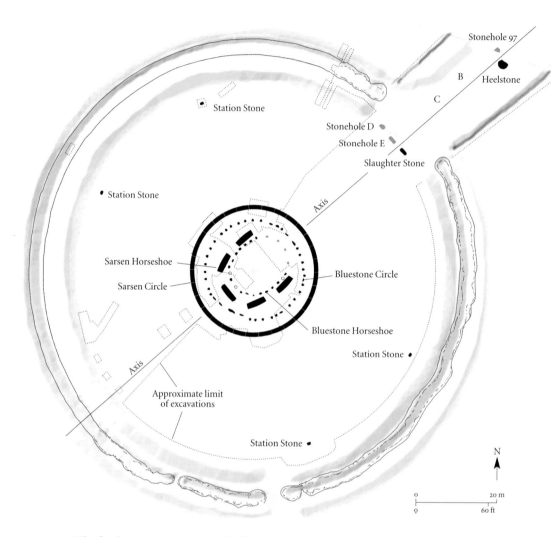

Stonehole 97

B   Heelstone

C

Station Stone

Stonehole D

Stonehole E

Slaughter Stone

Station Stone

Axis

Sarsen Horseshoe

Bluestone Circle

Sarsen Circle

Bluestone Horseshoe

Station Stone

Axis

Approximate limit
of excavations

Station Stone

N

0   20 m
0   60 ft

90 *The final sarsen monument with the Bluestone Circle and Oval/Horseshoe arrangement. The presence of two stoneholes and the fallen Slaughter Stone suggests that three sarsens were once standing at the entrance to the earthwork; however, the mirrored symmetry seen in the rest of the monument implies a pair of stones, one on either side of the axis.*

occurrence of bluestone within them, relatively close to the monument, is noteworthy but not entirely surprising (similarly fragments were picked up during excavations for the Stonehenge car park). Despite all the barrows opened by Stukeley and Cunnington in the Stonehenge landscape, these are the only certain references to bluestone fragments, and even then the context of two of the three is uncertain.

There is, however, a second group of bluestone fragments found close to the western end of the nearby Cursus by John Stone and (William) Edward Young in the 1930s and 1940s which may be much more relevant to the history of the Stonehenge bluestones.[74] The discovery of these fragments at a location over 1 km from Stonehenge led Stone to propose the former existence of a 'bluestone structure of late Neolithic or Grooved Ware age in the vicinity' (Grooved Ware being the distinctive decorated late Neolithic pottery type which developed a few hundred years before the Beaker period and overlaps with it, typically from around 2800 BC to perhaps 2200 BC). More recently, the reported discovery of bluestone fragments at Woodhenge[75] raises the possibility that bluestone monuments might have been erected at opposite ends of the Cursus (although apparently terminating at a long barrow sited at the north end of King Barrow Ridge, if projected eastwards beyond this point the Cursus leads straight to Woodhenge, 1.5 km distant).

The Y and Z Holes

Anyone writing about Stonehenge is destined to employ the word 'enigmatic'. If allowed to use it only once, I would reserve it for the Y and Z Holes. These are a series of substantial pits of near-identical shape arranged in two concentric groups outside the Sarsen Circle, the Z Holes being closest to the stones. They were named Y and Z because the outermost ring of pits, the Aubrey Holes, had initially been designated as X Holes. Just as the Q and R Holes heralded the arrival of the first stones, in the Y and Z Holes we appear to witness the last known 'structural' event at Stonehenge (Phase 3vi: currently accepted date 1640–1520 BC); the interval between the building of the first bluestone array and the cutting of the Y and Z Holes may have been as long as that from the construction of Salisbury Cathedral to the present day. The current view is that both rings are contemporary, the final concentric features at Stonehenge. The relatively stone-free soil in their secondary fills has been interpreted as an accumulation of wind-blown deposits gradually filling up the long abandoned holes.[76] Examples of almost every material, both natural and artifactual, present elsewhere at Stonehenge have been found in them, much of it of later date (including pottery of the Iron Age, Romano-British and Medieval periods, coins and horseshoe nails, and even human remains).

Discovered in 1923 by Hawley, the Y and Z Holes were clearly visible as large patches of 'humus' against the freshly exposed chalk surface, which upon excavation proved to be the uppermost fills of two rings, each probably containing 30 pits. The circuit of both rings of pits is irregular, and it has even been argued that they represent a spiral – an unnecessarily complicated and demonstrably wrong interpretation. There is no doubt, from both their morphology and geometric relationship, that this is a contemporary group which eventually suffered a common demise. Stratigraphically the holes post-date the Sarsen Circle: Y7 was cut into the backfilled construction ramp of one of the uprights (Stone 7), and a sequence of events is provided by the fact that not one later feature has been found cutting into any of the 35 excavated holes, further supported by radiocarbon dates obtained from antlers deliberately placed in the base of Y30 (1675–1520 and 1880–1690 BC), lying immediately west of the axis of the monument, and from Z29 which returned an earlier radiocarbon date of 2030–1740 BC.[77]

The Y and Z Holes display a wedge-shaped profile both on their long axes and across their widths, the sides tapering down to a flat base. The mean dimensions of the Y Holes are 1.7 by 1.14 m tapering to 0.97 by 0.54 m at the base, with a depth of 0.9 m. The Z series are fractionally larger and deeper, typically by some 0.1 m. There appears to have been a need to maintain the axial base dimensions, so within the smaller holes the end taper is reduced and the sides become near vertical. Hawley concluded from the outset that these curious cuts 'never held stones, as the sides and edges would have been ruined either by inserting or extracting them'.[78] The occurrence of largely intact antlers in the primary fill of two of the holes also refutes the idea that they ever held uprights. The present slope of the ground at Stonehenge still follows the trend of the Neolithic topography, and the average difference in depths between the shallower Y and deeper Z Series could imply a desire on the part of the builders to maintain a relatively level datum for the base of each of the holes. This may be a further reflection of the 'structural' preoccupation displayed within the internal geometry of the pits, especially when considered with the quite particular and puzzling 'footprint' within the bottom of each hole. Although neither Hawley nor Atkinson thought that

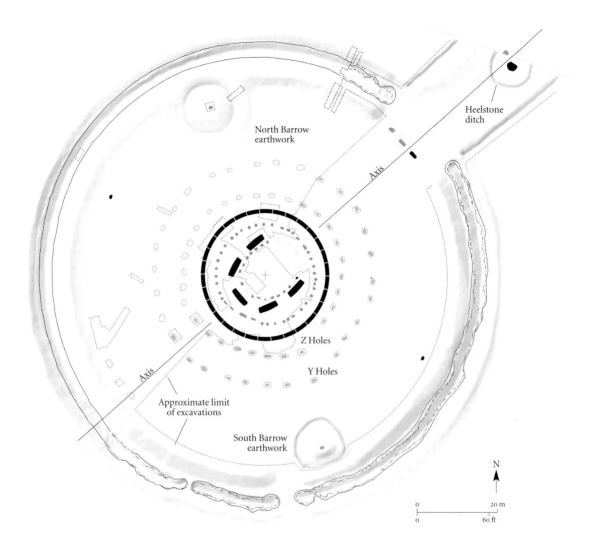

91 *The final structural event at Stonehenge: the digging of the enigmatic Y and Z Holes. Ring ditches were dug around the Heelstone and two of the Station Stones (North and South Barrows); there is no firm dating for these events, which may even post-date the Y and Z series.*

uprights had ever been present, and no imprint of stones was found in their bases, Atkinson nevertheless thought they had been intended to hold the bluestones.

On first impression it appears that each pair of Y and Z Holes was set to 'face' its nearest sarsen upright; closer examination shows this to be simply the result of the geometric concurrence (of 30 settings), for they become locally out of phase where the stone widths vary. The pit centres of the Z Holes are offset between around 2.5 and 4.4 m and the Y Holes 8 to 11.8 m from the outer face of the Sarsen Circle, demonstrating that they were certainly not set out by measuring from the sarsen uprights. The obvious answer to the problem facing the prehistoric surveyors in establishing accurate concentric rings outside the Sarsen Circle would have been to establish them by striking a series of offsets from the stones themselves, but this was not done.

Of the outer Y Holes, 18 have been excavated, the positions of Holes 20 and 21 recorded but not emptied, and the remainder located by metal probe. Of the Z Holes, 16 have been fully excavated, another was partially investigated, and the positions of 12 determined by probing, making 29 in total; a substantial break in the circuit on the southeast side provides ample room for a 30th, which would numerically match the outer ring, but no hole has been found, although the area in which it is thought to lie is partly occupied by a fallen sarsen upright (Stone 8).[79] The eccentric outward sweeping arc of Holes Z11, Z10 and Z9, combined with the apparent absence of Z8, has been interpreted by some archaeologists as evidence that the Z Holes were dug after the partial demise of the Sarsen Circle, making it impossible to cut Z8 at all. It could even be argued that another fallen sarsen (Stone 9) was responsible for the

92 Atkinson's excavations of Y Hole 16 (left) and Z Hole 16 (right) in 1953.

outward displacement of Z9 and Y9, although it is clear from the plan that the adjacent holes (Z10 and Z11) are similarly radially displaced, despite the fact that in this case their nearest sarsen neighbours (Stones 10 and 11) are still standing, and so it seems more likely that this shift was the result of a surveying error in setting-out the holes.

It is also sometimes argued that the circuit remained unfinished. Hawley had found Z7 to be a 'shallow depression' whose excavation had been 'only partly carried out', while as a result of his work around Stone 8, Atkinson concluded that only 29 Z Holes had ever been dug: 'one feels that for some reason the builders suddenly lost their sense of purpose, struggled on for a little in a half-hearted way, and finally abandoned their work without even completing the full number of holes.'[80] This would be a more convincing view if an equal discord was reflected in the morphology of the pits. However, despite their relatively chaotic appearance on plan, which itself is not nearly so 'disorganized' as it may appear (see Chapter 7), there is in fact a remarkable coherence of form which hints at no less a 'sense of purpose' than with any other of the pits and holes dug at Stonehenge.

Beyond the earthwork

The Avenue

The Avenue (Phase 3c) takes the form of a broad bank and ditched earthwork, which extends from Stonehenge into the wider landscape, first running northeastwards for 0.5 km, descending gently into a dry valley, then curving eastwards and continuing for a further 1 km before making a further broad southeastward sweep towards the River Avon. Its exact place in the sequence of construction is not known, although both Hawley and Atkinson observed the southern bank overlying the infilled Heelstone ditch, and both the Avenue banks buried other earlier (albeit undated) abandoned features. The Avenue acknowledges the widened entrance of the monument, but narrows slightly as it approaches the causeway, implying that it was constructed after the entrance modification. The Avenue ditches are usually less than 1 m deep and up to 2 m wide, but within 2 m of the Stonehenge ditch the southern Avenue ditch had faded out, riding up over the outer counterscarp bank and leaving a scar in the chalk bedrock that was no more than a shallow tapering groove;

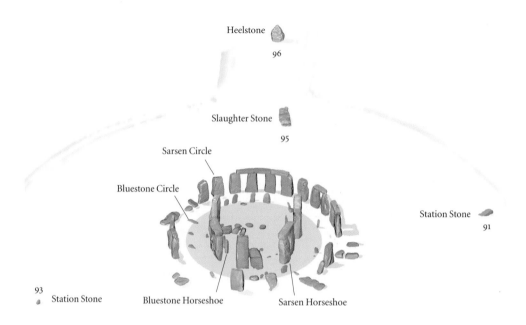

Heelstone

96

Slaughter Stone

95

Sarsen Circle

Bluestone Circle

Station Stone

91

93

Station Stone   Bluestone Horseshoe   Sarsen Horseshoe

93 *A computer-generated isometric view, looking northeast towards the Heelstone, showing all surviving stones.*

it appears that the counterscarp bank had been significantly eroded before the Avenue ditch was dug.[81]

Richard Atkinson saw the Avenue as 'a processional way' linking the monument with the river. Its discovery is usually attributed to William Stukeley, although it was John Aubrey who first used the term 'walk or Avenue', conjecturing that it served as the setting for an 'imaginarie Walke of stones which was there heretofore'.[82] Avenues leading to stone circles are rarely just earthworks, but are often marked by timbers or stones.[83] It is just possible that Aubrey had noticed the hollows of former stone settings along the Avenue, something which Roger Gale was in no doubt of when he complained to his companion Stukeley about their omission from his 1740 publication: 'I think you have omitted a remarkable particular, which is that the avenue up to the chief entrance was formerly planted with great stones, opposite to each other, on the side banks of it, for I well remember we observed the holes where they had been fixt, when you and I surveyed the place.'[84] One of Stukeley's unpublished sketches shows paired stones along the Avenue, together with at least one additional stone between the Heelstone and the Slaughter Stone.[85] No trace of any stones or stoneholes has been recorded within the Avenue subsequently, and despite geophysical survey at several locations, no conclusive evidence has yet been found,[86] although the detection of stone settings within former earthworks, infilled largely with natural chalk, can be an extremely difficult task, the deposits generally lacking the physical contrasts which might normally allow silted features to be detected by magnetic or electrical resistance survey techniques.

When the Avenue ditches were dug, chalk from the bank was cast over two of the four substantial postholes found by Hawley just west of the Heelstone

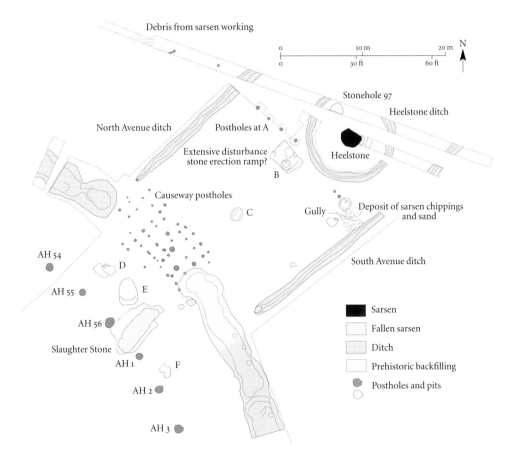

94 *Features excavated at the entrance causeway, and extending along the Avenue to the Heelstone. The extent of the early ditch/narrow entrance (subsequently backfilled) is shown.*

(Postholes at A), and possibly the Heelstone ditch. But despite the ditches having been investigated at various locations on at least 20 separate occasions, very little datable material has ever been found in them, and none of the few potsherds from primary contexts is truly diagnostic. Radiocarbon dating of the only four antler and animal bone samples considered to be derived from reliable contexts in the Avenue ditchfills have proved inconclusive, confirming only that it belongs to Phase 3 of the monument.[87]

This brief overview of the archaeology of the monument has presented some of the more important clues to the ideas and methods of the construction used by the   prehistoric communities who built Stonehenge. The following chapters expand on the remarkable achievements of its builders, and add a new dimension: illustrating the quite exceptional grasp of geometrical principles of its architects and surveyors. The cumulative evidence conspires to tell us that the internal integrity, precision and symmetry reflected in the design was of paramount importance, being clearly a vital and fundamental aspect of contemporary prehistoric cosmology.

CHAPTER 6

Astronomy or Architecture?

The concentric nature of Stonehenge is apparent even to the casual observer. The monument retains much of the original mirrored symmetry, which demonstrates the considerable care taken by the builders in setting out each of the arrays. The achievement of such precision is even more remarkable when the difficulty of positioning the huge sarsen stones and lintels to within tolerances of just a few centimetres is taken into account. There are two principal ways of interpreting this overriding concern for accuracy: 'astronomical', or 'architectural'. These themes are not necessarily mutually exclusive, but they are the root of all the major theories which have revolved around the idea of the 'purpose' of Stonehenge for over 200 years.

It has been argued that Stonehenge had a utilitarian function, even if only in the broadest sense. This model would see the various structural elements arranged according to rules which would be dictated by factors physical and external. If this is true, then we need to look for evidence and influences beyond the stones, either in the surrounding landscape or the celestial dome, for something that may elucidate the principles which dictated its construction. The idea that Stonehenge was an astronomical observatory, calendar or – a more recent theory – a 'computer', has been the major, and almost exclusive, focus of popular interest throughout the 20th century.

If we are to understand Stonehenge as fulfilling some kind of astronomical function, then the sequential arrangements of earth, timber and stone must be demonstrated to relate to specific astronomical events or phenomena, the principal, but not exclusive, preoccupation being the incorporation of a series of alignments. This pursuit has occupied astronomers and others for almost 300 years (notably Halley, Lockyer, Hoyle, Thom, Hawkins, Newham, Ruggles and North). From the amount of published literature which focuses on the supposed alignments of the stones, it might be supposed that this has already been adequately demonstrated, yet even those who have made extensive studies of the potential astronomical design of Stonehenge admit to uncertainties. Clive Ruggles, Professor of Archaeoastronomy at the University of Leicester, has summarized the situation:

> There is no convincing evidence that, at any stage, constructions at Stonehenge deliberately incorporated a great many astronomical alignments, or that they served as any sort of computing device to predict eclipses ... in short there is no reason whatsoever to suppose that at any stage the site functioned as an astronomical observatory.[1]

This statement has to be commended for its uncomplicated honesty, qualified, I must add, with the proviso that it would be unwise and clearly wrong to dismiss all astronomical ideas relating to Stonehenge.

My own opinion is that Stonehenge has only one alignment, i.e. the major line of symmetry established along the line of the summer-winter solstices; but having recognized a single important alignment, we should not immediately assume that all further aspects of the design, with its concentric elements and numeric sequences, are also of astronomical importance. By way of example, the east-west orientation of a Christian church or cathedral does not imply that a proliferation of sightlines exists within the building, nor that we should mentally join up every orthogonal element and read significance into them.

But if Stonehenge is a structure whose proportions and numeric elements reflect a careful design, what could have been responsible, if not 'astronomy', for its plan? What principles have dictated the setting and spacing of each successive timber and stone array, and is it actually reasonable to look for any continuity of design elements spanning a period of 1,000 or perhaps even 1,500 years?

The concentric and (above all) regular and precise symmetrical arrangement of the monument argues that the builders were preoccupied with its internal geometry and integrity. This is evident from the very earliest accurately surveyed circular earthwork and timber settings, and is repeated throughout each successive phase. It is difficult to see how the regular ring of Aubrey Holes of the earliest phase could have been laid out for any precon-ceived interrelated sighting or observation purposes. The Aubrey Holes circuit is simply a circular array which probably originally held a series of evenly spaced timber uprights. Apart from the archaeologically significant material they contain, these settings are important because they not only demonstrate the ability of the first Neolithic surveyors of Stonehenge to lay out and accurately subdivide a circle, but they also provide us with the earli-est of the enigmatic series of numbers associated with it: 56. Both 56 and 30 (the number of original sarsen uprights) have been argued to have a particu-lar astronomical significance, and therefore in the 'utilitarian' model of Stonehenge there would have to have been a clear and pressing need to include exactly these numbers independent of any design or aesthetic con-siderations between, or within, the various constructions. One might wonder why, if certain numbers such as 56 and 30 were astronomically significant, many other contemporary examples have not been found.

The choice we are presented with, therefore, is either that the number and spacing, not just the proposed alignments, of the various elements were established for a specific reason, or that these numeric elements are the result of a geometric plan and need have no external or astronomical significance at all. In this latter proposal both the numbers and spacing of each of the timber and stone arrays will have arisen as the direct consequence of the application of repeated formulae or design principles. This does not preclude the idea that these were desired numbers, but simply suggests that if they were essen-tial elements they were chosen to figure in the design of the monument for reasons of integrity, unity or aesthetics, rather than functional necessity.

One of the very real problems that archaeologists have with astronomical interpretations of Stonehenge or other prehistoric monuments is that there always appears to be something in the heavens that will align with just about anything else on the ground, if the spectator stands in the right place. I really have no idea if the stars Gamma Crucis, Rigel or Bellatrix were important to Neolithic people, but if a particular proposed sightline fails to align with a lunar or solar event, then these and a host of other bright points in the night sky are invariably offered as alternatives. How on earth are we expected to make judgments about the relative significance of all these options in a prehistoric context? A further difficulty is the introduction of imagined structural components or even artifacts for which there is no archaeological evidence whatsoever, such as a proposed series of six movable stones which could have been used to make the Aubrey Holes perform the role of a 'moon event' predictor,[2] or the absurd claim that our most outstanding and treasured Bronze Age gold artifact, known as the Bush Barrow lozenge (see below) was intended 'as an *aide-mémoire* for a calendar … placed horizontally at eye level and used like a plane table with an alidade, many of the markings on the lozenge could have been used as a 16-epoch solar calendar, with guidelines for inserting the inter-calary leap-day'.[3] Many archaeologists, bemused by this kind of speculation, myriad sightlines and calculations of angles of declination, reinforced with 'megalithic yards' and all kinds of 'mathematically verified' data, have simply ignored the impenetrable nonsense and with it much of the potentially useful archaeoastronomical arguments.

Why is the Bush Barrow lozenge so important in the context of Stonehenge? First of all because it is an example of the wrong use of ancient material to support theories which have no archaeological substance; the image of a 'Bush Barrow astronomer-king', with his elaborate and cunningly contrived gold surveyor's alidade, does nothing for the credibility of the archaeoastronomical case. Nevertheless, the lozenge truly does hold an important key to understanding the prehistoric mindset and contemporary knowledge reflected in the construction of Stonehenge. To demonstrate this requires a very careful examination of the evidence.

The Bush Barrow lozenge

Stonehenge was still standing in its final and most spectacular form, perhaps around 1750 BC or shortly after, when not far away to the south, on Normanton Down, a tall, physically distinctive Bronze Age man was interred within an earthen round barrow which still survives almost 3 m in height and 40 m in diameter. This mound is of a common type (bowl barrow), but its stature identifies it as a classic among the Wessex Barrows, renowned from the days of the antiquarians as containing a rich variety of objects which

TAB.XXXIII.
p.64.

Prospect from Bushbarrow

D

Sr Anns

a.Roundway hill .b . Oldbury D Stonehenge.

Stukeley delin

95 *William Stukeley's* Prospect from Bush Barrow *(1740). Bush Barrow is in the foreground, with Stonehenge just visible on the horizon.*

reflect the material wealth and status of this dynamic region during the height of the Stonehenge period and for several hundred years into the 2nd millennium BC. It appears that this mound, known as Bush Barrow since Stukeley's time, had lain undisturbed on the chalk downland for 3,500 years until Sunday 10 July 1808, when it was opened by William Cunnington. Included with the grave goods were two bronze daggers (the decayed wooden handle of one decorated with innumerable tiny gold wire pins inlaid in a zigzag pattern) and a large bronze spearhead. Near the skull lay a bronze axe head upon whose blade were imprinted traces of cloth, and there was also a mace made of exotic West Country fossil-rich stone, its shaft adorned with zigzag gold ferrules. Work on the less well-preserved material has largely confirmed that the man had been a warrior, for bronze studs which appear to have been part of a helmet have been recognized, together with the remains of what was perhaps a wooden shield.[4]

Amongst the accompanying objects were two decorated gold lozenge-shaped plates, one tiny (just over 31 mm across), and the other much larger, with 50 times greater surface area. This remarkable incised gold sheet, known as the Bush Barrow lozenge [101], is 185.5 mm long and 157 mm wide, its thickness around 0.1 mm increasing to 0.2 mm towards the edges. The outside edges had been tucked under the wooden support, and grooves impressed against the sides; traces of a layer of beeswax were sandwiched between the gold and the wood. The face carries a series of concentric lozenges engraved at equally spaced intervals, each defined by a series of four precise closely spaced parallel grooves. The smaller central zone carries two pairs of lines that divide the very centre into a pattern of a further nine small, equally sized lozenges. The border between the outside and first inner lozenge is filled with a series of single inscribed zigzag lines which create a pattern of nine interfaced triangles on each of the sides. Experiments undertaken to recreate this pattern show that the neat V-shaped rounded bottom grooves which outline the lozenges can be faithfully produced with an 'appropriately shaped and polished point'. The surface of the gold sheet is today slightly domed, due largely to interpretive restoration undertaken some years ago; slight 'bowing' of the outer two sets of incised lines has always been apparent, but is considered to be the 'incidental result of changes to the geometry of the object since manufacture'. The motifs were originally 'drawn' onto a flat sheet.[5]

Using computer-modelling, I analysed the design to establish the underlying geometric principles used in its construction, and to determine how it was first created 'on the drawing board'. For my CAD study I made an accurate drawing from a series of scanned images of the artifact in its pre-restoration condition[6] to create accurate vector models of the design. The dimensions were then checked back to the original published records. The finished computer drawing was subsequently tested to determine the most likely method used to configure the form of the sheet and the geometry inscribed on its surface. Even without the aid of detailed computer images, the accuracy and precision of the original marking out of the design is immediately apparent. It is self-evident that this must have been achieved with the gold sheet firmly fastened to a suitable base. The sheet must have been trimmed from a piece larger than the finished item. Two small pin holes visible on opposite extremities of the long axis of the lozenge may have been intended to secure it whilst being engraved (had they been for fastening the finished item to clothing or similar, there really ought to be holes on the other corners as well; also the 'pin holes' also appear to interrupt the incised lines, suggesting that the holes were made first).

The following figures [96 to 100] demonstrate how the design was created from a basic hexagonal model. The conclusion from the CAD analysis is that the Bush Barrow lozenge is not an elaborate sighting device, alidade, or prehistoric computer; it is a decorated ornament in the tradition of Bronze Age sheet metalwork, one that uses a beautifully simple geometric motif. But this is not the end of the story. If we consider the way in which the design was implemented, what we have is a remarkable insight into Bronze Age knowledge of both form and symmetry. Now that *is* something which has a direct bearing on the way we view Stonehenge.

Circles are the simplest forms to create. It is hardly surprising that roughly circular enclosures are the first types of earthwork that prehistoric communities constructed, often more or less following the contours around a hilltop. What makes certain works, including Stonehenge, special from the outset, is that they were surveyed, set out carefully to a predetermined plan; no ambiguity, no guesswork, and no compromise – what was desired was an accurate circular structure, and they set about building exactly that. In addition to the labour, tools, cordage and pegs required for such a venture, there was a real emerging knowledge of geometric principles. The precision and sophistication shown by Wessex artists and craftsmen in the embellishment of relatively simple geometric motifs on objects such as the gold bound amber discs and button cover found in one of Bush Barrow's neighbours on Normanton Down (Wilsford G8) [102] clearly demonstrates that they were familiar with the use of compasses to construct accurate circles, and there is a clear link between this draughtsmanship and the development of field surveying skills. The Bush Barrow lozenge shows that from the time of the construction of the first truly circular earthworks, ideas had progressed far beyond the geometry of circles to the understanding of relationships between the radii to create hexagons, the subdivision of angles, the setting out of accurate right angles and the investigation of other geometric forms including decagons and pentagons. It is a very small step from understanding this to looking for evidence as to how this knowledge was applied on the ground, and demonstrating that the same principles were being used and experimented with both in the earthwork and its internal structural features. Of course, the burial of the lozenge is relatively late in the sequence

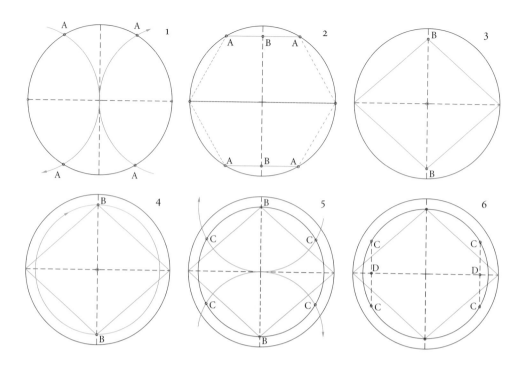

96 *The geometry of the Bush Barrow lozenge: 1–6. A baseline and circle are first scribed on a sheet of gold larger than the lozenge. From the intersections of the baseline with the circumference a radius is inscribed to create four additional points (A), forming the vertices of a hexagon. The midpoints of the two horizontal hexagonal facets (A–A) are then marked (to create Points B) (Stages 1 and 2). Joining Points B to the baseline intersections creates the master lozenge shape (Stage 3). Points B–B also establish the diameter of a second (inner) circle (Stage 4), on which a further four points are created (C) using the vertical axis (B-B), nominally a smaller hexagon rotated 30 degrees out of phase with the original (Stage 5). The vertical facets (C–C) intersect the baseline at Points D (Stage 6).*

of events, and in all probability by the time it was made most, although perhaps not all, of the design of Stonehenge had been established (there were still modifications to be made, such as the Y and Z Holes). Nevertheless, it is a point of arrival. We do not know how old the lozenge was when it was deposited. It was not as old as the sarsen structure, but the sophisticated geometric design can hardly have been a spontaneous product; the confidence of its execution proclaims it to be an evolved work based on long-established and well-practised procedures.

The Bush Barrow lozenge and successive monuments at Stonehenge share a further vitally important affinity: they were both planned on a drawing

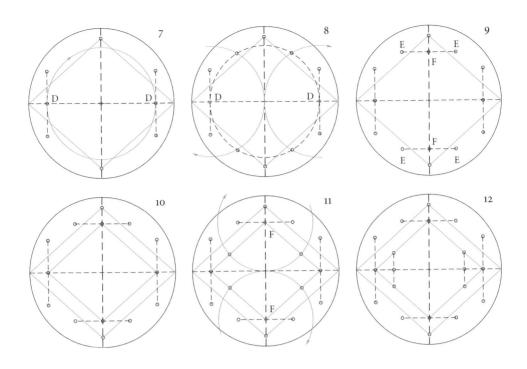

97 *The geometry of the Bush Barrow lozenge: 7–12. Steps 1–6 are repeated from D–D, establishing E–E and F–F, and creating the second (inner) lozenge.*

board. There is absolutely no way that the master design of the central sarsen structures or even the earlier arrangements can simply have been worked out 'on the ground' without first having been drawn on a prepared surface, perhaps smoothed clay or a chalk tablet. Surveyors familiar with the problems of both setting out and maintaining survey marks during phases of construction and subsequent works will recognize that some kind of drawing or model of the proposed monument must have existed. The clues are contained within the design of the monument, in determining where the survey pegs were originally placed, and by considering the dynamics of its construction.

It may appear ambitious to suggest that because we have dismissed any associations between the Bush Barrow lozenge and astronomy, which were always speculative at best, we can reject nearly all connection between the design of Stonehenge and astronomical alignments, but further computer analysis (discussed in the following chapter) confirms that the monument itself was no less a work which employed simple geometric principles.

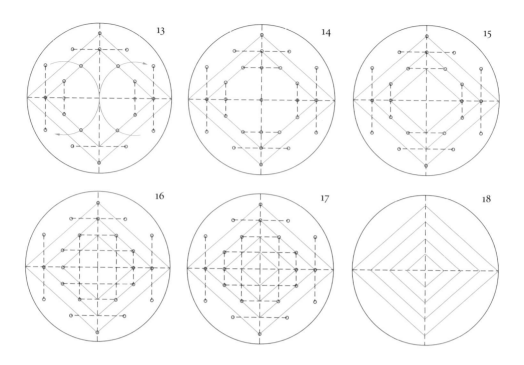

98 Above *The geometry of the Bush Barrow lozenge: 13–18. The now familiar steps create the third lozenge (Stages 13–15). Joining the inner nodes shown on Stage 15 provides the points of the fourth (innermost) lozenge (Stages 16–17).*

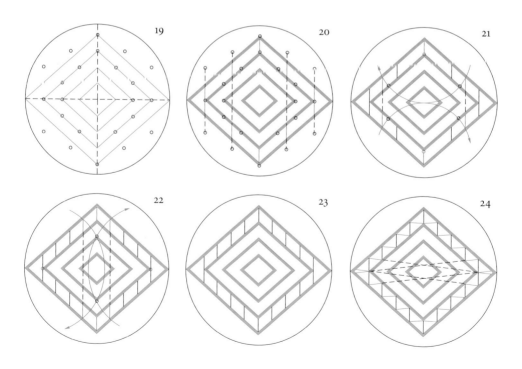

99 Opposite below *The geometry of the Bush Barrow lozenge: 19–24. The points used in setting out the lozenge design (19) are then used to establish the decorative elements (Stages 20–24). The reason for slight but significant details such as the overlap of the first pair of diagonals above and below the long axis becomes apparent, as do the relationships between the truly vertical incised border lines and the almost horizontal lines which converge slightly as the top of each vertical is joined to the base of its inner neighbour.*

100 Right *The geometry of the Bush Barrow lozenge: 25. The finished design with its decorative incised lines and central motif.*

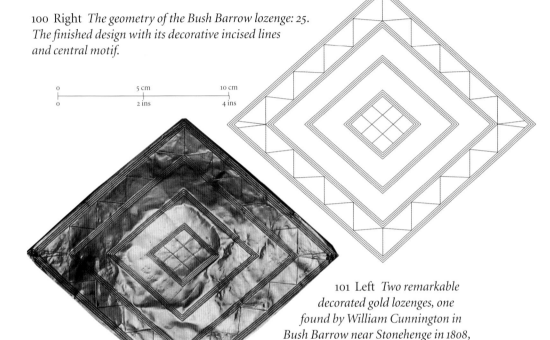

101 Left *Two remarkable decorated gold lozenges, one found by William Cunnington in Bush Barrow near Stonehenge in 1808, and the other by his grandson Edward almost 75 years later at Clandon, near Dorchester in Dorset, c. 80 km to the southwest, display similar geometric design principles, and may even have been made by the same craftsman or workshop (see p. 269).*

102 Right *Gold button cover base (left) and gold bound amber disc (right) found in a barrow c. 200 m from Bush Barrow showing considerable precision in their incised design.*

185

CHAPTER 7

The Prehistoric Surveyors

In the previous chapter, I suggested that the architects and builders of Stonehenge used elegantly simple geometric principles which employed motifs and designs that could easily be transferred onto the ground. This emphasis upon the architectural aspects of Stonehenge needs some justification. If the monument was designed on a drawing board, or its prehistoric equivalent, it should be possible to work back to the original concept of its design and the methods used in its surveying. In principle anything that could be constructed using a straight edge and some kind of compass or scribing device could be recreated by surveyors using pegs and cords. It is now time to look at the archaeological site plans and consider how this evidence can be retrieved.

When people began to build even the most rudimentary structures and set out the first fields and enclosures, important discoveries would have been made concerning the relationships of survey cord lengths, folded cords, and circles. There is even remarkable and unambiguous evidence that the principles of geometric design were understood tens of thousands of years before Stonehenge was built. In 2002, excavators at Blombos Cave on the Southern Cape shore of South Africa found two smoothed pieces of ochre (red haematite) [103] onto which had been incised a geometric lattice of interconnecting lines. These stones and their associated deposits have been determined by scientific methods to date to the Palaeolithic period ('Old Stone Age') and are over 70,000 years old.[1] The Blombos designs appear to be simply decorative, but it is quite clear that whoever created them was fascinated by the way a lattice with a long axial subdivision creates a series of regular triangles, lozenges and even hexagons. So here we have an example of the earliest known draughtsman employing these devices long before the universal language of geometry was to be put to practical use in the building of formal structures.

Two geometrically incised chalk 'plaques' [104], which were discovered in a Neolithic pit not far from Stonehenge during road widening, demonstrate that the people who lived on Salisbury Plain not long before Stonehenge was built were sketching on portable tablets of rock.[2] One of the plaques interestingly employs mirrored symmetry, which I believe is fundamental to understanding the geometric preoccupations of the later Neolithic and Bronze Age. Such relatively simple 'everyday' examples of ancient draughts-manship give no less an insight into the imagination of Neolithic people than the more painstakingly decorated massive slabs and stones found adorning major sacred structures, such as Newgrange in Ireland or the megalithic tombs of Brittany.

Establishing right angles, squares and triangles, striking perpendicular lines from a baseline, fixing regular points on the circumference of a circle and subdividing angles are all practical procedures which readily translate into cord-and-peg survey methods. Certain formulae would have been com-mitted to memory as part of the skill set of the prehistoric surveyor, and it is not difficult to imagine that this esoteric knowledge would have been handed down from generation to generation. Indeed, in writing this book one of the principles I set myself was that whatever I proposed as a solution to any of the prehistoric surveyor's problems had to be eminently practical. The test would be that I should be able to set out from memory alone all the key elements of the structure of Stonehenge on the ground, at full scale, and accurate to a few centimetres using only a single length of survey cord and a few pegs. I should stress, of course, that by 'key elements' I mean the principal positions where posts were erected and against which stones were set, not the actual footprints and vagaries of the individual stones.

Determining how the prehistoric surveyors arrived at these key survey points required much experimentation and 'reverse engineering', with con-stant reference to the actual archaeological evidence, and the practicalities which determined how a particular grouping may actually have been set out on the ground from an original 'drawing board' concept. The example of the

103 *Geometrical design incised upon a small piece of ochre (c. 6 cm long) of Palaeolithic age (70,000 years old) from Blombos Cave, South Africa.*

Bush Barrow lozenge presented in the previous chapter illustrates the application of prehistoric technical drawing perfectly. Looking through the computer files I found that I had experimented with well over 100 separate CAD models of the Bush Barrow lozenge before the relatively simple principles and details of its geometric design became apparent. The analysis of the various structures at Stonehenge presented a far more complex problem, as it could not be assumed that settings were always established directly in relation to immediate or even near neighbours, and positions might have been 'filled in' from survey points beyond the structure (just as the Bush Barrow lozenge had some original marking-out points outside the finished design). In fact, I imagined the problems to be far more challenging than they actually proved to be. One important revelation was how little use had been made of any external survey control points.

Currently no archaeological relationships have been found at Stonehenge to demonstrate the order of construction of the Sarsen Circle and Horseshoe – it could even be argued that there is nothing to prove that they even belong to the same phase of activity. The interpretation of contemporaneity is based on a series of assumptions succinctly summarized by Richard Atkinson: 'In the absence of any positive evidence that the sarsen structures are of different dates, one must accept their symmetry about a common axis and the similarity of their shaping and jointing as sufficient reasons for treating them all as parts of one and the same design.'[3] Atkinson was stressing the need to avoid what he described as the 'unnecessary multiplication of hypotheses', a maxim

104 *Neolithic decorated chalk plaques found in a pit close to King Barrow Ridge, approximately 1 km from Stonehenge. The plaque on the right clearly displays mirrored symmetry.*

particularly relevant in the use of archaeological evidence, and one I have tried to keep to the fore in my own interpretations of the geometry and setting-out of the monument. The burden of unfounded hypotheses that Atkinson alluded to has created a haze through which some of the most important aspects of the site's construction have become obscured.

Before examining the concepts behind the various arrangements within the earthwork, it is useful to look at the information presented by the plans of both the surviving features and those known from archaeological excavation and the photographic record:

1. The circular nature of the monument, which was retained throughout its life, with structural elements usually regularly spaced in various concentric arrangements and radially offset from a more-or-less common centre. In all probability this centre was always intended to be exact in respect of the earthwork;

2. In later periods a carefully planned symmetry about a common axis which passes through the entrance is apparent; even where the 'circularity' rule appears to be broken, e.g. in the two 'horseshoe' arrangements of bluestone and sarsen, the two halves are always mirror-images;

3. The four outlying Station Stones, set just inside the tail of the earthwork, often described as a rectangle, are placed accurately with respect to the centre of the monument and its axis;

4. The clear concern by the builders to maintain a high degree of precision within the construction was extended to include the elevation of

the monument. This is clearly indicated by the careful rebating of the underside on one of the sarsen lintels to ensure that it sat level with its neighbour;

5 Evidence of dressing is apparent on almost all the stones. Both the supporting uprights and the faces of the lintels of the Sarsen Circle and Horseshoe in particular were given a great deal of attention. In the curvature of the lintels attention was again drawn to the overwhelming desire to achieve harmony. Several of the earlier bluestones were elaborately worked, and the presence of two bluestone lintels reflects the methods of construction which were used in the sarsen structure: that the bluestones were reused on at least one occasion is important;

6 An immense amount of planning was required, and a substantial amount of prefabrication involved: the sarsen lintels were near perfect when fitted and were produced with accurately interfacing joints, but not all to the same pattern. These are considerations which have far-reaching implications with respect to the design and even the 'function' of the monument.

If a clear link could be established between the concentric structures and spacing, namely the overall symmetry of Stonehenge, could the geometric rules governing its design, and any possible methodology, be recovered? Where would one begin to look? Did the people who built the early earth and timber monument use different methods of setting-out than those responsible for the sarsen structure several hundred years later?

Let's start with the obvious, and ubiquitous, circle. There is only one way it could have been laid out on the ground, namely with a simple string and peg. This fact provides a thread of continuity from the first earthwork and posts through to the Y and Z Holes dug some 1,500 years later. Laying out a circle is hardly difficult, but as experimentation led to increasing sophistication and the empirical understanding of other geometric principles, a series of repeatable and reliable rules must have been discovered which would no doubt have been a source of great fascination. These geometric forms and their construction are now so familiar to us that we hardly consider them, but at some point in prehistory they were revelations, not forgetting that even as the first antler picks were breaking the ground at Stonehenge, over 4,000 km to the east in Mesopotamia the principles of geometry and mathematics had not only been discovered, but had been written down, and the formulae put to practical use.

How far had empirical understanding of geometry and its application to surveying progressed in later Neolithic Britain? There is ample evidence in the landscape for extensive works established long before Stonehenge, which could not have been laid out without some rudimentary understanding of the methods and principles of survey geometry. The ability to establish straight lines, rectilinear forms and symmetrical structures is seen in monuments such as the long narrow parallel-ditched (so-called Cursus) earthworks, some built as long as 6,000 years ago (making them among the earliest monumental structures in the world, see Chapter 1). Other Neolithic structures demonstrate that cord-and-peg surveying was known in Britain and Ireland before 3000 BC: for example, the magnificent (now restored) megalithic passage tomb at Newgrange, 50 km north of Dublin, for example, with its superb linear and curvilinear decorated kerbstones and its 'roof box', a device clearly designed to allow the midwinter sun to penetrate the centre, was carefully set out over 600 years before the first stone structures at Stonehenge.[4] There are many other examples of prehistoric surveying skills to be found in the British Isles; suffice it to say here that the knowledge needed to construct Stonehenge was already mature by the time the decision was made to build the sarsen monument. But Stonehenge was not only to be a structure of unique leviathan proportions – it was to bring together an unparalleled and extraordinary combination of design, survey and construction skills.

Clues to the surveyors' and builders' methods can be found in two key areas: first amongst standing or excavated features which preserve the most complete and accurate geometry, and secondly in minor deviations, showing that sometimes in practice the methods fell short of achieving what was clearly the intention.

The notion that a fixed unit of prehistoric measurement may have been used not only at Stonehenge but at other Neolithic and Bronze Age monuments was a preoccupation of many antiquarians, and of some archaeoastronomers. William Stukeley, writing in the 18th century, was convinced that the builders of Stonehenge had used a dimension which he referred to as a 'Druids' cubit'.

At the end of the 19th century, Flinders Petrie concluded that two units of measurement had been employed – one related to the earthwork and Station Stones, and the second to set out the central sarsens and inner bluestones (see page 79). More recently Alexander Thom proposed, on the basis of ground surveys of a large number of stone circles and of hundreds of megalithic monuments in the British Isles and Brittany, that a highly accurate unit, which he called the 'Megalithic Yard', had been in common use.[5] There is no agreement on whether any such universal system of measurement was used, and Thom's ideas have found little support among archaeologists, for it is difficult to see how an exact scheme of measurement (argued by Thom to be 0.829 m) could be extracted from the measurement of stones of largely natural form some of which have been variously displaced over four millennia or more, nor how, if it existed, such an accurate dimension could have been maintained between such geographically disparate locations. Elaborate claims as to how this could have been achieved have been made involving complicated calculations and contrivances that are hardly credible in a Neolithic context.[6] However, the discovery in Denmark of what has been described as a hazel-wood measuring rod in a Middle Bronze Age grave suggests that some standard, or at least transferable, system of measurement may have existed, even if only locally employed.[7]

The problems of maintaining 'millimetre' accuracy using rods, cords and pegs over ground which is often sloping or uneven would have been difficult in the extreme. But it is perfectly reasonable to ask whether Stonehenge was laid out using measuring rods, or whether survey control could have been maintained using cords stretched from a series of survey stations, whose locations were determined solely by a geometric model. I believe that the question answers itself: the real virtue of geometric-based construction is its 'scalability', i.e. no measurements (no units of prehistoric metrology) need be translated from the 'plan', as all the geometrically derived dimensions are self-scaling on the ground. In other words, to fix the setting of a polar array of a certain number of uprights on the site, the engineers could simply have scribed a circle of the required diameter, and then used a known method (i.e. a simple geometric formula) which would set out the desired vertices on the circumference; all the evidence which follows suggests this to have been the case.

Computers and maps

The first requirement in examining the design and layout of Stonehenge was to obtain the most accurate measured survey. Modern digital mapping of the surface features (the earthworks and stones visible above ground level), kindly provided by English Heritage from a 1989 survey, provided the basic framework for all my subsequent plans, and in addition provided some 1,600 spot heights which were extracted to create digital topographic models. All the significant excavation work had been undertaken in the days before computers, and so no original data exists in a form that can simply be introduced into a CAD programme. To obtain mapping of the buried archaeological detail from excavations undertaken between 1901 and the 1970s it was necessary to digitize the excavation plans; the positions of individual features were, where possible, checked against the 'hard' detail in respect of the positions of the nearest stones.

A remarkable paradox is that the most valuable data recorded prior to 1989 are the measurements compiled by the architect John Wood in 1740, when he and his son meticulously recorded hundreds of dimensions to an accuracy of half an inch (12.7 mm). This data was eminently capable of being converted into what is now the earliest digital version of Stonehenge; the computer plot of his work presented in this book is published for the first time. Wood's original plans are shown on p. 68 and p. 69, and my computer version on p. 195. I could find only a single mistake in Wood's transcription of his field notes, which meant that his map shows the position of the fallen and broken upright of the northern trilithon (Stones 59b and c) displaced too far to the southeast. However, it was clear from comparison between his annotated plan and text where the error lay, and it could be easily corrected.[8] Wood was prevented from accurately recording the shape of three of the bluestones (Stones 46, 47 and 48) as they were too 'incumbered with Dung and other Rubbish', and also the surviving upright of the northern trilithon (Stone 60) and the ground immediately in front of it, which were obscured by wooden huts. Whilst the accuracy of Wood's survey is outstanding, he could not have achieved the same degree of precision provided by modern surveying equipment. Nevertheless, there is no reason why his measurements cannot be used for comparative cartographic purposes, particularly as they provide unique information such as the position of the westernmost trilithon almost 60 years before it fell. Overlaying his plan on modern surveys shows that where stones have not been subjected to 20th-century engineering work the correspondence is remarkable, and it is clear that in the case of certain disputed stones the positions recorded by Wood over 250 years ago should take precedence over those of the 'modern' substantially restored Stonehenge. A comparison between Wood's survey and the modern plan is shown on p. 196.

For the rest of the map work used in my calculations I have relied on plans in the 1995 English Heritage publication *Stonehenge in its Landscape.*[9] Where dimensions are quoted or have been converted from feet to metres I have endeavoured to check the calculations back to the original excavation reports. Measurements have also been abstracted from the survey done by Flinders Petrie in 1877.[10] Small errors between disparate groups of buried features have to be accepted, and in any case are often unavoidable, as the Stonehenge plans are composite versions of many years of fieldwork records compiled throughout the 20th century by a number of different excavators.

Before looking in detail at any aspect of Stonehenge, whether visible or buried, I must stress that the inclusion here of dimensions to two decimal places does not imply accuracy to a centimetre on any plan, or that the subsequent computer calculations are the exact site dimensions; they are close as possible given the problems of the Stonehenge archive.[11] Fundamental errors that are all too often repeated are, first, the assumption that the currently published surveys of Stonehenge are accurate enough to be used for detailed calculations, which they are certainly not, and secondly – and more importantly – that even where good measured surveyed detail can be found, all the stones still stand in the exact positions in which they were set by the prehistoric surveyors. Furthermore, in deciding what to represent on the plan the modern surveyor of the monument is often faced with a choice as to which part of the often irregularly shaped stone finds its way on to the finished drawing. These choices are influenced by the effects of thousands of years of weathering and settlement, which means that the bases of some of the stones have often significantly shifted and been exposed or undercut by erosion. A further difficulty in retrieving a 'true' plan is that the ground surface is

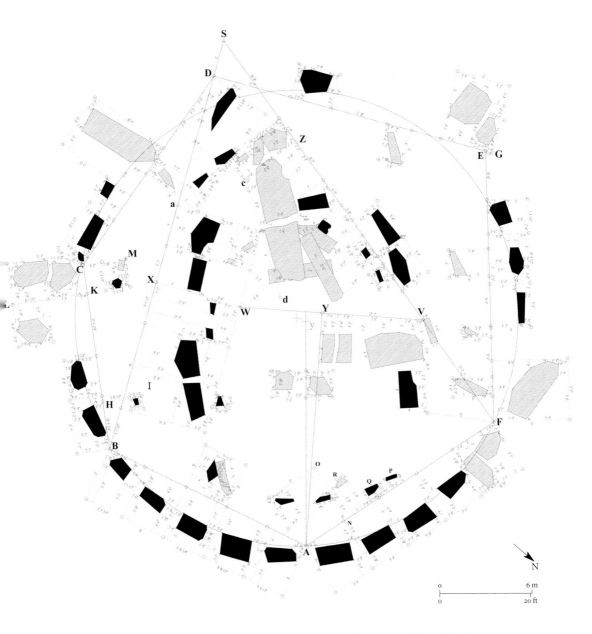

105 *A computer-generated version of John Wood's survey of 1740, using his original orientation, baselines, survey stations and chainage measurements (in feet and inches), with a correction to his single transcription error by which he displaced the positions of two fragments of the fallen upright of the northwest trilithon.*

106 *Comparison between Wood's survey and the modern plan. The * suffix indicates stones subject to 20th-century engineering works.*

markedly lower than when the stones were first erected. As if these are not complications enough, there is the cumulative impact of the various phases of remedial engineering work at Stonehenge to consider. Anyone who is unclear as to the amount and scale of what took place in the 20th century needs only to look at Julian Richards's book *Stonehenge: A History in*

Photographs,[12] a volume that chronicles the extent of the restoration work in the late 1950s and early 1960s, showing a number of the stones either out of the ground completely or in the process of being lifted back into position. These photographs should be studied before any sightline theories based on precise calculations derived from the present stone positions are contemplated.

In the present computer study, the CAD 'three-point circle' tool was frequently used to determine the potential centres of circular structures; this facility allows any three selected points to be included on the exact circumference of a computer-generated circle, the centre of which can then be instantly determined. A series of such calculations allows estimates to be made of slightly irregular works and permits 'trials' where certain stones or holes can be included or excluded in establishing the potential diameter of a circular setting. This facility is especially useful where some of the group are displaced from their original setting.

To summarize: the value of early surveys is complemented, not diminished, by the application of sophisticated modern methods of recording the stones. Existing plans of buried features derive from a variety of disparate archive material, but by using a combination of early cartographic sources and digital data it is possible to create drawings which can be cross-checked between the various records that have been compiled over a period of more than 250 years.

The Y and Z Holes

For my first detailed computer investigations I chose to examine the Y and Z Hole series. This may at first sight appear to be a curious choice, because these holes are the least accurately set out of the major concentric elements within the Stonehenge earthwork. There were two reasons for selecting them. First, they are the latest known features to have been created at Stonehenge; on present evidence they were dug at a time when quite complex geometric principles were clearly understood and employed, a fact which is unambiguously demonstrated from the precise designs which embellish contemporary artifacts. By examining a series of identical holes dug towards the end of the life of the monument one might expect to find something within the scheme of their setting-out that was a mature reflection of methods that may have been in use

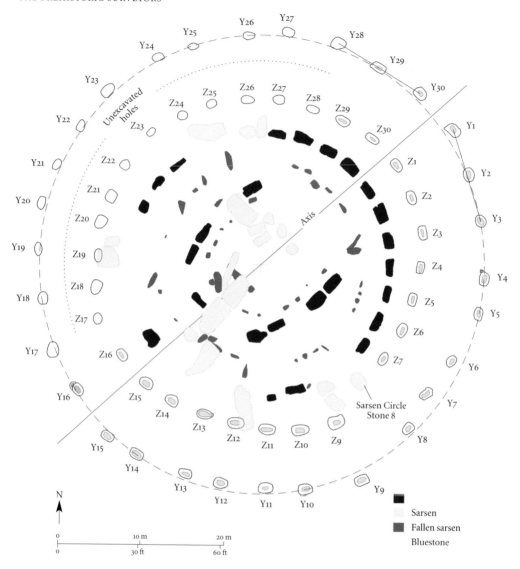

107 *Plan of the Y and Z Holes in relation to the stone monument.*

for centuries. Secondly, and very importantly, the Y and Z Holes include mis-takes, errors which permit an interpretation of the surveyors' methodology that cannot be easily retrieved from perfectly executed examples.

To provide an illustration, let us imagine the discovery of a ring of 30 post settings, all of exactly the same diameter, with each post standing precisely on a vertex of a 30-sided regular polygon (technically a triacontagon). How was the regular spacing of posts achieved? One can assume that the builders first scribed the circle and fixed the centres of six key timbers at the vertices of a hexagon; this would of course be struck using the radius string that was used to mark the circle. In our hypothetical model there is naturally no single axis present in the design or variation in the size or locations of the posts in plan, form, or by depth of setting or deposits within the postholes to indicate anything other than a regular ring. In the absence of further evidence little more can be said about this hypothetical case, other than recognizing that the builders aspired to perfection and were accomplished surveyors. Fortunately, in the archaeological record such occurrences are rare in the extreme; physical variations will be found, there will be a deviation from perfect geometry, or perhaps a small detail will emphasize one particular aspect of a structure. If, for example, the supposition that the builders began by setting-out a hexagon is correct, then a more accurate primary group of six posts might be found amongst the 30, or reciprocal groups of six accurate relationships identified around the circumference – perhaps a pair of larger settings framed an entrance or suggested an axis extending from the centre of the ring. It is this variability which provides the greatest number of potential clues, and hence the possibility of resolving the methods and intentions of the prehistoric surveyors.

The evidence of the surveyors' method provided by errors in the Y Holes

Many theories regarding the function and purpose of the Y and Z Holes have been advanced since they were first discovered by Hawley in 1923, but few begin with a critical examination of the archaeological evidence, nor how their seemingly erratic pattern arose. As a result we find explanations which include spirals and other untenable creations. I intend to start from the premise that there are no 'spirals' and no deliberate contortions, there are just two concentric rings of pits whose surveying went very badly wrong. Exactly why the surveyors were content to accept such poor patterns of spacing within this final spate of activity is a mystery equal to that of the question of their intended use, but obstructions caused by the presence of the sarsens, either standing or fallen, are usually cited as the reason for the errors, although it could equally be argued that the standards of excellence shown in earlier work had simply been neglected. Two obvious questions come to mind. As the centre was obstructed by the stone monument, how did the surveyors set out the Y and Z Holes without being able to scribe the circuits on the ground? And secondly, why did they not simply measure the required hole positions from the standing stones? The answer to the irregularity is revealed (below) using CAD modelling; why the simple option of offsetting from the standing stones was ignored remains one of the imponderables of Stonehenge.

I have focused on the outer Y Holes, as they demonstrate the greatest variations, and the wider spacing between the holes is susceptible to more accurate plotting on the CAD model; the contemporary Z Holes would have been laid out using the same methods. As the holes lack a vertical face against which any intended stones could have been accurately set, it is assumed that the original survey pegs marked the pit centres. Using the best available groundplan compiled from Hawley's original archive, a circle was first drawn to touch the maximum long-axis of each hole to determine its nominal centre; the fairly regularly tapering sides meant that these centres invariably fell within the basal footprint. Those pit locations which had been established by probing rather than excavation (Y17–Y28) were included in the drawing at this stage but not (with the exception of Y28) in subsequent calculations. Using the CAD 'three-point circle' tool, the centres were then selected for computation to give the best estimate of the circuit on which the Y Holes had been established; the few that displayed significant inward or outward radial deviation from the mean (e.g. Y7 and Y9) were excluded from the initial calculation, as were the two pits which flank the axis (Y30 and Y1). Calculations of the Y Hole radius ranged between 26.88 m and 27.15 m, depending on which of the holes was selected. A best-fit circle of c. 27 m radius passed through the centres of seven out of the 18 excavated holes, and within c. 30–50 cm of a further five, which was deemed acceptable, particularly taking into account inevitable minor errors in plotting their excavated locations from various site plans; the majority, including those known from probing, sit comfortably on or very close to, the circumference of this circle.

Stressing the conformity of the majority highlights the anomalous, most notably holes Y6, Y7 and Y9 (the first two lying significantly inside the circumference and the latter outside) and the 'portal' pair flanking the axis (Y30

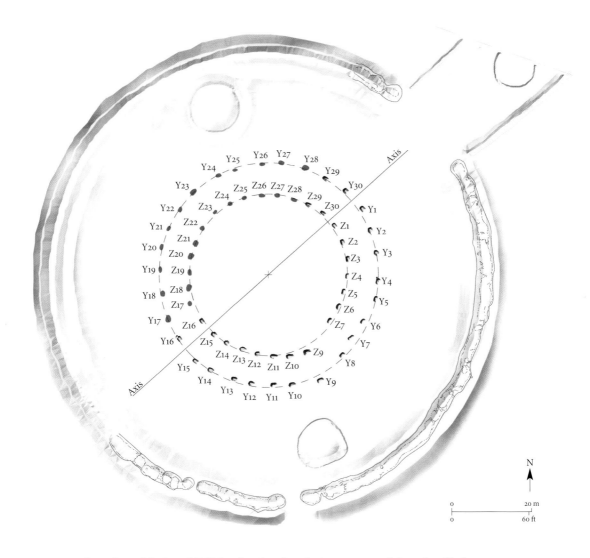

108 *Overview of the Y and Z Holes showing the relative accuracy of the pairs of holes on either side of the 'portal' settings (Y30 and Y1), and also demonstrating that the circuits on which the Y and Z Holes lie are more regular than often supposed.*

and Y1), their status emphasized by the deliberate deposition of five stag antlers in the base of Y30. These two holes were certainly dug further out from the rest, but, significantly, not equally so (Y30 by about 0.5 m and Y1 by 1 m). But if these 'key' pits were wrong, surely there would be little hope in finding symmetry within the rest? This appeared to be an unpromising start. These radial offset errors are not the only discrepancies in the layout: there are clearly major differences in the spacing between neighbouring pits. Thirty regular points set on a circle with the radius of 27 m should be 5.64 m apart. The distance Y2–Y3 is almost perfect, and what is interesting is that despite the significant outward radial displacement of Y1, the distance to its neighbour (Y2) is only a few centimetres short of the ideal, implying that the pit-to-pit distance was being maintained despite the radial shift. Similarly, Y29 and Y30 were also almost exactly the correct distance apart. So, if the distance between the holes was consistent what accounts for the radial displacement of the 'portal pair'? The CAD model reveals that these two holes actually sit on lines projected through Y28–Y29 and Y3–Y2, and the convergence of these lines at a slightly different point in respect of the axial symmetry of the monument has displaced the portals beyond the circle. Their forward displacement and slight lack of symmetry, although visible on the plan, would hardly have been noticeable on the ground. It is this relationship between the groups of three pits on either side of the axis which provides a further vital clue to the setting out of the Y and Z Holes.

To attempt to solve these problems we need to go back to the drawing board. The first principle, and one which is an important consideration in the construction at Stonehenge from the time of the introduction of the bluestones onward, is the use of mirrored symmetry in the design. Despite the deviations there is considerable regularity in the Y Hole circuit, which is particularly noticeable within the leading northeast group (where there is increased visibility from the centre of the monument through the splay of the Sarsen Horseshoe) [109]. A very important point of detail now needs to be stressed: the Stonehenge axis was always a clear sightline, but to place a series of 30 holes around the monument so that a pair falls on either side of the axis is not as simple as it may at first appear. The following model for fixing the 30 regular settings so that the lead pair falls on either side of the axis [110] assumes an open and unobstructed site, which of course was not the case with the Y and Z Holes, but this will nevertheless become important later when comparing an ideal procedure with the reality faced by the prehistoric surveyors, and will help explain the errors in the Y and Z Holes.

How, if the centre of the monument was largely obstructed, could the radial cords needed to fix the hexagon-pentagon relationship have been swept through the centre of the monument? Quite simply, apart from the few

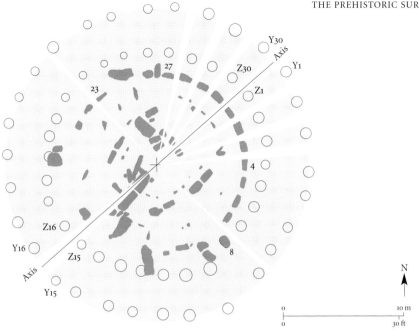

109 *The Y and Z Hole circuit was late, perhaps the last, in the sequence of events at Stonehenge, and the presence of the sarsen uprights now meant that no continuous circle could be scribed from the centre. Despite this severe restriction, a reasonably accurate arc extending some 30 degrees either side of the axis could have been established on the northeast side through 'windows' offered by the open arms of the trilithon Horseshoe between the uprights of the Bluestone and Sarsen Circles. From Stone 27 to Stone 4 of the Sarsen Circle, a series of radial lines run through gaps to pegs on the circumference would have defined one fifth of the circuit (accounting for the fact that these holes are the most accurately surveyed). On either side of this arc the use of survey lines would have been confined to the axis and two small corridors which were not exactly perpendicular to the centre (the true line being blocked by Stones 23 and 8).*

'windows' of visibility, the majority were not. It is possible, albeit difficult, to lay out a hexagon and pentagon without ever scribing a complete circle. What the surveyors appear to have done was to rotate the required survey cord lengths around key points on the desired circumference, and it is for this reason that the Y and Z Holes are somewhat irregular.

Is this no more than an interesting speculation? It would be so if the evidence from the plan did not show a whole series of reciprocal errors repeated around the circumference of the ring of holes demonstrating exactly how it was done. There are very good hole-to-hole relationships present within the

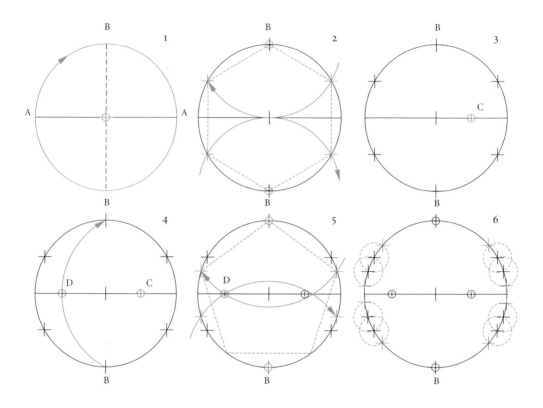

110 *The prehistoric surveyors' method of marking out 30 positions so that a pair falls on either side of the axis. The procedure begins by creating a circle on a baseline A–A and perpendicular (B–B), as shown on Stage 1. The vertices of a hexagon are found from points B using the line used to scribe the circle (i.e. the radial), and six of the intended hole positions now marked on the circumference. The surveyors needed to mark the 24 remaining positions. A simple method is to inscribe the internal angle of the pentagon within the circle, with one of its vertices coinciding with that of the hexagon. To create the angle of the pentagon, two further temporary survey markers are fixed on the baseline: the first at C (half the radius – the surveyors could simply have folded the survey cord in half); the second peg is found by transferring the distance C–B onto the baseline to locate peg D (Stages 3 and 4). The distance B–D is then transferred to the circle, intersecting at the four positions marked in red on Stage 5. The adjacent vertices of the hexagon-pentagon return the cord spacing of the required 30 settings. In the case of the Y and Z array, where the 'pentagon' vertices fall is significant: they mark the centres next but one to the holes flanking the baseline. In other words, this hexagon-pentagon gives precedence and greater accuracy to the setting-out of the second and third pairs on either side of the baseline, which would explain the relative accuracy shown by the Y Holes 28–29 and 2–3, and also the offsetting of the portal positions of 30 and 1, which had to be found from their neighbours in the absence of a continuously scribed circuit.*

whole group which at first appear random and erratic, but, when examined as a series which reflect the way in which the survey lines were stretched across the circumference, it becomes apparent that they are not. The errors occur in groups that cannot be explained in any other way. The single biggest problem would have been in trying to control the radial offset distances, and it looks very much as if the surveyors soon abandoned radial accuracy around most of the circuit; other spacing remained tolerably good because it was being transferred from point to point with their fixed lengths of survey line.

The Y and Z Holes represent more than just a numeric sequence; they are also illustrations of the use of geometric principles which had been established for hundreds of years, employed in the iconography of contemporary artifacts. The Y series encloses twice the area of the Z circuit, the

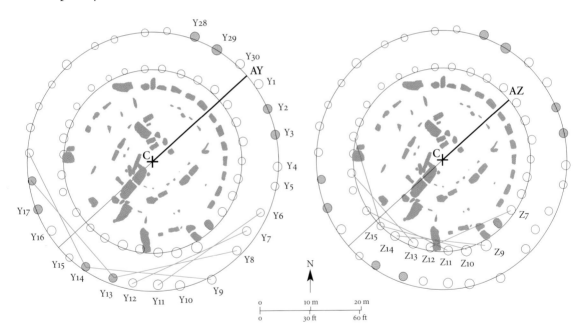

111 *Unable to swing arcs through the centre, and in the absence of a scribed circle, the surveyors resorted to using ropes run around the circumference to establish the spacing between holes. The rope lengths represent the radius of each of the circuits (C–AY and C–AZ), which logically returned the spacing between every sixth hole. This gave the correct distance between certain groups, but without reference to the centre circularity could not be controlled; deviations can be seen e.g. Y9, the most erratic of the series, was set out at the correct distance from the relatively accurate Y14 but failed to conform to the Y Hole circumference.*

product of inscribing a circle inside a square, and a second outside – the relationship is too precise to be coincidental. Similar geometry can be found at other prehistoric sites which employ concentric circles (Chapter 10).

I have not exhausted the evidence of the Y and Z plan positions. The CAD model has returned sequences that show certain groups relating more exactly with others, but there is little to be gained in going into further detail here. In the next two chapters I hope to show how the information derived from the Y and Z Holes has an important practical application in understanding the methods used in surveying the earlier phases of the monument.

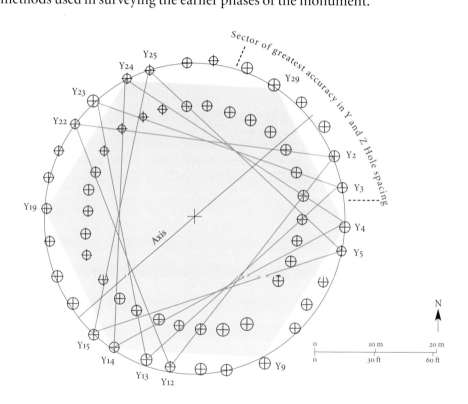

112 *Analysis of the Y and Z circuits using a computer model reveals that, despite their erratic appearance, reasonable accuracy can be found in certain groupings of holes: those in the northeast sector and, for example, others such as those identified by the hexagon. A recurring pattern of narrow-wide-narrow spacing can also be seen between 12 of the 30 Y Holes in three groups of four (Y2–5, Y12–15 and Y22–25). Because the centre was largely blocked by the sarsens, survey ropes could never have been stretched in the triangular configuration of the computer model, but this pattern nevertheless highlights repetition of errors transferred around the circumference.*

CHAPTER 8

The Geometry of the Early Monument

The Stonehenge earthwork began with at least one accurately marked out circle, and during its construction care was taken to follow the surveyors' marks – 'care' that is, but not what could be described as 'exactness'. Only half of the irregularly dug ditch circuit has been excavated, and so where its centreline is perceived to have lain depends upon which of the more non-concentric segments are included in the computation; estimations based upon the radius measured to the ditch centre within the quadrant flanking the causeway would give a diameter of 106 m. However, using a combination of information from photogrammetric and geophysical survey and other detailed topographic records to identify the course of the uninvestigated (western) half of the circuit, an average centreline would have a diameter closer to 108 m. Taking the three post settings apparently set along the spine of the largely unexcavated bank as its centreline gives a diameter along its crest of 97.5 m. As the earthwork is not quite regular, and has been subject to differential patterns of erosion, it is impossible to be exact.

There may well have been a prehistoric reference marker fixed within the centre of Stonehenge, but this area has been so extensively disturbed that we shall never know. However, temporary central pegs must undoubtedly have been used, even if only for brief periods during the marking out of the various constructions. Throughout its long history of use Stonehenge evidently had more than one centre, for the successive arrays are not precisely

207

concentric, nor would they be expected to be. There is a note of caution needed here: it is impossible to be sure how the various historic and often-quoted displacements for the various perceived centres of each phase of the monument have been arrived at. The only recent calculations are those by Wessex Archaeology in 1995.[1] Exact agreement cannot be expected between published dimensions compiled from plans derived from a variety of survey and excavation records which did not even share a common grid or coordinate system, particularly where a degree of interpretation has had to be made in respect of the significance of slight irregularities in the earthwork. Even after subjecting the best available English Heritage digital plans to CAD examination over a number of years, I can return only a series of reasonably accurate dimensions for both the ditch and bank and Aubrey Hole circuit; it is simply impossible to be as confident as some accounts suggest in citing relationships that supposedly existed between them and the later central stone structures. It is quite clear, for example, that the notion of an exact concentric relationship between the earthwork and Aubrey Holes, often argued to show that they are contemporary, is insecure.

The Aubrey Holes

As they lie on a circumference of a circle of considerable diameter, it is relatively easy to find a fairly accurate centre-mark for the circuit of 56 Aubrey Holes. A series of three-point CAD circles drawn through their centres shows them to have been set on a circle with a diameter within a very few centimetres of 87 m. The ideal spacing between the pits on a circle of this diameter would be 4.9 m. I must stress again that the dimensions quoted here have to allow for the history and disparate nature of the plotting and transcription of these features onto a composite plan; this does not affect their geometry, it simply means that the actual circuit cannot be calculated with absolute accuracy. There is some unnecessary confusion in the literature as to whether to measure the circuit to the centres or the inner edges of the holes. Clearly the centres of the smallest pits must be taken to lie on the circumference closest to the original surveyed circle; holes could have been enlarged and distorted but never reduced in size. Having determined the centre and ideal pit spacing, the second stage was to investigate whether individual pits showed a

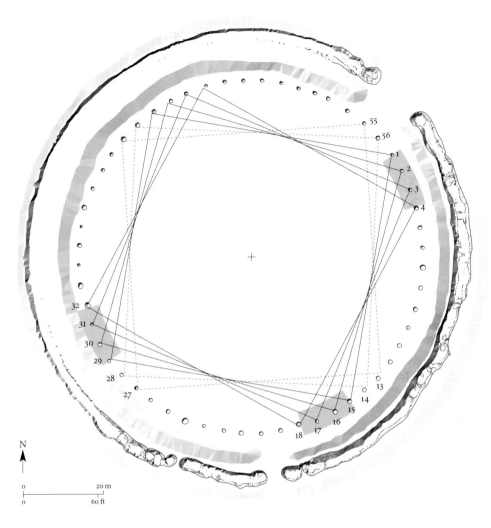

113 *Rotating a square about a common centre within the Aubrey Hole circuit to test for regularity between groups of reciprocal settings, which might indicate where the original surveyors' baseline and perpendiculars were established. Thirty-six holes have been excavated (AH 1–32 and 55–56); the location of the remainder is known only from probing. Using only the excavated examples restricts the test to six groupings, each providing reciprocal points on three sides of the square (the fourth corner in all cases lies within the unexcavated half of the circuit). It is interesting to note that the holes fronting the causeway (AH 55 and 56) show the least accurate geometric relationships with their reciprocals (13–29 and 14–28 respectively) and are unlikely therefore to have marked key survey positions and suggests that there was no axis or concern for the symmetry shown in the later monument.*

particular degree of relative geometric accuracy (or discrepancy) with respect to their neighbours (as seen in the Y Holes in Chapter 7).

There are certain obvious predictable relationships which need little explanation; clearly an axis between any two diametrically opposed pits could theoretically represent a baseline, but in reality only those opposing pairs whose diameters cross at the centre of the computed circle are contenders for having been master survey lines. The number of holes (56) divides into quarters and eighths, suggesting that survey control was established using the corners of squares or the vertices of octagons. Which of the holes, if any, lie at the corners of a square whose diagonals pass exactly through the computed centre of the circle? The easiest method to test this hypothesis is to draw a square inscribed within the Aubrey Hole circle and then rotate it so that each time one corner corresponds with a selected pit centre, then the others should also coincide with three further pits. Using only the 36 excavated examples (not those recorded by probing) restricted this test in practice to six groupings of three Aubrey Holes. Starting from the entranceway (clockwise) the first four holes (AH 1–4) are in near-perfect square relationship with their reciprocal partners (AH 15–18 and 29–32), but the two holes which front the causeway (AH 55–56) show a relatively poor geometric relationship with their reciprocals (AH 13, 14, 27 and 28) [113]. What does this mean with respect to how the pits may have been set out? To investigate this further required constructing a 'model' similar to that used to investigate the Y and Z Holes.

Certain groupings conform to more accurate 'square configurations'. Also important, although initially somewhat difficult to understand, is the fact that the accurate holes seem to cluster in groups, suggesting patterns similar to the 'localized' geometric accuracy displayed by several of the Y Holes. Perhaps something other than simply a square or octagon was being used to fix the points? There was one theoretical solution: if the spacing between 30 settings could be found by inscribing a pentagon and hexagon within a circle [110], it would follow that if a heptagon was inscribed within the circle that contained an octagon, then the survey cord length needed to fix the distance between the Aubrey Holes could be found. That, however, was surely impossible as the heptagon is a figure so difficult to draw that it would have demanded something quite extraordinary from our Neolithic surveyors.[2]

But somehow, using very simple methods, they had managed to find the spacing between the vertices of a 56-sided regular polygon.

Time after time the computer 'approximated' the required vertices using every conceivable (and some inconceivable) 'temporary survey points'. An approximation really would not do, as it would undermine the whole idea of the application of a simple geometric construction to Stonehenge. It had been done almost 5,000 years ago and there had to be a simple solution to the problem, one which could be easily transferred onto the ground with ropes and pegs. Nothing produced a practical solution, and browsing mathematics websites reinforced my pessimism. The regular triacontagon, with its 30 sides, and its neat 12-degree angles, and vertices that could frame pentagons, hexagons and decagons, readily opened itself to explanation, but the internal angle of a heptagon which would interplay with those of an octagon and return the correct cord dimension is, to three decimal places, a very inconvenient 128.571 degrees. Furthermore, there is general agreement that 'a regular heptagon is not constructible with a compass and straight edge',[3] meaning it could not be done without resorting to measured dimensions. I had already determined that there was no evidence for measured dimensions in the layout of the Y and Z arrays, where everything had been achieved by the application of geometric proportion; it made no sense to suggest that sophisticated metrology was used in the earliest phase only to be abandoned hundreds of years later. I experimented with the idea that somehow the radial rope had been subdivided to create a measure, but again this broke my self-imposed rule of uncomplicated cord and unmeasured peg-and-cord surveying. There was also one glaring paradox – if a 56-sided regular figure could be constructed in prehistory then so could a heptagon. Perhaps the ancient 56-sided figure had never existed in a truly regular form, and could not be marked out with the field equivalent of a 'compass and straight edge'. The answer had to be practical and empirical, and not essentially mathematical.

For two years or so I continued to look at other aspects of the Stonehenge geometry, returning every few months to the problem of the Aubrey Holes, but without success. What I had learned from the examination of the Y and Z Holes, however, was that the answer could lie in a small detail which could be

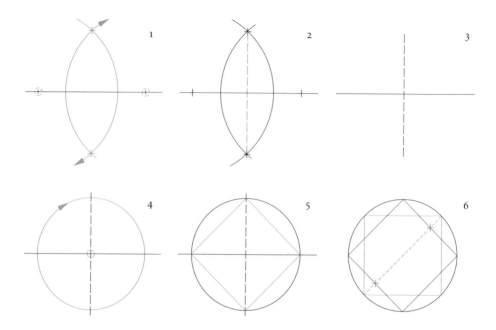

114 *Surveying the Aubrey Holes: a potential solution. Setting out 56 pegs (Stages 1–6). The sequence begins with a baseline and perpendicular (Stages 1–3). A circle is scribed which marks the corners of a square (Stages 4–5). A second square is created by projecting radials through the midpoints of the sides of the first square; the overlapping squares define an octagon (shaded in grey) (Stage 6).*

easily overlooked, I had now built up a series of simple 'Stonehenge rules' learnt from the CAD studies. All the layouts began with a straight baseline onto which a circle was scribed, and invariably the surveyors' construction points lay within the circle. There were key points to be found, usually on the baseline, which controlled how each array was established, and even in what order. Reference was often made to the centre peg and sometimes a cord dimension might be bisected, but above all there was nothing I had seen that could not have been set out with a single length of survey line, and was uncomplicated to the point that it could be set out, significantly, from memory.

I was sure that the surveyors must have begun with a baseline and perpendicular, from the centre of which a circle of the desired diameter was marked (Stages 1–4) [114]. The corners of the square thus created within the circle where it intersected the baseline and perpendicular gave the positions of the first four of the 56 holes (Stage 5). A second square set at 45 degrees to the first, now forming a regular octagon within the circle, provided a further four pit positions (Stage 6); this still left 48 to be found with an inter-pit spacing of 4.9 m.

It was necessary to find the survey peg positions from which an arc could be scribed to cut across the circumference of the circle at one or more of the remaining vertices. Not just any arc, but one in particular, one determined by reference to a survey mark that already existed or was created by the setting out of the squares or octagon. With so many Aubrey Holes to work from, the Stonehenge site plan on the screen soon began to resemble a well-worn dartboard, and the computer was returning potential answers which were becoming progressively more complex. On many occasions, after trying a series of convoluted geometric devices, I approached what appeared to be a solution only to realize that this cannot have been how it was done, at least not with a single rope and a few pegs.

I had allowed the computer only the basic tools to replicate 'cord-and-peg' surveying, thinking that this would approach the truth. This was before I realized that there was something missing; replicating the geometry and applying rules which restricted how it should be done had reduced everything to a mechanical process. A generation of archaeologists who studied at University College, Cardiff would well remember their remarkable mentor, Professor Michael Jarrett, admonishing some poor earnest data-laden undergraduate by loudly proclaiming that 'archaeology is more than a technical exercise'. I needed to bring the human dimension back into the work. On my complex computer drawing all the points had assumed nondescript and common values which are in fact naturally hierarchical when surveyed in the field. Which intersects would the surveyors themselves have regarded as significant? Without preconceptions I tried a different approach, this time by imagining the process of setting out the circles and squares in the field rather than simply looking at their groundplan on a screen.

The most obvious markers, other than the central peg, now appeared to be those where the sides of two rotated squares intersected; these eight points define the vertices of a second smaller octagon rotated 22.5 degrees out of phase with the first. They are clearly potential survey stations, but were they used, and how? An arc drawn through the centre of the circle from one of these points failed to intersect with any of the Aubrey Holes. Perhaps my surveyors had struck the arc to the circumference of the pit circle from this chosen point through one of the other inner octagon vertices? I tried each in turn; the results were close, but again not close enough. There were two other likely points remaining: the two points on the baseline where it intersected with the sides of my original square. The new arc struck from a vertex of the inner octagon (Point A) through one of these baseline intersects (Point a) swept across the circumference of the circle and passed exactly through two Aubrey Hole centres (Stage 7) [115]. I repeated this, assuming that it was a mistake, but there was no error: an arc centred on a vertex of the inner octagon had cut the midpoint of one side of the square in which it was framed, and passed through the vertices of two points of a 56-sided polygon within which the square was inscribed. It is interesting to note the way in which this arc defined the two new pit centres; on one side (clockwise) it passed through the fourth pit centre above the baseline, whilst on the opposite side (below the baseline) it cut the third [116].

Repeating the octagon-square arcs around the circumference of the pit circle ultimately produced a pattern of eight pairs of pit centres in addition to the original eight pits (the corners of the first survey squares), a total of 24 (Stages 8 and 9). In order to complete the circuit, all that was required was for the surveyors to scribe the centres of the 32 infill pits from their neighbours (Stages 10 and 11). The surveyors had achieved this empirically and, despite all the computer time I had devoted to the Aubrey Holes, in the end the solution

115 *Surveying the Aubrey Holes: a potential solution. Setting out 56 pegs (Stages 7–12). The vertices of the inner octagon become anchor points for the surveyor's rope. The distance A–a (points a being the midpoints of two sides of the rotated squares as shown on Stage 7) is transferred to the circumference. This process is repeated from each of the other octagon vertices (as in examples B–b and C–c (Stages 8 and 9)). Stage 10 shows all the positions struck from the octagon, an additional 16 points. The remainder would be infilled by finding the distance between any two surveyed pits and marking it on the circumference of the circle (Stage 11). The final figure (12) shows the 24 surveyed points outlined in red and the 32 infilled positions in black.*

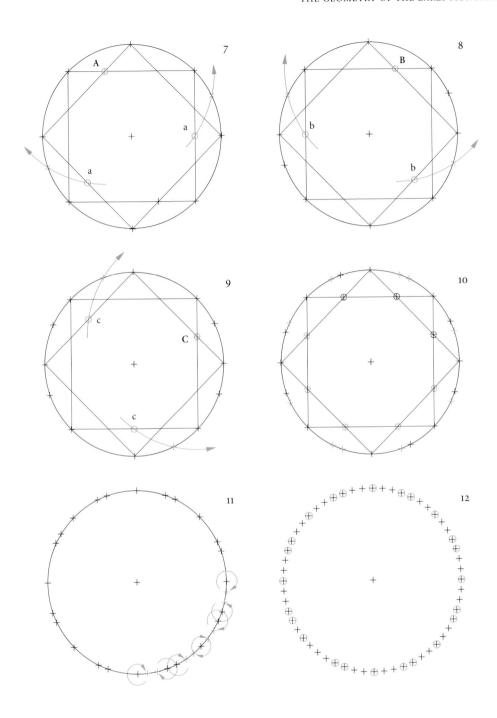

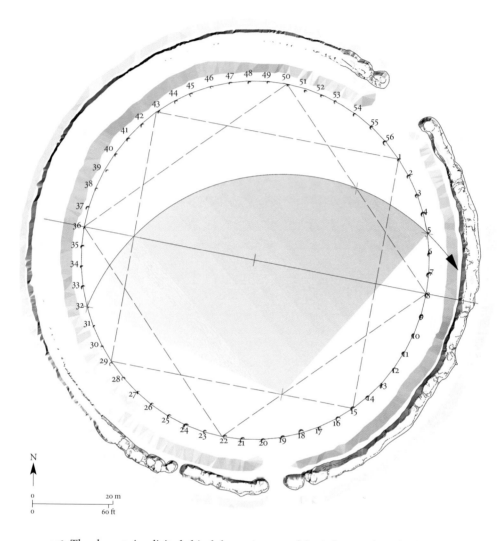

116 *The elegant simplicity behind the setting out of the Aubrey Holes. This figure shows how the prehistoric surveyors achieved accuracy and derived numeric sequences from the relationships between circles and squares. Square-and-circle geometry was also used in determining the spacing between many Neolithic and Bronze Age concentric arrays, both at Stonehenge and elsewhere (see p. 257).*

was also arrived at simply by experimentation. The heptagon theory was half correct. The regular symmetry of the original surveyors' baseline and square had to be broken, but it was not by drawing a heptagon directly, which was impossible, but by scribing a series of arcs which marked out the eight neighbouring pairs of Aubrey Holes midway between the vertices of the outer octagon. The first thing I did after I completed this Aubrey Hole model was to draw the elusive heptagon by joining up every ninth intersect; not because I needed a heptagon, but simply because I could.

Was the number 56 'desired' or was it 'discovered by design'? I prefer the latter, if for no other reason than it would have been simpler to lay out a circle of pits using the simple octagon-square rubric empirically; the alternative demands that their locations were worked out by Neolithic mathematics. Some may consider this possible, I do not. But if it simply reflects an interesting prehistoric discovery, does this mean that the number 56 was insignificant to the people who built Stonehenge, just something that happened to have resulted from experimenting with geometry? I will return to this point again in the final chapter. What is fascinating is how the surveyors used such simple methods which could as easily return the number 56 as they could 30, or indeed any desired subdivision.

Post settings in the interior

Apart from the Aubrey Holes, there are certain other features which are often grouped together on the putative plan of the early phase of the monument, amongst which are hundreds of disparate postholes. It is often suggested that within this pattern of holes can be seen a grand central timber structure which would have occupied much of the area which now contains the Sarsen Circle. Holes which conspire to form arcs, or potential arcs, or suggest 'alignments' and may therefore be related are shown on p. 95. They generally occur in short groups of threes or fours, though some are more persistent, especially those that lie furthest from the central sarsens; perhaps they simply appear to be more coherent because the chalk into which they are cut has not been riddled with later intrusions. However, Hawley removed the turf from over half the interior of the earthwork and had there been any real circularity within the larger outer holes, or even an approximation to a complete circle, it should have been visible. In short, no real evidence exists to group them into any major concentric array, nor has any particular geometric accuracy been noted in respect of their relationship with the centre of the monument.

The early axis

In the very earliest period there was a narrow northeast entrance into the earthwork, but no known single axis. So when was the Stonehenge axis fixed and why, and was there ever more than one? It is universally accepted that the axis of the monument represents the line of the midsummer–midwinter solstices, which is logical in that almost all major non-secular structures, whether prehistoric or modern, invariably display a significant axis of alignment which embodies some aspect of contemporary cosmology. There are several serious contenders amongst the various arrays at Stonehenge, and some thinly disguised pretenders, which might claim primacy in establishing the axis, or at least the first axis, of Stonehenge. The Aubrey Hole circuit clearly disqualifies itself from the outset by displaying a total disregard for 'symmetry about an axis'.

The early bluestone settings of the curious Q and R Holes, whose spacing (nine degrees) would have allowed concentric rings of 40 settings, show no obvious axis; even if there had been an attempt to create an axis by leaving out one of the sequence on the northeast side, the positions of the surviving group show that the array would have been asymmetric. The Q and R series is more closely related to the purely concentric circular arrays derived from square-and-circle geometry reflected in the Aubrey Holes and at other prehistoric sites. The surviving evidence for the Q and R circuits is largely unintelligible and unfortunately the geometry cannot be checked against the excavated remains with any degree of accuracy.

Approximations to what might be interpreted as a formal axis, perhaps more strictly speaking a 'bearing', can be recognized for the first time in the group of 'portal' trenches which appear to have been added to the inside of the R Hole circuit, from which they are morphologically distinct. Importantly, these trenches appear to be antecedents of the portal stones flanking the axis in the Sarsen Circle (Stones 30 and 1), thereby anticipating the axis of symmetry of the later monument. A further link can be seen in the spacing (12 degrees) between these portal trenches, which similarly indicates a 30-setting. One seemingly minor but fundamentally important detail now becomes apparent: the geometry of any settings or arrays that show mirrored-symmetry about an axis demands that the axis line itself is kept clear. In the case of settings with no axis, such as the Aubrey Holes and Q and R Holes, the placement of the surveyors' setting-out points was immaterial; the inset portals, on the other hand, show the first examples of survey set-out in which the geometry permitted an unobstructed axis.

Postholes on the causeway

There are numerous current interpretations of the causeway postholes (shown on p. 173). The view of many archaeoastronomers is that these posts form a series of sightlines which record various major solar and lunar alignments. The proposition is well presented, to the extent that even some archaeologists who are often sceptical of complex astronomical arguments accept the lunar sightline theory. One of the major unsolved problems is how these post settings related to the putative placement of three substantial sarsens: the (then upright) Slaughter Stone and the former uprights that at one time stood in Stoneholes D and E. Hawley thought that the posts were grouped in relation to these stone settings – indeed he used the fact that there appear to be gaps in the posthole array as a major part of his argument for there having been three portal stones: 'The lines of the postholes run towards the sites of these stones and as there are three groups of post-lines it seems very probable that there may have been a third stone.'[4]

The explanation of these postholes as a series of radially offset groups, either in relation to the portal stones or in fixing 'sightlines', is in danger of becoming an incontrovertible fact. This is not to say that the posts could not have functioned as astronomically inspired lines, but the argument is based on their having been established in a series of radial sightlines from the centre of the monument over a considerable period (quoted as six lunar cycles, i.e. 112 years).[5] The archaeological evidence shows that the posts were contemporary, belonging to a single planned phase of construction and associated with the short-lived original narrow entrance. The idea that they were exclusively, or even primarily, radial in their 'design' is insecure – they may appear to be a series of radial arrays, but CAD analysis shows that they were in fact laid out as a series of concentric rings in which the postholes relate to each other along the circumference of a series of six quite regularly spaced concentric arcs which accurately follow the circuit of the earthwork, with perhaps three radial interruptions as Hawley suggested (the group of three or four more substantial holes running contrary to the pattern is clearly unrelated and needs to be excluded from any putative 'sightlines'). As these arcs have diameters in excess of 100 m, the curvature of the post settings is almost imperceptible, but it undoubtedly exists; their circumferential accuracy can even be clearly seen on one of Hawley's rare photographs, which was taken looking across the causeway ditch terminals (p. 103). The subtle curvature of these postholes was also recognized by Thom,[6] but the obvious and relatively simple archaeological and structural implications were lost in his complicated interpretations of their potential function.

The most important point in the setting out of these posts is that their 'concentricity' has logical precedence over radial offset, in other words the series of six arcs had to be established before the timbers were set in a radial pattern. Seen as belonging to a single phase and function, these postholes are more in keeping with other circular geometry of the early monument such as the Aubrey Holes. The concentric arrangement of the posts implies that they were laid out at the same time and from the centre of the monument using cord-and-peg from a common survey mark, perhaps that used to mark out the earthwork. They are clearly early features that served their function, and were gone before any stones arrived on the site (including the group to which the Slaughter Stone belongs). Had these posts been set up over a protracted period of time for the purposes of fixing sightlines, there would have been no advantage in carefully locating subsequent flanking radial arrays on the curves of a series of difficult-to-survey arcs of circumference. Nor is it clear why an alignment used for any kind of sighting purposes would need to use up to six rings of substantial posts of varying diameters spaced only 1 m apart, an arrangement which would tend to confound rather than aid a sightline towards a distant object.

Other external post- or stoneholes

The four regularly spaced holes which lie outside the monument known as the 'Postholes at A', some 20 m beyond the medial line of the ditch, are thought to have been the settings for substantial timbers. The group lies 74 m from the centre of the monument, and several other holes have been found on more or less the same circuit (see p. 173). Although very little can be made of these posts, one interesting detail became apparent on the computer plot. The circuit on which these holes are set (i.e. 74 m radius) has a clear 'square-and-circle' relationship with the Stonehenge ditch. This may be coincidental, and could easily be overemphasized. I certainly do not intend to make anything of this fact on proportional relationships alone; it remains simply an observation. Nor would it be helpful to attempt to make anything of the remaining disparate, undated and isolated postholes and possible stone-holes on the causeway between the entrance and the Heelstone, as they are considered here too insecure to be firmly related to any known phase of activity.

The Station Stones

I have included the four Station Stones in this chapter despite the fact that they unambiguously reflect the axis and symmetry of the later 'wide entrance'. Two of the Station Stones survive (Stones 91 and 93); the second pair is known only from its stoneholes. The actual settings themselves are undated, although there is a strong argument that suggests that for logistical and practical reasons they must have been set out from the centre before the major sarsen construction stage (with which they share a common centre and very precise axial relationship). The geometric evidence for their earlier phasing is compelling enough to warrant consideration. It is often stated that the Station Stones were set on the corners of an accurate rectangle, which is correct, but this is only part of the truth. It has already been demonstrated above how the Aubrey Holes may have been set out simply by using two squares rotated at 45 degrees within a circle, the natural product of this square-and-circle geometry being an octagon. Were the Station Stones set out using a similar method? It certainly can be no coincidence that the positions of the stones and their missing partners are set exactly on opposing vertices of an octagon; this fact alone gives considerable insight into the rationale behind both their siting and their relationship with the rest of the monument.

There are reasons for thinking that it was the pit centres rather than the stones themselves which were set out by the surveyors, as all four stones

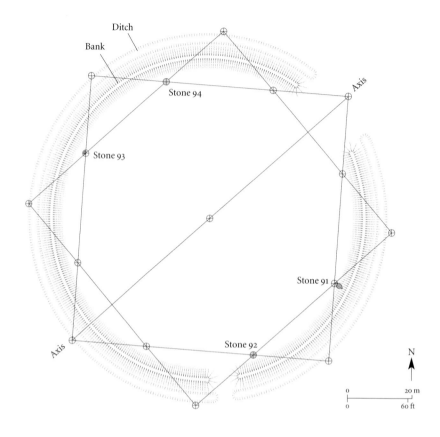

Ditch

Bank

Stone 94

Stone 93

Axis

Stone 91

Stone 92

Axis

N

0   20 m

0   60 ft

117 *The Station Stones: another example of square-and-circle geometry. The stone settings mark two diametrically opposed facets of a carefully surveyed octagon set out from the Stonehenge axis.*

appear to have been little more than naturally formed sarsens set in the middle of well-surveyed sockets. The notion that an exact (and curated) prehistoric measurement existed between marks on these stones is an unnecessary complication, for their location was clearly established by the application of an unambiguous geometric model. But one might rightly ask that if dimensions are unimportant, or at least only secondary products of geometrically proportioned survey methods, then how were the stones 'used' and what purpose did they otherwise serve? I believe the simple answer is the one that is so often cited, that a line taken between the Station Stones crosses in the centre of Stonehenge and that their paired symmetry echoes the axis of the sarsen monument. But how would anyone know exactly where to measure to or from, as the stones are irregular? In practice it probably did not really matter a great deal; simply looping the cord over the accurately positioned stones (this must also have been done with the survey pegs) and pulling the line taut between them would have made the intersection errors negligible. Of course all this assumes that the four stones are actually part of the internal geometric integrity of Stonehenge and were not located as sighting devices to distant objects, but the simple fact that they relate precisely and geometrically to each other provides the first and most vital clue in understanding their function.

A second, and no less important, point is that these geometrically accurate stones must themselves have been established by reference to some temporary markers. The obvious starting point is the baseline (axis) of the final Stonehenge construction, although there is no evidence to prove whether they were used to set out the axis in the first place, or to mark and respect an established alignment. Logically, the line which passes through the centre of Stonehenge was fixed first – it might be supposed that a circle was then laid out within which an octagon was inscribed. It looks simple, but there is a problem: the Station Stone octagon has no vertices on the Stonehenge axis itself. A simple geometric construction beginning with a square whose diagonal lies on the axis and whose angles meet the circle within which the octagon is inscribed would be 22.5 degrees out of phase with the Station Stone positions. If the axis baseline was used to establish the Station Stones, only one solution is apparent: the octagon upon whose vertices they lie must have been set out from a square whose corners lay outside the earthwork. Using this method the stoneholes would now be parallel with the baseline (axis). An axis foresight marker, acting as a temporary survey peg, could simply be placed on the causeway in a convenient position to ensure that it and the other three corners lay far enough beyond the outer ditch edge to be secure. Striking arcs from these pegs using the same cord length as the centre-to-foresight marker (i.e. the first square corner on the baseline) would place the Station Stones comfortably inside the tail of the bank. This implies that the diameter of the Station Stone 'circle' was a product of survey, not a predetermined dimension.

There is one proviso: the bank must have been substantially eroded so that good approximations to plan positions could be achieved by keeping the survey cords horizontal. There is plenty of evidence from the ditchfill to suggest that the bank had weathered relatively quickly; certainly by the end of Stonehenge Phase 2 (around 2500–2400 BC) the ditch was almost full and the bank must already have been reduced to a low mound which would not have seriously hampered cord-and-peg survey work.

In conclusion, the balance of evidence suggests that the Station Stones were designed to be set in exact geometric relation to a carefully surveyed octagon (whose dimensions were apparently determined by practical considerations rather than by formal relationships to any known features). Only four of the octagon vertices appear to have been marked, namely by the two surviving stones, and represented by the sockets of two others. The southwest–northeast diagonal of the square within which the Station Stones were set out represents the axis of the monument at this period. It was the length of the surveyor's line from the centre to the foresight on the northeast or southwest corner of this square which ultimately determined the position of the Station Stones. It may even be considered that the surveying of the Station Stones converted a 'casual' line or approximate bearing into the formal axis which dictated the symmetry of the later monument. None of this affects the importance of the solstice alignment of Stonehenge,[7] but does give precedence to the geometric setting of the Station Stones.

The Avenue

It is not possible here to pursue details of the Avenue earthwork into the wider landscape beyond the Heelstone. Along much of the straight section approaching the Stonehenge earthwork the ditches are perfectly parallel, but as they near the entrance causeway they converge, presumably a practical solution to match the width of the enlarged entrance, with no geometrical or surveying connotations. However, at a distance some 500 m beyond Stonehenge, where it deflects eastwards, the Avenue turns through 134 degrees. The internal angle of an octagon is 135 degrees. Coincidence? Perhaps.

CHAPTER 9

The Geometry & Construction of the Stone Monument

Oe of the most remarkable aspects of Stonehenge is the precision with which the massive sarsens were placed in respect of their circular and mirrored plan positions. The eye is distracted by the size and tapering sides of the uprights, some of which, although obviously worked, still retain much of the irregularity of the natural form of the stones. So it is difficult at first to appreciate that the Neolithic surveyors set out the stones to an accuracy of a few centimetres – but they did, using nothing more than a piece of cord and a few marker pegs. As explained previously, the Sarsen Circle and Horseshoe cannot have been simply 'sketched' on the ground; they were built according to a scalable, predetermined design that displays an internal geometric integrity entirely independent of anything outside the circle. How was this achieved and what dictated the design?

The Sarsen Circle

We might suppose that, given all the complications and enigmas embodied within the design of the monument, the circuit on which the Sarsen Circle lies is the least complex element. An accurate circle is easy to mark out, but this fact masks a far more sophisticated relationship between the Circle, the trilithon Horseshoe, and the numbers of stones in each array. These details are intimately and inseparably linked: the methods of survey which translated the design into the stone monument on the ground hold the clues not

only to the form of the final structure, but also to the techniques of the masons and sequence of construction. How was this achieved? The setting-out of the central sarsen structure began with a straight line, an axis of symmetry along the line of the midsummer sunrise–midwinter sunset solstice, already established by the previous bluestone construction. From the centre a circle was then drawn with reference to the Station Stones which, together with the axis, was used to establish the symmetry of the trilithon array. As the baseline/axis had to be kept clear, it had to pass exactly between six important stones: the four uprights of the Sarsen Circle (Stones 30, 1, 15 and 16) and the dominant tall twin uprights of the Great Trilithon (Stones 55 and 56); the basic surveying methods used in marking out the 30 survey points of the circle would have been similar to those outlined for the Y and Z Holes in Chapter 7.

But surely there is a logical error here, for the massive trilithons had to be in place before the Sarsen Circle? Yes they did, but here we need to draw an important distinction between the surveying and design stage which marked the stone positions and the construction of the monument itself. It is quite

118 *Elevated camera view, looking southwest.*

clear that the trilithons had to be erected first – this is not only logical but will be further apparent as the surveyors' translation of the structure unfolds below. The first clue to the harmony between the design, survey, construction and, not least, the logistics of the build is seen in the fact that it would not have been possible to scribe an accurate circuit for the Sarsen Circle once the Horseshoe trilithons were in place – a simple but vitally important fact.

There are construction methods and tools in use today which would have been entirely familiar to the builders of Stonehenge: examples of masons' lines, plumb bobs, survey pegs and ranging poles almost identical to those used to build the Egyptian pyramids can all be found within the pages of a modern survey supplies catalogue. Certain things have not changed; there is no reason to use methods or instruments that are more complex than the task demands. In setting out the Sarsen Circle it is evident that everything could be achieved by scribing intersecting arcs on the ground with a rope (as with a pair of compasses), whilst the use of what might be described as the 'field equivalent of a straight edge' was either not used at all, or was very restricted (simply pulling the cord tight provided the few straight lines which were required). Nor were measured dimensions needed, at least not in establishing the positions of the survey pegs – all the measurements returned can be explained as the natural products of proportionality derived from geometric constructions. However, there is a little more to fixing the position of the stones of the Sarsen Circle than marking a circle of 30 pegs, as each upright, had to support a lintel and needed to be placed precisely in the right place. There could be no room for error.

One of the first questions which might be asked is how was the diameter of the circle decided? To answer this it is necessary to think about the dynamics of the construction. The stones were not simply arranged to conform to some kind of regular approximation to symmetry; their placement was as exact as was humanly possible. The surveyors did not design Stonehenge, they did exactly what surveyors have done all through the documented history of construction, in that they marked out the plan of a structure whose form and proportional dimensions had been pre-determined. This perhaps needs further explanation. It is not an argument for the division of labour in Neolithic Britain; the surveyors may have also been the designers and builders, though undoubtedly there would have been a hierarchy of supervision and skill. What really needs to be separated is the design, the setting-out and the construction, just as in any major building project.

The designers and surveyors were working to a geometric model which could be expanded or contracted without affecting the overall integrity of the structural elements. Proportionality rather than absolute dimension was paramount. Before they reached the setting out and construction stage the 'off-site' design of the monument was already complete.

But was there a master dimension to which the structure was meant to conform? As the evidence so far has dismissed the idea of measured dimensions and emphasized geometric proportionality, it would be logical to look for instances not only within the intricacies of the structure itself, but within its setting in the earthwork. It is often pointed out that the Station Stone 'rectangle' (i.e. the width of its narrow side) appears roughly to bracket the monument; but only approximately, there is no exactness to the fit. There is, however, a far more interesting relationship to be found between the Station Stones and the sarsen monument, remembering that the Station Stones mark four vertices of an octagon, and knowing that the surveyors marked not the outer, but the inner face of the Sarsen Circle. A quite remarkable correlation between these elements can be seen, as shown on p. 230 [119]. Rather than accept that the sarsen monument is roughly contained by the four Station Stones, if we look at the diameter of the surveyed circle against which the ring of sarsens was placed we find that it is precisely half the length of the square framed by the Station Stone octagon; in other words, the Sarsen Circle is contained within a square exactly one quarter of the size of the square framed by the Station Stone octagon, again emphasizing the proportionality of the design. It appears therefore that the Station Stones controlled not only the centre point and axial symmetry of the sarsen monument, but also directly influenced the size of the circle itself; such an accurate relationship is more in keeping with the carefully laid out geometrical framework displayed not only by the Station Stones but also seen within the central structure itself. Having established that the prehistoric engineers wished to create a circle of this size, we now have to consider how this was put into practice.

If proportionality influenced the diameter of the Sarsen Circle, what determined the number of stones used in its construction? The answer to this difficult question really depends very much on whether one chooses to believe that numeric sequences were all important and pre-determined, as some would suggest, or whether the available stone, form, integrity and geometric design of the monument presented elegant solutions which translated into natural and easily surveyed arrays. I believe the answer is that engineering and structural requirements played a vital if not overriding part in the spacing and numbers of the uprights; and, certainly in the case of the Sarsen Circle, that it was the notion of supporting a circle of carefully dressed stone lintels that was at least as important, if not more so, than the numbers of supports themselves. Why 30? Because this number was easy to set out to a geometric formula, and offered a simple solution to balancing the desired circumference of the Circle to the dimensions of the available stones, not just the uprights but the 30 lintels, each of which had to be of uniform length

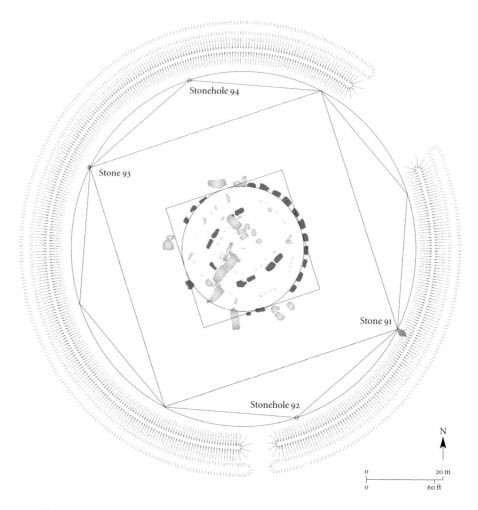

Stonehole 94

Stone 93

Stone 91

Stonehole 92

N

0 _____ 20 m

0 _____ 60 ft

119 *The proportionality of the sarsen monument in relation to the Station Stone octagon. The side of the square within which the inner face of the Sarsen Circle lies is half the length of the square contained within the Station Stone octagon, and occupies exactly one quarter of its area.*

and form. There were natural proportions to be found within the range of sarsens on the chalk downs which dictated the maximum dimensions of any of the stones used in the construction. That the engineers were working to the very limit of the available resources is amply illustrated by a number of compromises which had to be made. Stone 11 of the Sarsen Circle was only barely wide enough to support its lintels, and others cracked or broke during construction but were nevertheless pressed into service. It clearly proved difficult to find a good match for the magnificent and exceptionally large Stone 56 of the Great Trilithon of the Sarsen Horseshoe, so much so that its twin had to be 'counterbalanced' by leaving a substantial unworked mass on its base, with all the engineering difficulties that this must have presented, and also Stone 56 itself had to be buried to an exceptional depth so that its height would match that of its ungainly partner. In all, the evidence suggests that the Downs had been scoured for the best of the stones, and there was nothing larger or better proportioned to be had – even among those selected there were faults which demanded engineering solutions. The demand for 40 uprights (30 for the circle and ten trilithons) together with their 35 lintels simply exhausted the supply of the more substantial readily available 'local' stone. So how did the dynamics of the resource, the design, and numeric 'solution' come together?

To understand the Sarsen Circle it is necessary to examine the details and order of its construction. Clearly the supporting uprights had to be accurately set in place, and the relative positions of their tenons established in respect of the sockets (mortises) on the undersides of the lintels, before the latter were also manoeuvred into place. The inter-stone tenon-socket relationship is not regular and exact, nor does it matter, for it could be corrected relatively easily, and sometimes it was necessary to do so, for there are mistakes which show that mortise holes had been made in the wrong place and had to be re-cut to match a tenon (see p. 145). What had to be precise, however, was the curvature of the lintels and the carefully cut tongue-and-groove end joints in their radially splayed ends. Like the survey markers, these simply cannot have been worked out as construction progressed; the joints needed to be cut and trial-fitted on the ground, and not just in pairs; each one in the group had to fit exactly with its neighbours. The Sarsen Circle is not a series of stones that were conveniently fitted together during the course of construction, with all the difficulties that would present; it is clearly a carefully cut prefabricated construction in its own right, which is why I emphasize the point that the purpose of the uprights was to support a near-perfect ring of lintels; it was the lintel ring that dictated how big the circle of supports needed to be, and where exactly to place the pegs for the uprights, and not the other way round. The idea that they were somehow fashioned into shape by trial and error so that they eventually fitted the ring of sarsen uprights is simply incredible.

I suggest that the surveyors worked to an exact and pre-determined plan, and that the work on setting-out the uprights would have begun only after the lintel ring had already been formed and the carefully fitting joints and curvature perfected. It follows that if the lintels were cut first then they could be designed around the size and quality of the sarsens available as uprights. To create the lintels a template of some kind must have been used; the fact that five of the six surviving lintels show a standard deviation of only 0.06 m from an average dimension of 3.4 m clearly demonstrates they were intended to be identical. If a number of attempts was needed to make a stone fit the prefabricated lintel ring it would not have been a problem; there was no need to raise the final structure until all 30 lintels were perfect and interlocking. The builders could have then been sure of the final fit before the difficult and demanding task of construction began. The straightening of uprights and replacement of lintels proved a difficult task even with modern cranes employed during the restoration work of the 1950s and 1960s. The Neolithic engineers would have wanted to lift the six-ton lintels once and once only, although this task is not as difficult as most accounts would have us believe. A recent experiment in the Czech Republic has shown that each could have been manoeuvred into position, using a wooden ramp, by as few as ten men in three days.[1]

One further remarkable constructional achievement to be noted is that, despite the slope of the ground, the tops of the sarsen lintels were set almost perfectly level, both by varying the depths of the holes into which the supports were set and by dressing the lintel tops where necessary. Setting the lintels in place, perhaps better seen as a process of bracing the lintels and uprights together (for ultimately they form a type of interlocking structural ring beam), would only have taken place after the bearing surfaces of their supports had been prepared, and probably not until the uprights had settled. A further task needed to be undertaken before the lintels could be lifted into position; the paired tenons had to be shaped on the top of the uprights ready to receive the lintel mortise holes. Preparing a level surface to a datum

120 An A-frame plumb line of the type used in ancient Egypt. The sketch is based on an example found in the tomb of master builder Sennedjem, found at Deir el-Medina, near Thebes (19th Dynasty, c. 1300 BC); clearly earlier examples existed. By placing such a device across the top of neighbouring uprights it was possible to ensure level surfaces.

common to the tops of each sarsen upright, though laborious, would have been technically quite simple. The heights would have been checked, probably using a simple triangular framed level and plumb line similar to devices known from ancient Egypt.[2]

Once the lowest upright in the circle had been identified, its height would have been transferred round the circuit by pounding the tops so that they were all level. Small sarsen chippings found in concentrations next to the foot of some of the uprights seemingly represent waste material from such activity.[3] Just as the mortise holes were pre-cut on the lintel bases at a regular spacing from each end, the paired tenons on the uprights could also be predetermined, as they would always lie a fixed dimension on either side of the centre (regardless of the width of the uprights). Although this can only be checked against the better-preserved examples where they are not concealed by the lintels, the tenons appear to have been offset around 0.45 m each side of the vertical axis of the upright, i.e. their centre-to-centre spacing is around 0.9 m. The need to re-cut some mortise holes shows that sometimes when things went wrong in working the tops of the uprights, there was no alternative other than to modify them to fit (see p. 145). Careful preparation of the stone foundations in advance meant that the amount of work needed on the top of the uprights was kept to a minimum. It is often assumed that once the stones were set in their foundations it would have been impossible to raise their height. This is erroneous, as alternately levering the stone from side to side and introducing material into the hole would gradually have worked the base upwards. Whether it was necessary to raise them up or to reduce their height (by pounding their tops), the builders would not have wanted to do this once the tenons had been prepared.

121a Right *The sarsens were brought from the chalk downs, c. 30 km north of Stonehenge. The largest stones (up to 45 tons) were selected as uprights for the Sarsen Horseshoe and Circle, smaller stones (of around five to six tons) were selected for lintels. Prior to transport they were worked to reduce weight, and one surface was dressed to present an even surface to the wooden rollers or guides. The stones were conveyed to a location close to the site, but not yet brought within the earthwork.*

121b Opposite *Suggested sequence in the surveying and construction of the sarsen monument.*

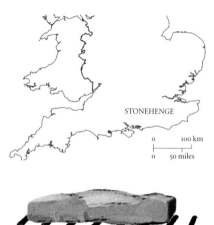

STONEHENGE

0   100 km

0   50 miles

The Sarsen Horseshoe

The astonishing feat of engineering which lies behind the design and construction of the five trilithons is awe-inspiring. These massive lintel-capped sarsen uprights once stood in five pairs, arranged in precise and accurate mirrored symmetry and dominating the centre of the final major construction. The form and design of this central array have occasioned considerable speculation both amongst antiquarians and later archaeologists. In 1880, Flinders Petrie, having just completed his own detailed measured survey of the monument, could only comment that 'the trilithons are not on a circle, and the scheme of their placing is obscure'.[4]

Having argued not only how the various elements were set out, but why certain numeric sequences that are relatively easy to survey were employed in marking out the various concentric settings (from the Aubrey Holes to the Y and Z Holes), the ultimate test would be to find a link between the Sarsen Circle and the most elusive of all the Stonehenge geometric constructions, the 'Horseshoe' plan of the trilithon array. With their mirrored symmetry the trilithons appear at first sight to embody a series of measured, rather than geometrically surveyed, dimensions. Perhaps the Horseshoe array was an exception, and the prehistoric surveyors measured the position of each of the paired settings from points fixed along the axis of the monument. But nowhere else on the site, at any period, was there a need for measured

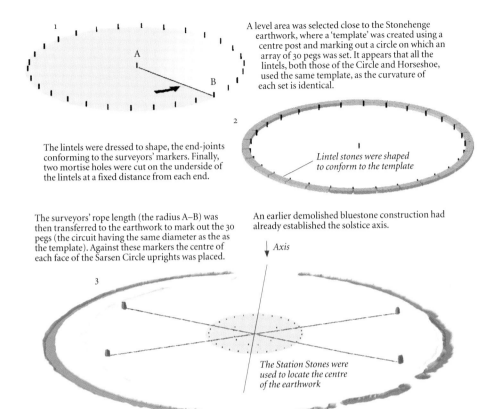

A level area was selected close to the Stonehenge earthwork, where a 'template' was created using a centre post and marking out a circle on which an array of 30 pegs was set. It appears that all the lintels, both those of the Circle and Horseshoe, used the same template, as the curvature of each set is identical.

The lintels were dressed to shape, the end-joints conforming to the surveyors' markers. Finally, two mortise holes were cut on the underside of the lintels at a fixed distance from each end.

Lintel stones were shaped to conform to the template

The surveyors' rope length (the radius A–B) was then transferred to the earthwork to mark out the 30 pegs (the circuit having the same diameter as the as the template). Against these markers the centre of each face of the Sarsen Circle uprights was placed.

An earlier demolished bluestone construction had already established the solstice axis.

Axis

The Station Stones were used to locate the centre of the earthwork

The markers for the trilithons were then set out from the circle of pegs (to a pre-determined geometric plan, see p. 242). All the pegs were then knocked down flush with the ground level to protect them from damage. The working area was restricted and, to avoid obstructing the centre of the site, foundation holes were dug and stones erected one at a time or in pairs. Construction began with the Great Trilithon which was raised from inside, its flatter, smoother face to the southwest; the survey markers for these two major uprights were thus unique, having been placed on the 'outside' of the stones.

The flatter surface faced the centre (apart from the Great Trilithon)

Tops finally levelled and tenons formed

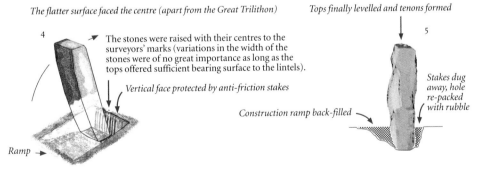

The stones were raised with their centres to the surveyors' marks (variations in the width of the stones were of no great importance as long as the tops offered sufficient bearing surface to the lintels).

Vertical face protected by anti-friction stakes

Construction ramp back-filled

Stakes dug away, hole re-packed with rubble

Ramp →

Only after raising the uprights and ensuring the tops were level could the tenons have been created. Levelling was largely achieved by varying the foundation depths of the uprights, but their irregular form and varying widths meant that the final exact placement of the tenons could only be decided when the stones were standing. The positions of the tenons were established by placing them on either side of a plumbed line from the top of the stone to the survey marker position on the ground. They would then exactly match the pre-cut mortises on the lintels.

235

dimensions, or evidence of their use. The layout of the Sarsen Horseshoe presented a challenge as my proposition required that the setting out had been achieved by reference to a simple geometric model without measurements.

The problem was daunting, for not only was it necessary to show how the Sarsen Horseshoe may have been designed using geometry, but any explanation had also to acknowledge the fact that the Horseshoe was clearly constructed before the Sarsen Circle. With the Circle it is easy to see how the surveyor's cord was used to set out the survey marks against which the stoneholes were excavated, but could a cord have been used in the same way to fix the positions of the stones of the mirrored arms of the Horseshoe?

If there was an answer to the problem of the trilithon geometry, I had first to recreate the plan of the survey pegs which had determined their positions. In the case of all but the Great Trilithon, wherever investigation had taken place there were either construction ramps on the outer side of the stoneholes or friction stakes on the inner face, confirming that, like the majority of the encircling sarsen uprights, they too had been set up from the outside and their smoother (inner) face placed against the survey mark on the edge of the stonehole. The central Great Trilithon appeared to be a special case, not only because of its size, but also because of certain unusual aspects of its construction; also, as it straddled the axis, there was no need to 'mirror' its placement. The surviving, now straightened, western stone (Stone 56) is so enormous that it needed to be set in a pit some 2.5 m deep, not just to provide a firm foundation, but also to ensure that its top matched that of its relatively shallow-founded (now-fallen) twin. As Gowland's excavations revealed a clean wall of chalk against the outside (southwest) face of Stone 56 and a probable ramp[5] on the opposite side; it is clear that the stone had been erected from the inside of the monument, and that the survey marks must have been placed on the south side of the uprights for the Great Trilithon; a small but vitally important detail, to which we can then add the equally significant fact that uniquely among all the sarsens their better and flatter faces look outwards, away from the centre of the monument.

Temporarily leaving aside the problem of the Great Trilithon, I created a computer 'model' of the other two pairs of opposing trilithons. Comparison with John Wood's 18th-century plan clearly shows that when the western trilithon (Stones 57, 58 and 158) was re-erected in 1958, it was displaced 20 to 30 cm too far to the southwest, no longer showing a true symmetrical relationship with its diametrically opposite twin. By creating a mirror-image plot using the less-disturbed uprights on the southeast side of the axis (Stones 51, 52 and 152, and 53, 54 and 154), it soon became clear that it was possible not only to find the 'ideal' survey marks for the restored trilithon, but also for the fallen upright of its neighbour (Stone 59). At least now there was something to work from – not the irregular bulk of the stones, but a series of precise survey points representing the peg positions against which the stones were originally placed, just like the pegs used to set out the uprights of the Sarsen Circle. (Most attempts at unravelling the geometry of the Horseshoe often show arcs drawn through the centreline of the stones instead of their inner faces, demanding that the Neolithic engineers would have had to struggle to adjust the huge and irregular sarsens to a theoretical line running through the middle of the deep foundation pits and the stones themselves – a notion that is inconceivable.)

The ten newly computed positions marking the anticipated trilithon survey pegs were added to those of the Sarsen Circle. Somewhere within the matrix of computer cross-hairs was the elusive answer to the arrangements of the trilithons; but where? The survey peg locations on either side of the baseline which marked the bases of each side of the mirrored trilithon arrays were tested against conjectured oval configurations and intersecting arcs of circles, including the classic paired overlapping circles of classic *vesica piscis* geometry.[6] There were times when the estimates and proposed survey cords almost coincided with my model survey pegs, but not quite, never exactly. Moreover, none of the arcs which included the opposing pairs of lesser trilithons ever embraced the Great Trilithon; or rather, those that did invariably had a centre anchored at a seemingly random location. No points from which the Horseshoe could have been set out were found on a line perpendicular to the centre of the monument. Even a cursory inspection of the plan shows that the Horseshoe is not central to the Sarsen Circle, but displaced southwestwards along the axis, so that a line drawn across its open arms crosses the axis some 8.4 m from the Circle, whilst to the southwest the distance is only 6.4 m.

The problems were, by now, very familiar ones that had tempted me on many occasions to take the easy option and suggest that maybe the prehistoric surveyors had themselves settled for some kind of 'best fit', which would give me licence to conclude that close was good enough – but this would compromise the fundamental proposition that Stonehenge was a geometrically inspired construction. The trilithon enigma presented more than an opportunity to reinforce the elegant simplicity and method behind the design of the monument; it had now become, like the Bush Barrow lozenge, a real challenge, or, what in sporting parlance might be described as a needle-match. I admit this freely. I knew that the arrays of 30 were, in all probability, not only set out by procedures involving the accurate use of the surveyors' radial cords, but also that the numeric component of both the Sarsen Circle and Horseshoe made sense within the context of 'hexagon-based geometry'. I was, however, puzzled by the fact that whilst the numbers five and ten present in the trilithon group (ten uprights in five paired arrays) were natural 'steps' in arriving at 30 settings, the trilithons themselves did not reflect any kind of spacing which might have resulted from hexagon or radial cord survey methods. The complicated survey models had to be abandoned. I remember imagining asking my ancient surveyors just how the design could possibly have been created with just one length of rope: 'Show me, because I have absolutely no idea.'

Removing the outlines of the actual stones from my screen, I concentrated on the key positions of the survey markers. Working this time from a survey peg model which had been drawn from John Wood's 1740 plan, I noticed something quite remarkable. Normally my computer models were rotated, so that grid north was at the top of the screen. When working with the reconstruction based on Wood's dimensions I was observing the image as he conceived it, with the axis running vertically on the computer monitor. When I switched off Wood's base plan, leaving only the pattern of 40 small survey marker cross-hairs, the CAD screen took on an entirely new dynamic. Without a line drawn to represent the axis (even this had been switched off), there was no longer any need at all to see the trilithons reflecting 'curves' struck from stations on either side of the axis. Looking at Wood's plan in this way emphasized the relationship between the opposing mirrored uprights rather than the neighbouring trilithons of the outstretched arms of the Horseshoe, demonstrating that they could have been set out in a series of broad sweeps across the axis from each end (see pp. 242–43). I had been seeking to create additional survey control pegs from which the trilithon array might have been established, yet there were already plenty of pegs available: those which marked the Sarsen Circle. Why should more be needed?

Anchoring the computer-generated radial survey line which the surveyors had used to mark out the Sarsen Circle to the pegs flanking the northeast axis (i.e. the peg locations for Stones 30 and 1) in turn, a radial arc from peg 30 sweeping through the centre of the monument towards the centre of Stone 5 of the Circle cut exactly through the marker peg for trilithon Stone 52; the reciprocal from Stone 1 swept from the centre towards Stone 26, cut through the marker for trilithon Stone 59. A pattern soon emerged: the prehistoric surveyors had used the marker pegs of the Sarsen Circle to control the survey of the Horseshoe array; every one of the trilithons had a reciprocal relationship with an upright in the outer circle. Time after time arcs swept across the screen, intersecting with survey marker pegs. At first the computer was only finding arcs on which the trilithon uprights lay, not the vital closing intersects which would tie down their exact positions. I had become so absorbed in the 30-peg based geometry of the emerging Neolithic survey that I had switched off the solution to the missing intersects. The answer lay in the two pegs of the axis; it was so obvious that in the pursuit of more complex answers it had escaped my notice. With the emerging pattern of the Horseshoe unfolding, I switched back on the axis layer. A new series of arcs centred on these positions and drawn between opposing pegs of the Sarsen Circle revealed the previously elusive intersects with the earlier arcs, exactly marking the original prehistoric survey positions of the trilithon uprights. It is worth noting that the perceived 'curvature' of the mirrored trilithons on either side of the axis is not substantially reflected in the relative positions of the uprights. The inner faces of the paired supports are virtually in line with each other, and a pair of survey pegs central to each would have been all that was required to position the stones, the emphasis on curvature given by their carefully dressed lintels.

Only the survey markers of the Great Trilithon fell short of a 'perfect' series. From at least the end of the 16th century, until its restoration in 1901, the surviving upright (Stone 56) was leaning considerably inwards. It would not have been possible to determine exactly where the stone originally stood. When Petrie carried out his survey in 1877 he shaded an area southwest of the leaning stone suggesting where its outer face might have been when the stone was upright, an estimate which moved its plan-position a distance of some 30 to 40 cm outwards from the centre of the monument. My computer model of the survey pegs predicted that the outer face of Stone 56 should in fact lie between 40 and 60 cm southwest of its present position, much as Petrie had suggested. Switching on the modern base map, which shows the stone as restored in 1901, revealed something even more remarkable: that my survey marker fell within the centre of the stone as it stands today and not on its outer face. Taking the opposing pairs of the other trilithons as reference points, it was possible to check their mirrored positions against the axis, but the Great Trilithon has no such independent reference point; its position on the baseline and, more importantly, its restored position along the axis could not be verified against any such detail.

There is no certainty that this stone, which had been leaning for centuries, had been put back where the Neolithic surveyors intended it to be, but to have the confidence to assert this needed proof beyond that indicated by the computer model alone. The account of the work carried out before Gowland set the stone upright in 1901 needed to be re-examined, and the surveys made by Wood (1740), the Ordnance Survey (1867) and Petrie (1877) had to be compared with Gowland's careful drawing [122a] of the stonehole before the engineering work began. Rather than trust survey dimensions that may always have been measured relative to the fallen, broken and displaced stones, I struck two circles from the centre of Stonehenge on each of the historic maps: the first was drawn to touch the innermost part of the leaning trilithon, the second the outermost. The object was to compare its various plotted positions in relation to the undisturbed eastern trilithon (Stones 51, 52 and 152). These circles showed a good agreement on the three pre-1901 maps, but all mismatched the modern survey. There was now little doubt that the standing stone of the Great Trilithon had been restored in the wrong place. But there was more to this exercise than identifying discrepancies in re-setting the stone; if a displacement could be confirmed, then it demonstrated

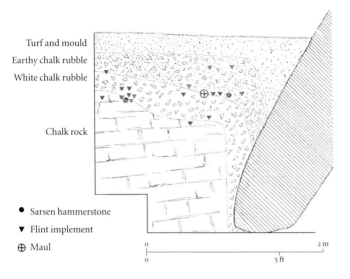

Turf and mould
Earthy chalk rubble
White chalk rubble

Chalk rock

• Sarsen hammerstone
▼ Flint implement
⊕ Maul

0   2 m
0   5 ft

122a Left Detail prior to engineering work as shown in Gowland's drawing of 1901.

122b Below The displacement of the Great Trilithon upright (Stone 56) following straightening in 1901.

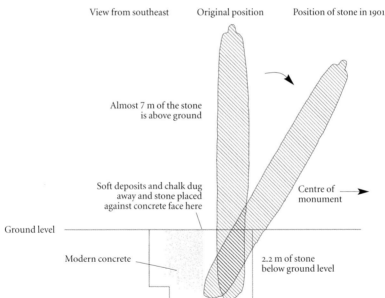

View from southeast   Original position   Position of stone in 1901

Almost 7 m of the stone is above ground

Soft deposits and chalk dug away and stone placed against concrete face here

Centre of monument

Ground level

Modern concrete

2.2 m of stone below ground level

that the prehistoric survey methods and geometric principles which had been used to mark out all the other stones in the sarsen arrays had also been used to fix the original position of the Great Trilithon.

In 1902 Gowland published the plans and section drawings of his restoration work. Amongst his drawings are records of the deposits that lay against the southwest face of the stone where three successive blocks of chalk were

123 The marker pegs against
which the centre face of each of
the 30 Sarsen Circle uprights was
to be erected were set out (see
p. 203 [109]). The numbers refer
to those conventionally used for
the Stonehenge stones. However,
construction began with the
Sarsen Horseshoe (below).

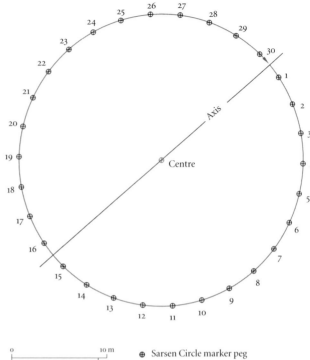

N

| 0 | | 10 m |
| 0 | | 30 ft |

⊕ Sarsen Circle marker peg

124 The prehistoric
surveyors laid out the Sarsen
Horseshoe using the markers
for the circle and two at its
intersection with the axis
(A1 and A2). This figure
illustrates the relationship
between trilithon uprights
53–54 and 57–58, the axis
and pegs marking the Sarsen
Circle. Arcs centred on axis
position A1 extended from
pegs 19 and 20 (or 11 and 12)
cross those scribed from axis
position A2 from 7 and 8 (or
23 and 24). The intersects of
the surveyors' ropes which
fixed the remainder of the
trilithon uprights are shown
on [125].

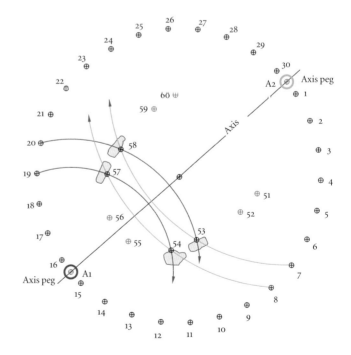

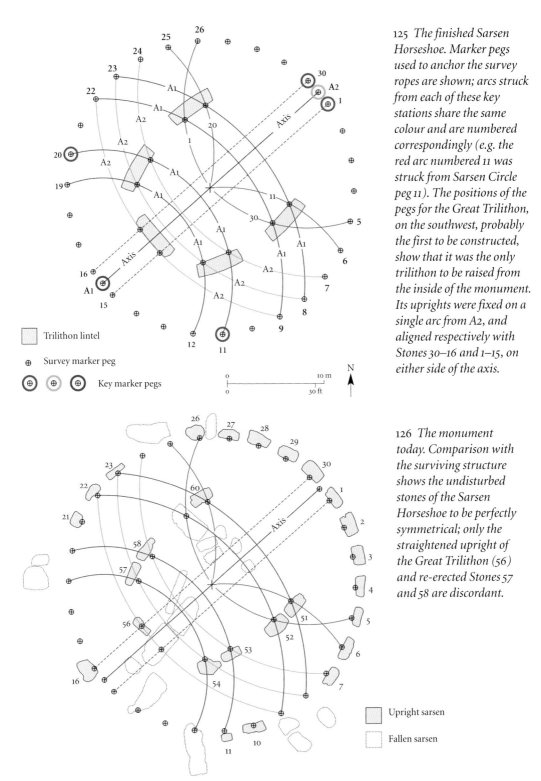

125 *The finished Sarsen Horseshoe. Marker pegs used to anchor the survey ropes are shown; arcs struck from each of these key stations share the same colour and are numbered correspondingly (e.g. the red arc numbered 11 was struck from Sarsen Circle peg 11). The positions of the pegs for the Great Trilithon, on the southwest, probably the first to be constructed, show that it was the only trilithon to be raised from the inside of the monument. Its uprights were fixed on a single arc from A2, and aligned respectively with Stones 30–16 and 1–15, on either side of the axis.*

Trilithon lintel

Survey marker peg

Key marker pegs

0   10 m
0   30 ft

N

126 *The monument today. Comparison with the surviving structure shows the undisturbed stones of the Sarsen Horseshoe to be perfectly symmetrical; only the straightened upright of the Great Trilithon (56) and re-erected Stones 57 and 58 are discordant.*

Upright sarsen

Fallen sarsen

243

cut away to reach the bottom of the Neolithic foundation hole [122a]. As each section was removed it was replaced with concrete to form a wall against which the outer face of the stone was to be subsequently set. The section drawings show that, deep below the turf, the leverage exerted by the massive stone as it tilted into the centre of the monument had pushed its base outwards, causing it to 'bite' into the chalk on the (southwest) side of its foundation cut. When the stone was re-erected it was winched upright not to where it had been originally set, but against a vertical face representing the maximum displacement of its toe [122b]. This is perfectly understandable: Gowland's task was to correct the tilt; the relatively small dislocation of the 45-ton trilithon was not important in the scheme. The result is that today the stone stands perhaps as much as 60 cm southwest of the position in which it was first erected, and is rotated approximately nine degrees anticlockwise from the perpendicular of the axis. These are small but very significant details.

The design behind the most elusive of the Stonehenge constructions had been finally revealed by a careful examination of the methods used by its surveyors. It is a remarkable prehistoric expression of form that uses the interplay of overlapping arcs to create a symmetrical array, a geometry encompassing elegant and harmonious relationships which includes the empirical employment of the mathematics of diffraction patterns [127]. I have no doubt this is worth exploring further – I was simply intrigued that the Neolithic draughtsmen and surveyors had discovered these spatial relationships and used them in their architecture.

The answer to a further puzzle was now apparent: despite their massive size, the gaps between the trilithon uprights were less than between the uprights of the Sarsen Circle. In truth, there was no element of choice in their centre-to-centre spacing, which had already been dictated by the design. The mistake that

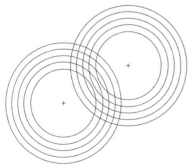

127 *The elusive geometry of the Sarsen Horseshoe was inspired by the proportionality of the intersects of overlapping circles (a 'diffraction grating').*

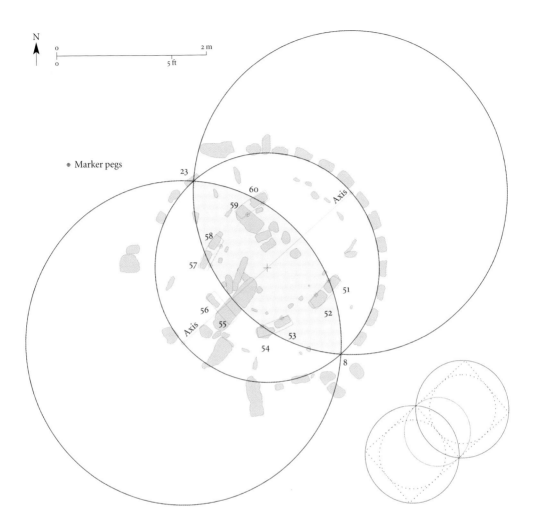

128 *The zone within which the two pairs of mirrored trilithons on either side of the axis were placed (shown in grey) is defined by an elegantly simple geometric configuration in which arcs struck from the Sarsen Circle at either end of the axis pass through the two perpendicular points (represented by the two marker pegs for Stones 8 and 23). Each of these overlapping circles has twice the area of the Sarsen Circle, indicating a further square-and-circle relationship in the design.*

129 *Survey experiment to re-create the prehistoric surveyors' marker pegs for the Sarsen Circle and Horseshoe. Chalk dust was used to highlight the line after the circle had been lightly scored into the turf using a rope anchored to a central peg. Above Looking along the axis towards the Great Trilithon. The marker position for Stone 52 of the eastern trilithon was set out using ropes whose lengths and anchor points are shown on p. 243.*

131 Opposite below *The complete life-size layout was accomplished by two people in 2½ hours. No measurements were made other than establishing the length of the rope used to mark the radius to ensure that the experimental circle conformed to the inner face of the Sarsen Circle. Despite irregularities in the ground, the accuracy of the groundplan was generally within 2 cm (with a maximum error of 8 cm) of the 'ideal' shown on pp. 242 and 243, similar to small discrepancies found within the actual monument itself.*

I and others had made in previous attempts to unlock the enigma of the trilithons was in assuming that the solution lay within the relationships between the trilithons themselves, when in fact their locations were determined entirely by the survey pegs set out for the encircling ring. The reason why their geometry has remained so problematic is quite clear, as it is hardly possible to guess how a regular circular set of survey markers could have been translated into an inner horseshoe. The surveyors' system was actually very simple, but not at all obvious, and looking at the plan locations of the

130 Above *Oblique aerial photograph, Noke, Oxfordshire, September 2007.*

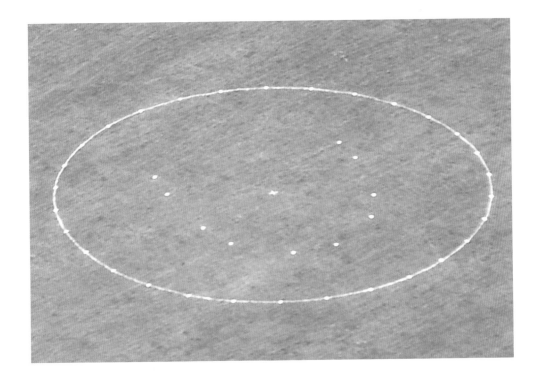

trilithons in isolation would never have returned the solution. To understand how it was done had meant 'getting inside' the method used to set out this and other arrays. The accuracy seen in surveying the Sarsen Circle was now apparent within the trilithon settings; importantly it also allows the true intended Neolithic structural alignment to be confirmed with some precision. I also believe that the survey relationships demonstrate beyond reasonable doubt that the Sarsen Circle and Horseshoe are contemporary phases of construction, as all judicious accounts based on the archaeological evidence from Stonehenge have always suggested.

The Bluestone Circle and Horseshoe

The geometric integrity of both the Bluestone Circle and Horseshoe is poor, which is hardly surprising as they appear to have been set up simply in imitation of the sarsen monument. The computer model of the few stones which can be trusted as approximating to their original positions shows displacements of up to *c*. 1 m from the ideal circle-oval line of symmetry. There is no case for regarding this group as part of a discrete independent geometric array, planned in the same way as the Sarsen Circle and Horseshoe; they were reused from an earlier structure, the architectural details of the stones largely neglected, irregular stones being juxtaposed with more elaborate examples (including former lintels employed as pillars for a new circle and oval arrangement). These stones are set in poorly surveyed positions, lacking precise survey marks, which is good reason to consider them as having been conceived as part of an entirely separate and less ordered phase of activity. In all probability they are exactly what they appear to be: an afterthought or embellishment, making use of otherwise redundant bluestones from an earlier dismantled (pre-sarsen) array.

What little detail can be determined from the Bluestone Circle and Horseshoe is architecturally, rather than geometrically, significant, such as the placement of two prominent leading stones which flank the axis on the northeast at a wider-than-average spacing. This lead pair sits neatly behind the axially aligned multiple 'portal trenches' of the buried R settings, interpreted by Atkinson as preserving the first solstice alignment known from Stonehenge. But the later circle and oval configuration needed no careful surveying, the axis having been already fixed by the sarsen structure, which itself almost certainly continued the outline of the earlier monument to which the stones from the Q and R Holes, the Station Stones and probably the Heelstone belonged. The re-use of the bluestones respects this tradition and certainly can be viewed as a concern for maintaining the fabric, if not the form, of the earlier work. It is significant that there are no credible 'sightlines' within this group, as just about all are blocked by the sarsen uprights; they are clearly, and simply, a monumental array. Of interest is the distance between the Great Trilithon and its nearest neighbour, the grooved bluestone (Stone 68), which is 1.6 m compared with the *c.* 1 m spacing of the other trilithons, the increased difference being no more than the result of the modern displacement of the Great Trilithon upright when it was straightened.

The Slaughter Stone and Heelstone

It is not known exactly where the Slaughter Stone or Heelstone belong in the sequence of construction of Stonehenge, although it is probable that the Heelstone setting is actually much earlier than any of the worked sarsens. Reasonable guesses as to where these stones fall in the monument's chronology are based largely on the way in which they and their putative neighbours relate to the symmetry of the Stonehenge axis. Radiocarbon dating has firmly placed the fill of the hole adjacent to the Slaughter Stone (Stonehole E) within Phase 3 of the monument, i.e. to the major sarsen structure rather than earlier period. The presence of the distinctive casts of wooden rods laid flat in the bases of both Stonehole E (next to the Slaughter Stone), and Stonehole 97 (next to the Heelstone) provides a link, albeit tenuous, which may merit an investigation of a possible survey relationship between the two pairs of stones.

Both Stonehole E and the setting for the Slaughter Stone lie on the median line of the earlier Stonehenge bank, which could mean that their placement is one of convenience or symmetry, rather than a dimension determined by the surveyors. They could, of course, have been stone replacements for earlier timbers, a suggestion which may be supported by Hawley's observation that the causeway postholes appear to gravitate towards them. If they were simply set on the median of the axis of the bank there is no point in looking for 'concentric' relationships between these stones and the other two outlying (Heelstone) settings, but if they marked the sites of earlier, more precise timber arrangements then perhaps some association may have existed. On present evidence, it is safer to say that whatever governed the positions of the Slaughter Stone and Heelstone was determined by factors that are currently not known, or are at best speculative. The axis of the stone monument passes to the northwest of the Heelstone, between it and its putative twin, but to talk in terms of 'accuracy' would be misleading, as the Heelstone is a rough and unworked sarsen boulder. Perhaps they are better explained as 'framing' the axis.

It is not known how long the twinned Heelstone array stood or what the dressed Slaughter Stone 'portal' may have resembled, although the 'portal' appears not to have had a lintel. The archaeological evidence is equivocal, as the digging of a ditch around the Heelstone, which fails to acknowledge and even cuts through the stonehole of its counterpart, was believed by both Hawley and Atkinson to predate the bank of the Avenue associated with the widening of the entrance and the construction of the sarsen monument. But the stone monument is perfectly symmetrical on either side of the axis, and what cannot be readily explained is why the Heelstone would have had its neighbour removed when mirroring of the stones was seemingly of paramount importance: either the relationship between the Avenue bank and the Heelstone ditch is insecure, or we have to accept that the 'symmetry rule' had been broken. If, as seems more likely, the Heelstone ditch was overlain by material spread from the Avenue bank rather than underlying the bank itself, the more geometrically coherent Heelstone pair, and probably the twinned entrance portals, may have survived much later in the life of the monument than is generally imagined.

Reassessing Stonehenge

I intend now to discard many of the conventions and rules that I have tried to adhere to in presenting the facts in earlier chapters and instead engage more freely with the evidence. Looking inwards into the archaeology and design of the monument has, I would argue, taken us closer to what actually happened, and how it was achieved. Yet the inevitable question has to be confronted, 'what was the purpose of Stonehenge?' It is a commonly held notion that virtually every detail can be explained by some supposed alignment, the case being so obvious that it needs no further clarification. Throughout the book I have used the word 'designed', because no reasonable approach to Stonehenge could see it arranged to fulfil or respect any requirement, astronomical or otherwise, without it first being carefully planned 'offsite'; only thereafter was the idea translated into a formal structure. It might be suggested that this presents no problem, for would not the Neolithic astronomer-priests, or whatever people like to call them, have told the builders where to put the stones so that they would relate in some way to the movements of the heavens? Surely that is why the monument is set on the solstice axis, and why the Station Stones and the trilithons, the most dominating set of sarsens on the site, must also have been positioned in relation to the movements of the sun and moon? The problem with what appears obvious is that it gains merit and eventually becomes fossilized by repetition. After all, the sun was known to go around the earth until first Copernicus, recognizing the truth of the Greek Aristarchus of Samos's nearly 2,000-year-old treatise, and then Galileo pointed out that although it might be obvious, it was not the correct conclusion.

How does this affect the astronomical arguments? The fact that Stonehenge was created from a premeditated geometric design is vitally important because it has to do with the idea of primacy – it tells us precisely what determined the position and interrelationships between the stones and other important details. The archaeological evidence shows us first and foremost that the monument was set out to an exact and carefully conceived plan. The dimensions, numeric sequences and proportional relationships that are often deemed to have been established by external reference can better be explained as owing nothing to anything beyond the earthwork, not in the landscape, the celestial dome or anywhere outside the circle. However, once conceived, the structure, its placement and orientation, i.e. where and in which direction it was set up, were of great importance.

But if the Aubrey Holes, Station Stones, Sarsen Circle and Sarsen Horseshoe are all geometric arrays, where does this leave the astronomical interpretation? Precisely, one might say, where it belongs, as one component of the monument but not the sole reason for its creation. The midsummer sunrise–midwinter sunset alignment is undisputed, but to put it in context, it must be presumed that the people who possessed the skill to build Stonehenge would clearly have been no less concerned with its siting. It may be that from the outset the architectural detail was expressly designed to harmonize with the cycle of the year to which the axis relates, but that is quite a different idea from interpreting the individual stones as being exclusively aligned on the movements of the sun, moon and stars. So what determined the orientation of the monument?

In 1912 John Abercromby, author of the first major work on Bronze Age pottery, made a very perceptive observation when he concluded that 'from the analogy of Greek temples, of cathedrals and mosques, it is evident that the central part of worship lies in the opposite direction to the entrance, to which the worshippers, when at prayer, invariably turn their backs. So some other reason than sun worship on June 21, must be found to account for Stonehenge .…As the position of the most sacred part of the *cella* lay at the southwest end, the faces of the celebrants would be towards the direction of the sunset at the midwinter solstice.'[1] There is no doubt from the excavation record and from my own analysis of the plan and survey methods that the Great Trilithon, the largest central structural element, was erected from the inside of the monument, with its better-dressed face towards the rays of the midwinter sun. The logical sequence of construction demands that the trilithons were constructed before the Sarsen Circle, and the fact that Stone 56 was erected from the inside of the monument shows that the Great Trilithon was the first to be completed, emphasizing that the pivotal event was indeed the winter solstice, marking the end of the short cold days and long winter nights and heralding the birth of a new year.

But why were the remainder of the stones set out to a carefully premeditated and harmonious geometric scheme? Perhaps the single most telling detail is that the prehistoric surveyors had every opportunity to place any of the stones, not just those which register the axis, in exact relation to the celestial events they are often purported to represent, but they did not. When we look at the Station Stones, for example, they are in perfect geometric harmony, but they only approximate to the cyclic movements of the sun and moon that the astronomical model would have them mark. Likewise, the surveyors' pegs that fixed the positions of the Sarsen Circle and Horseshoe were all determined in relation to the symmetry of the architect's design. Not a single stone could be moved out of its carefully planned premeditated position, or shifted in respect of celestial events, nor was there any need to, for this is not why they were placed where they were, nor was it part of the function of the stones to record astronomical phenomena or predict solar or lunar eclipses. True, there is certainly a nexus to be found within the Stonehenge arrays, but even the relatively simple arrangement of the four Station Stones tells us that it is internal rather than external, one of geometric integrity not external decree.

For whatever reason, the symmetry of the construction takes precedence in every aspect of the sarsen monument. If the design of Stonehenge tells us anything, it is that we need to explore other dimensions and appreciate the wider intellectual skills, those reflected not simply in the construction, but within the realm of dynamic ancient creativity not bounded or restrained by a perception of people being passive observers of astronomical events. But when we let go of popular current theories we are faced with a difficult task; for there are no guarantees that the designers of Stonehenge lived in a world whose cosmology might be grasped through any property inherent in the structure that we recognize today. Circularity, for example, can mean whatever one chooses it to mean. Does it contain or exclude, mirror or mimic? How can we know what it truly symbolized at Stonehenge? Nevertheless we naturally search for meanings; they offer the possibility of a common bond with past societies, even though the terms of reference may be different, and ours are inescapably confined to the here and now.

It is possible to stand the whole current Stonehenge idea of a 'gathering place' (for whatever purpose) on its head. Instead of a location where people observed the heavens or indulged in ritual activities, perhaps it was actually a celebration of human skill and artistry, a construction presented to the spiritual world, or whatever it was that they believed inhabited the domain in which they had discovered the universal rules of harmonic form. Perhaps as such it was a gift to this other world. Once constructed, far from being a gathering place, it was taboo, the stonework finished and perfect, cremation burials now long since ceased; it stood in stately magnificence and solitary splendour, the people who constructed it never again permitted to cross the threshold into the inviolable *sanctus sanctorum* of the enclosure. Only the sun entered and retreated as the cycle of the year progressed through the seasons; the 'Avenue' was symbolic, reserved for the passage of deities and the spirits of ancestors who were buried within the now ancient earthwork. This is why there is so little artifactual material at Stonehenge and why so few barrows were constructed in close proximity. Is this outrageously speculative? Perhaps so; it is simply an illustration which indicates why we need to be wary of any explanations which flirt with ideas that substitute words such as 'ritual', 'sacred' or the imagined world of 'ancestors' for tangible evidence. Similarly, the idea that people waited for two or three decades, the better part of a Neolithic lifetime, to witness a particular celestial event which may not even have been visible, 'cancelled due to bad weather', casts doubt on the notion of Stonehenge as a monument in constant use as an astronomical observatory.

However, given the right clues we can explore possibilities that might bridge the gulf between hard fact and mere speculation. The details locked within the design of Stonehenge tell us what the builders knew, and how they applied their skill to create a unique structure, and also that this knowledge was part of a cultural tool kit whose hallmark is manifest within other monuments. What are the implications? What is the significance of the carefully constructed 'diffraction grating' pattern displayed by the trilithon arrays, and how could it possibly have been arrived at? There are no coincidences here; the only way this spatial arrangement could have been set out was by the careful pre-selection of certain Sarsen Circle pegs as master control stations; some were used and others ignored to achieve a deliberate mirrored symmetry which flows along the axis but not its perpendicular.

The people who built the earth and timber monument were among the first surveyors; they were fascinated by the relationships, the proportionality of squares and circles and the numeric sequences that could be derived from the interplay of these forms. This is not only evident at Stonehenge [132] but also in the design of other concentric late Neolithic structures such as the Sanctuary at Avebury, Wiltshire, and the henge monument at Mount Pleasant, Dorset [133].[2] Logically there is no single axis of symmetry to be found within purely circular settings, but as monuments became more complex and new skills and knowledge were acquired, the Neolithic surveyors appear to have developed their ideas into sophisticated and often extremely accurate plans which frequently embody mirrored symmetry. What is not clear is whether this is a reflection of a shift in contemporary beliefs, an iconography translated into structural form expressing a newly emerging cosmology, or whether it was the discovery of the simple geometric principles themselves that was to open a door to a world of mirrored form which was to become immensely significant, ultimately leading to the design and construction of Stonehenge.

In 1998 a remarkable discovery was made on the coast at Holme-next-the-Sea in Norfolk.[3] Shortly before 2000 BC the stump of a substantial newly felled oak tree had been buried, its trunk inverted so that the roots were exposed to the sky, and then surrounded by a 7-m diameter ring of over 50 posts [135]. It was evidently part of a more extensive complex because other prehistoric timber settings were found nearby. At the time it was created the site had been several miles inland. The timber had survived for 4,000 years because the ground in which it had been set had always remained wet; the stump was

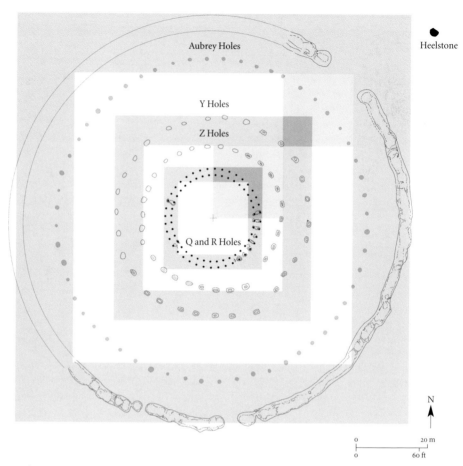

Aubrey Holes

Heelstone

Y Holes

Z Holes

Q and R Holes

N

0   20 m
0   60 ft

132 Above *At Stonehenge a thread of continuity can be recognized in the way the prehistoric surveyors used square-and-circle geometry to partition the space within the enclosure. Disparate and temporally unrelated settings were established using square-and-circle geometry from the centre of the monument. There are times during its unique, protracted and complex structural history when other geometric rules were applied. But at other sites where contemporary or near-contemporary arrays were being set out, the proportionality and harmony of square-and-circle relationships were paramount features of their design.*

133 Opposite *Examples of square-and-circle proportionality are seen in the design of two major prehistoric concentric monuments. Both are broadly contemporary with the earlier (pre-sarsen) activity at Stonehenge. At the Sanctuary, near Avebury, Wiltshire, the design appears to be almost exclusively based on the square-and-circle geometry. The majority of the concentric elements at the henge monument of Mount Pleasant, Dorset, seemingly a longer-lived site, show a similar pattern. Importantly, at Mount Pleasant, there are settings at the cardinal points just inset from the outer ring of postholes which show near perfect relationship with the innermost arrays.*

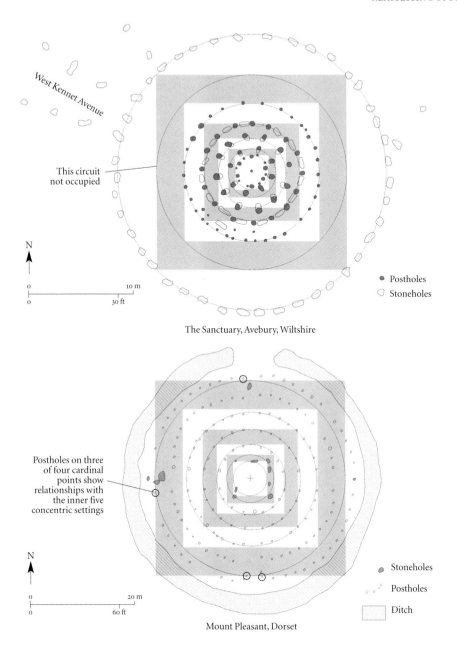

The Sanctuary, Avebury, Wiltshire

This circuit
not occupied

West Kennet Avenue

N

0   10 m
0   30 ft

● Postholes
◌ Stoneholes

Posthotes on three
of four cardinal
points show
relationships with
the inner five
concentric settings

N

0   20 m
0   60 ft

◉ Stoneholes
∘ Postholes
▨ Ditch

Mount Pleasant, Dorset

in such remarkable condition that the marks made by no fewer than 38 individual axes could still be recognized. The considerable effort required not simply to fell the oak tree, but to dig up the roots and rebury it upside down suggests that the motivation was something more than the desire to create a kind of elevated platform; it seems as though the act of inverting the tree had

134 *Midwinter sunset.*

some significance in itself. Whatever its purpose, we can see in this so-called 'Seahenge' structure a further example of what appears to be prehistoric dualism, the division of the world into two domains. Here again we have symmetry, not essentially in plan, as with many Neolithic and Bronze Age monuments, but that suggested by the horizontal plane, above and below ground. The juxtaposition of root and stem hints at a cosmology concerned with light and dark and the harmony of opposites. We can only speculate as to what this means, but time and again the mirrored theme recurs at so many sites that it must have implications for Stonehenge, the classic and most astonishing of all the symmetrical monuments.

But there was not only proportion and symmetry to be found, there were also numbers, and any numeric series arrived at as a result of prehistoric experiments would have been regarded as significant, even mystical. It has already been explained in connection with the Aubrey Holes that it would have been very difficult to start with the idea that 56 postholes were essential, and then task the surveyors with marking them out accurately on the ground; rather they discovered a method that returned this number based on their emerging knowledge of square-and-circle geometry. The association between any geometric figure and a cycle of events in the natural world will not have gone unnoticed – it was magical, if you like, that what they had drawn to a simple set of 'discovered' rules could equate with, for example, two lunar cycles of 28 days; right from the outset 28 or 56 will have become important. Here was something they undoubtedly established by experiment long before marking it on the ground, a link between their 'mathematics' and the perceived harmony of the wider world. It was prehistoric science, with workable rules and repeatable results.

This is not entirely guesswork on my part. There is one historic source relating to the number 56 which strongly suggests that this may be true. There are innumerable references to basic geometric forms in ancient texts, but little reason to mention the more complex – that is, unless there was something very special about their associations. Remarkably, the eminent Greek writer

135 *An early Bronze Age timber setting exposed on the seashore at Holme-next-the-Sea, Norfolk, is popularly known as 'Seahenge'. The focus is the inverted stump of a huge oak tree, felled c. 2000 BC, remarkably preserved in waterlogged ground. The ring originally stood several miles inland, but has now been encroached upon by the sea.*

Plutarch (c. AD 45–120) does draw attention to the mysterious significance of a 56-sided polygon:

> It is plain that the adherents of Pythagoras hold Typhon to be a daemonic power; for they say that he was born in an even factor of fifty-six; and the dominion of the triangle belongs to Hades, Dionysus, and Ares, that of the quadrilateral to Rhea, Aphroditê, Demeter, Hestia, and Hera, that of the dodecagon to Zeus, that of a polygon of fifty-six sides to Typhon, as Eudoxus has recorded.[4]

It is interesting to explore this remarkable statement further, as he also comments:

> There are some who give the name of Typhon to the Earth's shadow, into which they believe the moon slips when it suffers eclipse.[5]

According to Plutarch, this account of the cosmic struggle between light and dark was already an ancient myth known to the Greek astronomer and mathematician Eudoxus some 500 years earlier. Here a clear association has been made between the number 56 and lunar eclipses.[6] This is fascinating. Yet, what is important in this context is the fact that Eudoxus mentions a 56-sided polygon and that this is not a direct reference to a number but rather to a geometric construction which was clearly known as such, and was capable of being drawn in antiquity. Hence its significance is clearly more than whatever astronomical implications might be read into it; it is an astonishing relic of what was already an ancient tradition of square-and-circle geometry within which the secret of how to draw this elusive figure had been discovered.

By the time the sarsen structure was built at Stonehenge the surveyors had learnt to use quite complex hexagon-based constructions which involved not only the use of the radial string (to create a hexagon within a circle), but also the ability to use an axial line which formed the basis for the construction of a pentagon, the interspace between the hexagon and pentagon vertices providing the correct 30-hole spacing around the circumference (see p. 204). Not only is this apparent in the setting-out of the stones, but also in the numbers contained within the finished arrays, where everything can be easily derived from the basic hexagon framework. In very simple terms, we have added to the tradition of square-and-circle survey the 'hexagon-and-circle' and its derivatives – devices which are also clearly evident within the sophisticated geometry of artifacts of the later Stonehenge period, particularly those found in the Bush Barrow. That prehistoric knowledge included the ability to draw a regular ten-sided figure can be further seen in the geometry of the Clandon Barrow lozenge, using the 'decagon-and-circle' to establish both the form and decorative panels (Appendix p. 269).

Does the suggestion that numbers came first and their potential worldly or sacred associations second work with 30 as well as 56? Certainly it does if considered from the same perspective. The relationship between the radius of the cord that draws a circle and the fact that it also divides the circumference into a hexagon demands to be considered important; the real curiosity is why it appears to have been absent from the earlier geometry. To people who could draw a regular 56-sided polygon a hexagon must have been a simple matter. How this hexagon-based survey method and its numeric consequences, as revealed both on the drawing board and computer screen and displayed within the sarsen monument, might be translated into any pattern of 'real world' events is open to debate, and certainly to further study, if indeed there are any such associations to be made.

I consider the use of 30 sarsen uprights to have been one of utility. The number of supports needed was something determined by structural necessity, a reflection of the dimensions of the available stones and one of engineering convenience. Thirty was a good number to choose; it was easy to set out and use a radial cord to control a substantial part of the construction. The same cord could be used to create an accurate template outside Stonehenge against which stones for the circle could be matched and prepared before they were transported to the centre of the site. This argument for an element of prefabrication is based on the notion that the purpose of the 30 sarsen uprights was to hold aloft their most important 'device', the near-perfect ring of lintels. Setting out the Circle would have been relatively simple, but the amount of 'drawing-board design' and planning required to lay out the groundplan of the trilithons is astonishing; there is nothing simply structural here, the overriding concern was to position the uprights and their five lintels in a precise geometric relationship with the Sarsen Circle.

136 *View looking southwest along the axis,*
with the Slaughter Stone in the foreground.

This interplay between the three-dimensional aspects of the design, the precision of the lintel curvature and the heights of their tops was absolutely crucial to the design of the monument, to whatever end.

The application of a series of simple geometric procedures would have ensured that every aspect of the monument's design could be controlled and scaled from concept to the masonry work and final construction. The use of the radial cord to transfer a fixed and proportional pattern of survey markers from template to site guaranteed that the trilithon structure matched its pre-determined plan, that the dressed lintels would fit exactly, and that relationship between the Circle and Horseshoe was maintained.

Having considered Classical documentary sources which refer to a 56-sided polygon and its unambiguous associations with Typhon, we need only to read a few lines more of Plutarch's work to find this statement concerning the number 30:

> Then again, the Moon herself obscures the Sun and causes solar eclipses; always on the thirtieth of the month …[7]

Arguably, taking these statements at face value, if it is possible to link the 56 Aubrey Holes with lunar eclipses, it would be reasonable to suspect that there may have been a connection between the number 30 and solar eclipses. I can already imagine hands going up at the back of the class: solar eclipses do not always happen today on the '30th of the month'. This apparent conflict arises because Plutarch, who was writing a century after the introduction of the Julian calendar (a modified version of which is still in use today), was referring to historic sources at a time when months were still measured by a lunar calendar, the interval between two new moons being about 29.5 days;

solar eclipses only happened on days of the new moon, when the moon is directly between the earth and the sun. In his text, Plutarch has substituted the 30th of the month for the archaic 'day of the new moon', despite the fact that the new calendar was now out of phase with the lunar cycle.

On the same page he offers us a year of 360 days (neatly divisible into 12 months of 30 days), leaving five (the number of trilithons) remaining days which were recognized by the Egyptians as the birthdays of the gods:

> Hermes … composed five days, and intercalated them as an addition to the three hundred and sixty days. The Egyptians even now call these five days intercalated and celebrate them as the birthdays of the gods.[8]

The real problem with so many of these ancient sources is that one can find suggestive associations relatively easily. However, such references are intriguing, as ancient societies worldwide were naturally concerned with lunar and solar events, and many developed calendars based upon them. The possibility that the architectural design of Stonehenge reflects a desire to express or rationalize the passage of time is an entirely reasonable suggestion, albeit not susceptible to proof.

When I introduced the Stonehenge myths and legends in Chapter 2, I raised the question of whether it was conceivable that folk memory could possibly extend back as far as the Bronze Age. Contained within the pages of the *Rig Veda*, the most sacred of Hindu texts, is an unbroken tradition of Vedic Sanskrit hymns whose origins almost certainly overlap with the dates of the use of Stonehenge. Many archaeologists, including Stuart Piggott who worked alongside Richard Atkinson at Stonehenge, have considered the *Rig Veda*'s historical importance, not in respect of the stones but because it provides an unambiguous example of the power and resilience of oral tradition. It conveys memories of a prehistoric but sophisticated world, even though its contents were not written down until the 5th or 6th centuries AD.[9] This text is fascinating for many reasons, not just because it contains references to events and ancient technology, often in quite beautiful verse, but because it underlines something very important about the way we might view prehistory in the light of oral tradition. Leaving aside the pessimistic view that everything woven into the fabric of Stonehenge folklore is worthless, there is some merit in looking again at exactly what we have been told.

What happens if we strip away the names of the key players – those who have clearly been introduced to give a veneer of credibility by later (medieval) writers who drew on some of the earliest documented figures in British history – then consider the geographic framework, and finally the comments on the structural details? We are told that the stones were brought from 'Ireland' and that they formed part of a pre-existing structure that was difficult to move. They had originally come from the 'remotest confines' of Africa and had been brought to Ireland by 'giants' when they 'inhabited that country'. These are not any stones, but ones of exceptional quality, and only 'a man of the brightest genius, either in predicting future events, or in mechanical con-trivances' could move and re-erect them, for it needed great skill and artistry.

The idea of external influences being directly responsible for Stonehenge, certainly those as robust or as literal as proposed by a brief flirtation between a chronologically displaced Stonehenge and Mycenae, first proposed by Stuart Piggott in 1938, has long been abandoned. However, we must be care-ful in assuming that the monument owes its unique design and innovative construction exclusively to the imagination of an increasingly sophisticated local population. The notion that Stonehenge embodies exotic ideas may be unfashionable, but the evidence of trade conspires to illustrate that links between contemporary prehistoric communities were extensive. In the past few decades and certainly since the introduction of radiocarbon dating, the date of Stonehenge has been constantly pushed back in time, as has the date when the technology of the first metalworkers first appeared in the British Isles; currently the earliest known copper mine in northwest Europe (with associated habitation), in Co. Kerry, Ireland, is broadly contemporary with the early years of the stone monuments at Stonehenge.[10] These events can hardly be coincidental, although despite tantalizing discoveries such as the Boscombe and Amesbury Beaker graves, with their suggested 'incomer' status, these early prospectors and adventurers are not proven to have been responsible for the construction of the stone monument, which currently appears to be a few generations older than the earliest of the known Beaker interments.

Doubtless, contacts with the fabled 'Africa' (for which we can read the more exotic shores of the Mediterranean) must have existed, and with them the opportunity for the transference of many skillsets, from navigation and rope-making, essential for any seafaring venture, to mathematics and geom-etry, and masonry construction, all of which had already been applied in the Middle East for over half a millennium before the sarsen structure was built at Stonehenge. It is perfectly reasonable to see knowledge arriving from the Mediterranean and developing along the trading routes which passed raw materials and artifacts between peoples; this does not need to be literally read, as the stories suggest, as moving the stones themselves. This is nothing new: Aylett Sammes, a contemporary of John Aubrey, suggested the movement of ideas rather than the stones themseves over 330 years ago.[11]

Geoffrey of Monmouth in the early 12th century AD described Merlin as a wise and eminently practical man who knew how to deconstruct the stone circle using 'clever machines', and who then proceeded to supervise their transport, shipping and re-erection at Stonehenge. He is presented as having been skilled in 'mechanical arts' rather than the 'magic' with which he is associated in the modern mind. Indeed, William Camden, at the end of the 16th century, was to portray him, perhaps perceptively, as 'that great Mathematician', a concept which remained constant throughout all subsequent editions of his *Britannia* up to the end of the 18th century.[12] Perhaps the most intriguing observation in the Stonehenge myth is the oblique reference to the structural details of Stonehenge: 'if they are placed in position round this site, in the way they are put up over there, they will stand forever.' The expression 'in the way they are put up over there' is interesting. Is this ancient knowledge of the way the stones were fitted together using their mortise and tenons jointing, a technique unique among megalithic structures? It is very unlikely that Geoffrey of Monmouth knew about the stones' interlocking devices, nor would there have been any reason to describe them as stones of exceptional quality, exotic or revered.

A curious argument is sometimes advanced that because the medieval illustrations depict the iconic sarsen structure built of local stone, and not the Welsh bluestones to which the legend clearly alludes, that the legends repeated by Geoffrey of Monmouth and his contemporaries were clearly fabricated. It takes only a moment to realize that this gives more credibility, not less, because Geoffrey and his contemporaries could have had no knowledge of the exotic provenance of the bluestones, nor the possibility that they had been taken down from somewhere west of Stonehenge and re-erected on site. It would be well-nigh impossible for a medieval chronicler to have invented these separate and archaeologically demonstrable facts.

We must not reject such legends as mere fabrication, for if we do, as Piggott pointed out, we could be in danger of throwing out our only contemporary account of a Bronze Age structure.[13] It would be hardly surprising to have such a survival of oral tradition, relating as it does to the most remarkable example of prehistoric stonework in Europe. Nor should we be too concerned with the idea of what we consider to have been possible in the past, simply because we do not understand how something was done. The stones were transported and manoeuvred into place, it's a simple fact, and I have not overly speculated about how it was engineered, being more concerned about the 'why'; but to the medieval mind it was impossible that they were moved and erected by men 'of this period'; they must have been the work of ancient 'giants'. Before anyone could begin to understand Stonehenge it was necessary first to discover prehistory; when the idea finally emerged, and the true antiquity of our human ancestors was recognized, it was at the same time both a revolution and a constraint, one that opened up a temporal dimension, but polarized perceptions of the past, conjuring up fearful images of ancient preliterate 'howling savages'.[14]

It has taken a long time to eliminate the perception that prehistory is synonymous with primitive culture, a notion long abandoned by archaeologists, but one which remains a pervasive part of the popular perception of our distant ancestors. The skill and imagination of the Neolithic people who built Stonehenge would stand any test of intellect we might apply today. I have presented here a brief insight into their world. In using the evidence on the ground to explore how the design of Stonehenge was laid out by the prehistoric engineers, I have learnt something about what the communities who built the monument *knew*, an intangible but vital part of the insight into the wider dynamics of the monument's construction that will perhaps help to contribute to greater understanding of what it may actually have meant to its builders. Perhaps eventually we will have to conclude that its unique structure served an equally unique and elusive function, but there is still much to explore, and I suspect that day is a very long way off; until then Stonehenge will continue to hold its fascination and present a challenge to future generations.

Appendices

Radiocarbon dates

At Stonehenge only a relatively small amount of material suitable for radio-carbon dating has been recovered from reliable contexts. The samples of greatest importance are recognized as those associated with specific phases of construction, such as the creation of the early earthwork, the introduction of the stones, and the final series of pits which mark the end of the known activity (in all a period which spans almost 1,500 years).

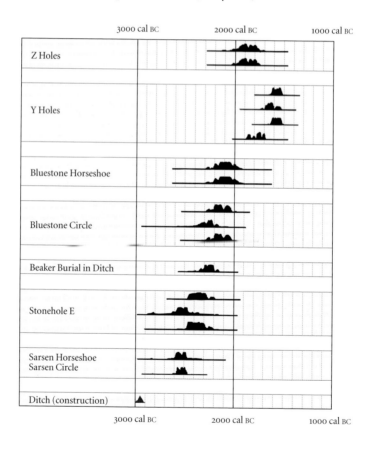

137 *A summary of the distribution of more reliable radiocarbon dates from Stonehenge, based on the data presented in the English Heritage publication* Stonehenge in its Landscape *(Cleal et al. 1995) in conjunction with more recent reviews of the integrity of specific contexts by Bronk Ramsay and Bayliss 2000, Bayliss et al. 2007 and Parker Pearson et al. 2007.*

The Clandon Barrow lozenge

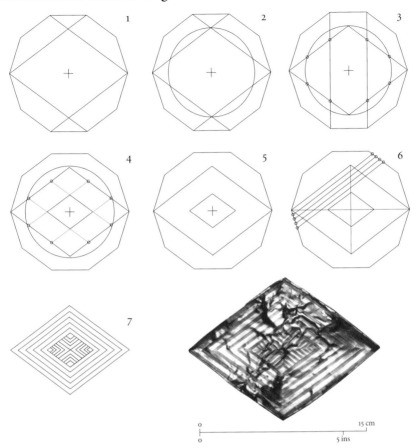

138 *The design of the Clandon Barrow lozenge (shown in colour on p. 185) is based on the ingenious use of a regular 10-sided polygon (decagon) which was then used to control the proportion and spacing of its concentric design, a device also used by the Stonehenge surveyors in setting out the 30 uprights of the Sarsen Circle. The geometry behind Stage 1 is shown on p. 204. Stages 2–5 establish the outer shape and central panel; Stage 6 shows how the midpoints of two facets fixed the spacing of the four decorative incised lines. Stage 7 shows the finished design.*

The smaller Bush Barrow lozenge

139 *Both the Bush Barrow lozenges were based on hexagonal geometry. The illustration shows how the form and proportions of this lozenge, shown here at actual size, were established (the grey shaded area shows the hexagon-based design behind the larger of the Bush Barrow lozenges, see pp. 182–85).*

Notes

Introduction: Seeking Explanations

1 Hawkins 1966. The quotations are taken from the publishers' summary of the evidence presented in the Fontana/Collins 1973 edition: 62–63.
2 North 1996: xxxix.
3 Newall 1956: 140. The transport and erection of the stones have been investigated in two television programmes: BBC2 *Secrets of Lost Empires* 1994 (in which various engineering experiments were attempted), and Channel 5 *Stonehenge, the Ultimate Experiment – Live* 2005 (in which a life-size model using polystyrene blocks, known as 'Foamhenge' was built). The results are summarized by Richards and Whitby 1997 and Richards 2007: Chapter 10.

Chapter 1 Landscape & Opportunity

1 RCHME 1979; Richards 1990; Exon *et al.* 2000; Bewley *et al.* 2005.
2 Cleal *et al.* 1995: 56.
3 Carruthers 1990: 250–2.
4 Oswald *et al.* 2001.
5 Kendrick and Hawkes 1932: Chapter VII; Wainwright 1990.
6 Cleal *et al.* 1995: 113.
7 English Heritage website: http://www.eng-h. gov.uk/mpp/mcd/sub/henen7.htm.
8 Harding 2003.
9 Meaden 1997.
10 McOrnish 2003.
11 Burl 1987: 62.
12 A recent reassessment of the dating of five southern British long barrows: West Kennet, Wayland's Smithy, Fussell's Lodge, Ascott-under-Wychwood and Hazleton North, has been carried out by Whittle *et al.* 2007.
13 *ibid*: 16, referring to the skeletal material found in Fussell's Lodge long barrow by Paul Ashbee, 1966.
14 Roaf 1990.
15 Parker Pearson *et al.* 2006. The Stonehenge Riverside Project 2003–2010; interim reports for the 2004 and 2005 seasons and summary interim reports for 2005 and 2006 are published on the Sheffield University website: http://www.shef. ac.uk/archaeology/research/ stonehenge. For previous excavations at Durrington Walls see Wainwright and Longworth 1971.
16 Stonehenge Riverside Project (note 15). *Summary Interim Report 2006*: 4.
17 Revealed in 1850 when a storm eroded the overlying sand dunes, and extensively excavated by V. Gordon Childe in 1928–30. Clarke and Maguire 2000.
18 Stonehenge Riverside Project (note 15). *Summary Interim Report 2006*: 10.
19 Darvill 2006: 109.
20 Stonehenge Riverside Project (note 15). *Interim Report 2005*: 4.
21 Fitzpatrick 2002 and 2003; Wessex Archaeology website: http://www.wessexarch.co.uk/projects/ amesbury/archer.html.
22 Fitzpatrick 2004a, 2004c.
23 Fitzpatrick 2004b; Wessex Archaeology website: http://www.wessexarch.co.uk/projects/wiltshire/ boscombe/may2005/.
24 Budd 2000.
25 Baker *et al.* 2003.
26 Piggott 1938.

Chapter 2 Myth, Legend & the Early Antiquarians

1 Roseman 1994; Cunliffe 2002.
2 Diodorus Siculus *Histories* II: 47.
3 Cunliffe 2002: 116–120.
4 Arnold 1879: 11–12.
5 Geoffrey of Monmouth *Historia Regium Britanniae* Book 8. Translations taken from Giles 1848 and Thorpe 1969. For a discussion of Geoffrey's sources see Piggott 1941a and 1941b. In the latter, Stuart Piggott drew attention to the similarities between this legend and that of Bran Fendigaid (Bran the Blessed) who led an army to Ireland. Bran, a hero in early Welsh literature is mortally wounded; his head is returned to Britain, where it is carried on a long, eventful and protracted 80-year journey through Wales and into England. Like the Stonehenge story it is interwoven with shadowy mythical and pseudo-historical figures, and eventually finds its place in the fabric of Arthurian literature. See also Loomis 1930.
6 Geoffrey of Monmouth *Historia Regium Britanniae* Book 12, final chapter (20).
7 *ibid*.
8 Piggott 1941b: 319.
9 Johnson 1908: 11.
10 Grinsell 1975.
11 Atkinson 1979: 185.
12 Heck 2007: 14.
13 *ibid*: 10–15.
14 The destruction of the stones at Avebury is documented by Burl 1979: 36–54.
15 Hearne 1710; Smith 1964, republished by Chandler 1993.

16 Rastell *c.* 1530.

17 Lambarde 1730: 314–15.

18 Eiseley 1962.

19 With numerous revisions and subsequent editions (six in Camden's lifetime). First translated into English by Philemon Holland in 1610, with a second edition by Holland in 1637; substantial additions were made by Edmund Gibson in 1695 and 1722, and by Richard Gough (published in three volumes) in 1789.

20 Poem entitled *To William Camden.*

21 Letter of 6 June 1716. Piggott 1950: 37.

22 William Camden's *Britannia,* Philemon Holland (ed.) 1610: 254.

23 Plautus, *Pseudolus:* 21–30.

24 Bolton 1624: 181–2.

25 The translation is from William Camden's *Britannia,* Philemon Holland (ed.) 1610 Edition: 251.

26 Chippindale 2004: 36.

27 British Museum Add.28330, p. 36a; Bakker 1979.

28 Possibly Stones 13 and 14 or 15 and 16.

29 Wheatley and Ashby 1879: Plate XXII.

30 William Camden's *Britannia*, Richard Gough (ed.) 1789: 92.

Chapter 3 Fieldwork, Excavation & Speculation

1 Chippindale 2004: 47.

2 Jones 1655: 75.

3 *ibid*: 59–60. Jones describes the stone monument in the 1620s as follows: [The Sarsen Circle]: 'The stones which made the outward Circle, seven foot in breadth; three Foot and an half thick, and fifteen foot and an half high: each stone having two tenons mortaised into the *Architrave*, continuing upon them, throughout the whole circumference. For, these *Architraves*, being joynted directly in the middle of each of the perpendicular stones, that their weight might have an equall bearing, and upon each side of the joynt a tenon wrought (as remains yet to be seen) it may positively be concluded thereby, the *Architrave* continued round about this outward circle.' [The Bluestone Circle]: 'The smaller stones of the inner circle, one foot and an half in breadth, one foot thick, and six foot high. These had no *Architraves* upon them, but were raised perpendicular, of a pyramidal form. That, there was no *Architrave* upon these, may be hence concluded, the stones being too small to carry such a weight, the spaces being also too wide, to admit of an *Architrave* upon them without danger of breaking, and being but six foot high, there could not, possibly, be a convenient head-height remaining for a passage underneath, especially, considering fully the greatnesse of the whole work.' [The Sarsen Horseshoe]: 'The stones of the greater

Hexagon, seven foot and an half in breadth, three foot nine inches thick, and twenty foot high, each stone having one tenon in the middle.' [The Bluestone Horseshoe]: 'The stones of the *Hexagon* within, two foot six inches in breadth, one foot and an half thick, and eight foot high, in form pyramidall, like those of the inner circle.'

4 *ibid*: 76.

5 Long 1876: 83.

6 Neave 1943; Burr 1766: 4–16.

7 Darvill 2006: 156.

8 Fowles 1981: ix.

9 Webb 1665. A compilation of all three components of the controversy: Inigo Jones's *Stone-Heng*, Walter Charleton's *Chorea Gigantum*, and John Webb's *Vindication* was published in 1725, and reprinted with a new introduction by Stuart Piggott in 1971 by Gregg International Publishers.

10 Fowles 1981: 20.

11 *ibid*: 75 and 128–29.

12 *ibid*: 87. Descriptions of more recent saw pits suggest they had typical dimensions of around 3–3.5 m × 1.2 m × 1.8 m deep.

13 *ibid*: 89.

14 *ibid*: 25.

15 *ibid*: 32.

16 William Camden's *Britannia* 1695, E. Gibson (ed.): 108–9. A facsimile of this edition, with an introduction by Stuart Piggott, is published by David and Charles Reprints, 1971.

17 *ibid*: 109–10.

18 Britton 1847: preface. A facsimile of this edition, with an introduction by K. G. Ponting is published by David and Charles Reprints, 1969.

19 Later engraved by Elisha Kirkall for inclusion in a second edition of John Webb's *A Vindication of Stone-Heng Restored*, published in 1725.

20 Stukeley 1740: 5.

21 *ibid*: 56–7, 64–6.

22 *ibid*: 13.

23 Lecture entitled *Newton* by Professor Robin Wilson, Gresham College, Holborn, London, 30-01-02. www.gresham.ac.uk

24 Stukeley 1743: 54. For biographies of Stukeley see Piggott 1985 and Haycock 2002.

25 Mowl & Earnshaw 1988; Spence *et al.* 2004.

26 Lukis 1885: 276.

27 Wood 1747: 98.

28 *ibid*: 60.

29 *ibid*: 35.

30 *ibid*: 53.

31 *ibid*: 43.

32 Mallgrave 2005: 8.

33 Wood 1747: 56–7.

34 Lukis 1885: 275.

35 *ibid*.

36 Chippindale 2004: 92.

37 Smith 1771: Introduction, v.

38 Smith shows the whole outline of the leaning Stone 14 resting on Bluestone 38. He excused Wood's misalignment of Stone 60 because in 1740 it was partially hidden by Gaffer Hunt's hut which had been built alongside it. Hunt is said to have 'attended there daily with liquors, to entertain the traveler, and shew him the stones', keeping a cellar 'under the great stone [Stone 59a], next to the hut' (Smith 1771: 58). By the time of Smith's visit the hut had been removed, revealing a fallen bluestone (Stone 72). It is unclear how far Gaffer Hunt's activities extended in the vicinity of these stones; there was at least one hut and an adjoining shed in which horses were tethered (Wood 1747: 36), but as Wood did not record the third fragment of the fallen lintel (Stone 160a), an element also added by Smith in 1771, it is probable that this area was also obscured at the time of his survey.

39 Extract reprinted by Legg 1986: 107–11.

40 'Account of the Fall of some of the Stones of Stonehenge, in a Letter from William George Maton, M.B.F.A.S. to Aylmer Bourke Lambert Esq., F.R.S. and F.A.S. dated May 30th 1797', Easton 1800: 76–80. Both John Hassell's *North Prospect of Stonehenge*, drawn at the very end of the 17th century, and the survey work carried out by John Wood in 1740, less than 60 years before this trilithon collapsed, show a westward lean which anticipated its fall.

41 Hutton 1788; Repcheck 2003.

42 Ferguson 1872: Chapter 3.

43 Hoare 1812: 142.

44 Cunnington 1975: 10.

45 *ibid*: 39.

46 Letter to John Britton, 12 April 1803 quoted by Cunnington 1884: 147.

47 Long 1876: 85.

48 Long 1876: 56–57.

49 Hoare 1829: 6.

50 Hoare 1812: 20 (footnote).

51 Davis and Thurnam 1865; Thurnam 1869; Thurnam 1871; Piggott 1993.

52 Cunnington 1975: 76.

53 Daniel 1981.

54 Wilson 1851.

55 Lubbock 1865: 52–3.

56 Information provided by Joseph Browne (guide, guardian and illustrator of Stonehenge) to Dr John Thurnam, who added that: 'Before the hole was filled up, I buried a bottle, containing a record of the excavation;' quoted by Long 1876: 86–7. Inigo Jones, William Stukeley and William Cunnington are all recorded as having previously dug in front of the altar.

57 Cunnington 1869: 348.

58 Chippindale 1978: 111.

59 James 1867.

60 Darwin 1881.

61 Petrie 1877; Petrie 1880: 22–23. For a biography of Petrie see Drower 1985. The translation of the mortise and tenon from woodworking to stonework at Stonehenge had been proposed by an architect 15 years earlier (Masey 1867).

62 977 BC was calculated by Broome 1869: 202–4 and 1870: 36, 39 and Appendix.

63 Lockyer & Penrose 1902.

64 Fergusson 1872.

65 Maclagan 1875: 70.

66 Maskelyne 1878.

67 Ramsay 1858; Long 1876: 70.

68 Long 1876.

69 Barclay 1895: 61–73.

70 Harrison 1902.

71 Chippindale 2004.

72 Harris and Goto 2003.

73 Read 1922.

74 Gowland 1902; Judd 1902.

75 Seven interim excavation reports were published: Hawley 1921, 1922, 1923, 1924, 1925, 1926 and 1928. In addition there is a considerable body of correspondence and diaries whose whereabouts are documented by Cleal *et al*. 1995: 580–83.

76 Atkinson 1979: 63; Hawley 1925: 21–22.

77 Newall 1929.

78 Hawley 1929: 16.

79 Thomas 1923: 250.

80 Darvill 2006: 137–39 summarizes the debate.

81 Piggott 1951.

82 *ibid*: 283.

83 Libby 1952; Burleigh 1981.

84 Hawkins 1973.

85 Thom 1971; Thom & Thom 1978.

86 Cleal *et al*. 1995: 11–12 and Appendix 3: 536–38 which provides a concordance of all the 20th-century excavation trenches.

87 Cleal *et al*. 1995.

88 Mr Richard Wort recalling his memories of Frank Stevens at the A303 Stonehenge Improvement Inquiry in April 2004; website: http://www.planning-inspectorate.gov.uk/ stonehenge/documents/PM20April.doc.

Chapter 4 The Early Earth & Timber Monument

1 Cleal *et al*. 1995: Table 64 p. 522 and 531.

2 Flagstones was partially excavated in advance of the Dorchester bypass, Woodward 1988, Healy 1997: Melbourne was discovered by aerial photography, Palmer 1976: 39; Oswald *et al*. 2001: 133–5, 150. Both earthworks are approximately 100 m in diameter.

3 Antlers found at the base of the ditch have provided nine reliable radiocarbon determinations from which the date of the construction of the Stonehenge earthwork has been calculated.

4 Hawley 1928: 153.

5 Smith 1965. The fact that each concentric ditch ring encloses an area approximately double the circumference of its internal neighbour, hints at an early preoccupation with surveyed measurement.

6 Solid chalk has a density of *c.* 2,500 kilograms per cubic metre. The Stonehenge ditch circuit (minus the causeways) is 325 m long. Assuming that not more than four cubic metres could have been extracted for every metre of the circumference, the maximum chalk extracted per metre of the ditch would be in the region of ten tons. The estimate for Avebury was calculated by Burl 1979: 175.

7 Hawley 1928: 157. He noted that 'the greater number of them has been found on the east and southeast' and that 'the people they belonged to seem to have had a superstitious reason for selecting the eastern area'.

8 *ibid*: 158.

9 Piggott 1936; Cleal *et al.* 1995: 130, 136 (Segments 7 and 17).

10 Hawley 1928: 160. Cleal *et al.* 1995: junction between Ditch Segments 19 and 20.

11 The complex sequence of events, together with section drawings and profiles of all the excavated segments are detailed by Cleal *et al.* 1995.

12 Evans 1984: 13–21.

13 The calculation is based on the excavated dimensions of the ditch and the results of experimental archaeological works constructed in the 1960s on Overton Down, near Avebury (some 35 km north of Stonehenge), from which both the natural angle of repose of loose chalk and its 'expansion' factor upon excavation have been calculated: Bell, Fowler and Hillson 1996.

14 Atkinson 1979: 24, 170.

15 Cleal *et al.* 1995: 108.

16 David and Payne 1997: 80.

17 Wood 1747: 43.

18 David and Payne 1997: 80–1.

19 Hawley 1923: 18. In a diary entry for 1922 Hawley notes, with an honesty typical of his records, that he did not find the posthole which lay on the centreline of the ditch terminal in the course of excavation; it was revealed as the result of a storm which washed down the chalk face and revealed the 'outline' of the deposits infilling the post socket. Diary entry 2-11-1922, quoted by Cleal *et al.* 1995: 144. Hawley had changed his method of working from the top downwards in an attempt to avoid the problems of dealing with the complex

interleaved ditch deposits. This is clear from his own account, for in his second season he stated that 'the curved layers were not suitable for vertical [i.e. top to bottom] excavation'. His earlier methods had not revealed the presence of later cuts made into the ditch fills and cremations were coming up randomly and unpredictably with the rubble shovelled up in the horizontal spits. He could now say 'that in advancing, a section of the ditch was always presented to view' (i.e. he now could see a top to bottom vertical face through which later cuts and cremations could be recognized).

20 Hawley 1924: 32.

21 *ibid*.

22 Cunnington 1930: 103–4.

23 Atkinson 1979: 26.

24 Cleal *et al.* 1995: 522.

25 Webb recorded that 'there hath been the heads of Bulls, or Oxen, or Harts, and other such beasts digged up, or in, or near this *Antiquity* (as divers now living can testifie)'; Jones 1655: 75 (with further references on pp. 100 and 105). In his second edition he refers to 'an abundance of them' excavated in the 1620s by the Duke of Buckingham 'and divers other Persons, at several other Times', Webb 1725: 123. William Stukeley reported that the then landowner, Thomas Hayward had also 'found heads of oxen and other beasts bones, and nothing else', Stukeley 1740: 32.

26 Cleal *et al.* 1995: Pl. 6 and Fig. 290 (auger hole 8).

27 Hawley 1921: 30.

28 Cleal *et al.* 1995: 96.

29 Maud Cunnington noted that these three holes (AH 1, 55 and 56) were amongst the minority of a group of only six that are not recorded as having contained cremations, which might imply that they were infilled when the entrance was widened, long before the remainder of the holes became the focus for such burials, Cunnington 1930: 105.

30 Gibson 1998: 48.

31 For example: Castleden 1993: 67–70. See Cleal *et al.* 1995: 151 (Fig. 70) for the difficulties in identifying contemporary concentric rings from the excavated evidence.

32 Hawley 1925: 24.

33 Newham 1972: 26.

34 Cleal *et al.* 1995: 160.

35 Evans 1984.

36 Atkinson 1979: 29–30; Cleal *et al.* 1995: 272.

37 Known as the 'Hel Stone', at Long Bredy Hut, southwest of Dorchester. Described as 'about seven feet and a half high by seven feet wide and is a rudely shaped gibbous mass and indebted, most probably, to its unwieldy size for its preservation through long ages past': Warne 1872: 111; for further discussion see Heavey 1977.

38 Aubrey quoted by Long 1876: 143; Stukeley: Lukis 1882: 139, quoted by Newall 1966: 93.
39 Hoare 1812: Map of Stonehenge and its Environs.
40 Stukeley 1740: 37.
41 Pitts 1982.
42 Diary entry dated 2-6-1920, Cleal *et al.* 1995: 284.
43 Burl 1994: 91.
44 Stonehenge Riverside Project. *Interim Report 2005*: 12–23 and 88–104, available on the Sheffield University website: http://www.shef.ac.uk/archaeology/research/stonehenge. Field 2005 discusses the tradition of erecting sarsen monoliths in the early Neolithic period on the nearby Marlborough Downs.
45 Hawley 1925: 23. This hole seems to have underlain the Stonehenge Avenue bank, but unfortunately no direct stratigraphic relationship was evident as, according to Hawley, the bank was 'almost level here'.
46 Hawley 1928: 174; WA contexts 3603, 3606 and 3607. This 'groove' was described originally by Hawley (1925: 25) as a 'trench with wide sloping sides about 9ft [2.75 m] wide'. Atkinson re-examined part of this area in 1956 and demonstrated that this feature predated the Heelstone ditch and interpreted it as a construction ramp for the Heelstone; a small (early Neolithic) Windmill Hill pottery sherd recovered from near the base of this trench was noted as 'the first example of this variety to have been recorded from Stonehenge', Atkinson 1979: 203–4.

Chapter 5 The Stone Monument
1 Cleal *et al.* 1995.
2 Atkinson 1979: 51; Darvill and Wainwright 2002, 2003; Darvill 2006: 136–41; chemical and magnetic susceptibility analysis has identified the most likely outcrop as Carngoedog, Williams-Thorpe *et al.* 2006.
3 Darvill 2006: 139.
4 Burl 1999: 118.
5 Judd 1902, Kellaway 1971, Thorpe *et al.* 1991 and Burl 1985 and 1999: 107–23 have argued in favour of glacial transport, whilst Thomas 1923, Green 1997 and Scourse 1997 have found no geological evidence for glaciation.
6 Hawley 1922: 44. His reference to Chilmark ragstone is probably the local Greensand.
7 Bowen and Smith 1977; Howard 1982: 119–124; Green 1997: 260-3.
8 Free 1948; King 1968. John Aubrey described the techniques for splitting the sarsens as follows: 'Make a fire on that line of the stone, where you would have it crack; and after the stone is well heated, draw over a line with cold water, and immediately give a knock with a Smyths sledge,

and it will break, like the Collets at the Glass house'; Fowles 1981: 38. See also William Stukeley's ms. sketch of fire-setting at Avebury, dated 20 May 1724, The Bodleian Library: Gough Maps 231, fol.5 [ill 65].
9 Ixer and Turner 2006.
10 *ibid.*
11 Gowland 1902: 57.
12 Atkinson 1979: 58 (footnote).
13 Stone 3, although as it only cuts the packing of the Q Hole (Q4) it is not completely impossible that both were standing at the same time.
14 Atkinson 1979: 58.
15 Castleden 1993: 137.
16 Atkinson 1979: 205.
17 Cunnington 1929a: 13.
18 Cleal *et al.* 1995: 188.
19 For a discussion of the distribution and significance of bluestone chippings see Atkinson 1979: 63–65 and 99–101.
20 Cleal *et al.* 1995: 177; Atkinson 1979: 91 emphasizes the fact that the sherds derived from the 'refilling' of the hole following the dismantlement of the stone setting; there is no reliable radiocarbon evidence.
21 Dimensions are taken from English Heritage digital data; the thickness is given by Atkinson 1979: and the weight estimated by Ixer and Turner 2006.
22 Writing in 1802, William Cunnington (1883: 147) noted that 'the sides of the altar stone still retain the marks of the tools with which it was originally wrought'. For observations by Atkinson and Piggott see Atkinson 1979: 211–2 and Daniel 1959: 51.
23 Cleal *et al.* 1995: 210–11 (context no: WA 3359).
24 *ibid*: 181 and Fig. 86 (context no: WA 3639).
25 *ibid*: 532–33. For more recent reappraisals see Bronk Ramsey and Bayliss 2000, Bayliss *et al.* 2007: 43–50 and Parker Pearson *et al.* 2007: 618–28. The only reliable radiocarbon dates are based on a single determination from Stonehole 1 of the Sarsen Circle (2580–2470 cal BC) (95% probability) and another from either Stonehole 53 or 54 of the Sarsen Horseshoe (2600–2400 cal BC) (95% probability). As the trilithons could not have been erected after the Circle was completed, the overlap suggests a probable date for construction in the middle of the 3rd millennium BC.
26 Long 1876: 62–63 records a visit by John Thurnam and other members of the Wiltshire Archaeological and Natural History Society in September 1865 relating that they 'obtained a ladder … and took it to Stonehenge on the summit of the omnibus, and had it placed against the large trilithons. Several of those present mounted it … it is curious that on the upper surface of the impost of the largest trilithon [Stones 53, 54 and 154] there are two superficial round holes as if incipient mortices'.

Atkinson 1979: 43 describes similar shallow holes on the fallen lintel of the Great Trilithon (Stone 156) which 'has a pair of shallow irregular impressions towards the ends of its original upper surface' which are 'best regarded as unfinished mortice holes'.

27 Letter to the Editor of *The Times*, Saturday 17 September 1892, from Rev. Arthur W. Phelps.

28 Gowland 1902: Fig.12; Cleal *et al.* 1995: 198.

29 Atkinson 1979: 213.

30 *ibid*: 44–7; Atkinson *et al.* 1952.

31 Cleal *et al.* 1995: 30–33; Crawford 1954.

32 First noted by John Wood in 1740, Wood 1747: 60–61.

33 Petrie 1880: 9–13.

34 Hawley's diary entry for 10-9-1924, quoted by Cleal *et al.* 1995: 194.

35 Hawley 1922: 42; Newall 1929: 80.

36 Cleal *et al.* 1995: 192.

37 Cleal *et al.* 1995: 30–33; Crawford 1954; more recent work in 2002 by Wessex Archaeology and Archaeoptics Ltd., using laser technology to scan the stones, has resulted in the discovery of several new and otherwise imperceptible carvings, Goskar 2003.

38 Duke 1846: Duke interpreted them as 'astronomic gnomons and stations': 142–43.

39 Wood 1747: 43–44.

40 Cleal *et al.* 1995: 273. Colt Hoare and Cunnington found nothing of interest when they dug into this barrow at the beginning of the 19th century; Hoare 1812: 146.

41 Atkinson 1979: 33.

42 *ibid*: 78.

43 Burl 1994: 93 emphasizes this point, which becomes obvious when Philip Crocker's plan of 1810 (Hoare 1812) is compared with those drawn after the early 1920s.

44 In a letter to John Britton on 12 April 1803 he wrote that: 'To ascertain whether the 'slaughtering stone' stood erect, I dug round it, and also into the excavation where it originally stood when erect …. By digging I found the excavation in which the end … was placed', noting that on the end of the stone 'you may see similar irregularities as you must have noticed on the butt ends of the upright stones of the fallen trilithon [Stones 57, 58 and 158 which fell in 1797]. Let any persons who have doubt, examine the stone, and they will be convinced' (quoted by Long 1876: 56–7). Writing to Rev. James Douglas in spring 1810 Cunnington described his last visit to Stonehenge: 'I made the men dig under the prostrate stone so as to examine it thoroughly, and I have now Sir R. Hoare, Mr Crocker, and an Irish gentleman to attest the fact that the aforesaid stone was placed originally in an erect position. That part of the stone which stood in the ground

was rough, but those parts which were exposed were stippled like the others' (quoted by Cunnington 1975: 151). Hoare 1812: 144 stated that he and Cunnington had dug sufficiently deep 'as to be able to examine the undermost side of the stone, where we found fragments of stag's horns'.

45 Hawley 1921: 34.

46 Hawley 1921: 36.

47 Cleal *et al.* 1995: 524.

48 Hawley 1924: 36.

49 Atkinson 1979: 31.

50 Cleal *et al.* 1995: 285–86.

51 Jones 1655: 57. The fact that Jones gave the height rather than the length and also the thickness of the half-buried stone is sometimes taken as evidence that it must have been standing. But the stated 'height' of 20 feet [just over 6 m] corresponds with the Slaughter Stone in its fallen position, had it been standing it would probably have only been 15 or 16 ft high [4.6–4.9 m]; the thickness could easily have been determined by probing or digging alongside it.

52 Stukeley 1740: 33.

53 Hawley 1924: 36.

54 Burl 1994: 88.

55 Atkinson 1979: 31.

56 Stukeley 1740: 30.

57 Judd 1893: 11–12; the search for the stone is referred to by Lockyer 1906: 94, and geophysical survey results published by David and Payne 1997.

58 Inigo Jones (1655: 63) noted that several had disappeared in the intervals between his visits at various times during the second quarter of the 17th century: 'Those of the inner circle, and lesser *Hexagon* [Bluestone Circle and Horseshoe], not only exposed to the fury of all devouring Age, but to the rage of men likewise, have been more subject to ruine. For, being of no extraordinary proportions, they might easily be beaten down, or digged up, and at pleasure, made use of for other occasions. Which, I am the rather enduced to beleeve, because, since my first measuring the work, not one fragment of some then standing, are now to be found.' Hawley found evidence for the removal of at least four stones from the Bluestone Circle in the western quadrant, probably in the 17th century judging by the debris left by the stone robbers. John Wood's plan of 1740 provides evidence of further damage and deterioration, which continued into the 19th century: 'a constant chipping of stone broke the solitude of the place' wrote one correspondent (a 'Vacation Rambler', Glastonbury) to the editor of *The Times* in 1871, noting with dismay 'the demolition that has been affected by the hand of man' since his first visit some 30 years previously.

59 Hawley 1926: 8.

60 Atkinson 1979: 51.

61 Cleal *et al.* 1995: 212.

62 *ibid*: 533.

63 Gowland 1902: 55.

64 The possibility of an oval setting was first suggested by Hawley 1928: 172–73. Excavation by Atkinson in 1956 found three further holes, two of which cut through the infilled stoneholes of the abandoned R portals (termed R1 and R38 by him); because of the significantly greater spacing of this 'northern arc' compared with the stones of the horseshoe he suggested that this group may have formed part of an earlier arrangement in which the dressed bluestones had originally stood; Atkinson 1979: 209–10. For a plan and discussion of the evidence see Cleal *et al.* 1995: 212–18.

65 Atkinson 1979: 54; North 1996: 430.

66 Atkinson 1979: 55.

67 Recorded for the first time by William Long in 1876: Long 1876: 233; uncovered to a depth of 0.7 m beneath ground level by Newall in 1950: Newall 1952.

68 A glimpse into the complexity of the relationships of the various bluestone arrangements can be seen from one of the excavation trenches dug by Atkinson in 1956 between the stonehole of one of the collapsed trilithons (Stone 58) and a fallen fragment of its neighbour (Stone 59a), where he discovered a bluestone stump (Stone 70a), originally part of the Bluestone Horseshoe, standing upon a bluestone 'plinth', showing clear stratigraphic evidence for two earlier settings, the bases of which both bore stone impressions; Cleal *et al.* 1995, Cutting 35: Fig. 90 and 243–44.

69 Cleal *et al.* 1995: 207.

70 This omission is particularly puzzling as six years later when he found a bluestone fragment in a much later round barrow Cunnington was quick to see its potential significance, writing in a letter to Colt Hoare in September 1807 (quoted by Cunnington, R. 1975: 113–14): 'The most natural conclusion will be that these pieces were scattered about on the plain, before the erection of the Tumuli under which they have been found. If this conclusion is just, it gives higher antiquity to our British Temple than many Antiquaries are disposed to allow.'

71 Cunnington 1922 and 1924.

72 Cunnington 1889: 106, in which 'deep trenches, reaching to the natural chalk below, were dug to the total length of eighty-two feet', and large numbers of 'ponderous stones' encountered.

73 Stukeley 1740: 46; Newall 1929: 79; Cunnington 1929b: 224–25; Wiltshire County Council Sites & Monuments Record SMR No. SU14SW728 (Amesbury 4; Colt Hoare No. 16).

74 Stone 1939: 366 and 1948: 16–19.

75 Accounts of the discovery of bluestone fragments during recent excavations have been published on the internet, although at the time of writing (December 2007) neither their identity nor their precise archaeological context has been confirmed.

76 Atkinson 1979: 35.

77 Cleal *et al.* 1995: 524.

78 Hawley 1923: 27.

79 Hawley 1925: 30. This broken stone (2.3 m long and 1.2 m wide) lies flat with its long axis radially across the Z Hole circuit; the hole could lie directly beneath it, although a hole of average dimensions would be wider than the area covered by the footprint of the fallen sarsen. When Hawley investigated the chalk surface around this stone in 1923 he was clear: 'nor was it secreted under the fragments of fallen Stone No. 8.'

80 Atkinson 1979: 83.

81 Hawley 1924: 30.

82 Fowles 1981: 76, 80.

83 Cleal *et al.* 1995: 303.

84 Lukis 1885: 268, letter from Roger Gale to William Stukeley, 28 May 1740. Stukeley's manuscript notes, which he later crossed out, state that: 'There is not one stone left therof, yet a curious eye without difficulty will discern a mark of the holes whence they were taken tho' the ground is so much trod upon, and moreover the course of a horse race traverses I about the middle' (from Manuscript 4.253, Cardiff Public Library, quoted by Burl and Mortimer 2005: 78).

85 Manuscript Gough Maps 229 Folio 16r, Bodleian Library, Oxford. It is difficult to interpret the significance or accuracy of Stukeley's observations from this sketch as he also shows a double concentric ring immediately inside the main earthwork which bears little resemblance to excavated features, although this could be no more than a (rather fanciful) reconstruction combining the 'cavities' recorded by Aubrey and the Slaughter Stone into his outer ring, and the four Station Stones into the inner.

86 Bartlett and David 1982.

87 Cleal *et al.* 1995: 534.

Chapter 6 Astronomy or architecture?

1 Ruggles 1997: 203.

2 Hawkins 1973: 177–83.

3 Thom, Ker and Burrows 1988: 492 and 493.

4 Hoare 1812: 202–5, Pls. XXVI and XXVII.

5 Kinnes *et al.* 1988; Shell and Robinson 1988. A similar gold lozenge is known from Clandon Barrow, Martinstown, Dorset, and decorated rectangular gold sheets have been found in barrows at Upton Lovell, Wiltshire and Little

Cressingham, Norfolk. See Taylor 1980 and Clarke *et al.* 1985 for this and other items of Bronze Age goldwork from the British Isles.

6 Kinnes *et al.* 1988: 32.

Chapter 7 The Prehistoric Surveyors

1 Henshilwood *et al.* 2002; Henshilwood 2006; Jacobs *et al.* 2006.
2 Vatcher 1969; Harding 1988. Similar incised and quite precise geometric motifs have also been found on a stone at the Neolithic village of Skara Brae, Orkney, which is broadly contemporary with the settlement at Durrington Walls; Clarke *et al.* 1985: 3.18, 56.
3 Atkinson 1979: 78.
4 O'Kelly 1982.
5 Thom 1967, 1971.
6 For example North 1996.
7 Burgess 1980: 342.
8 The error arose because one of Wood's survey markers (Y) was sited close to his computed centre of the circle (y); when he transcribed his measurements the wrong baseline to survey marker A was used resulting in Stones 59b and c being plotted from the baseline y–A instead of Y–A, which generated a southeastward displacement in the region of three feet.
9 Cleal *et al.* 1995.
10 Petrie 1880.
11 Cleal *et al.* 1995: 9–22.
12 Richards 2004.

Chapter 8 The Geometry of the Early Monument

1 Cleal *et al.* 1995.
2 Compass and Straightedge Constructions in Geometry – What is possible and impossible and why. Professor Tony Peressini, Department of Mathematics, University of Illinois. http://mtl.math.uiuc.edu/modules/module13/ what_to_do.htm
3 Hawley 1924: 36.
4 Newham 1972: 15.
5 Thom *et al.* 1974: 87, Fig. 11.
6 Thatcher 1976; Atkinson 1976.

Chapter 9 The Geometry & Construction of the Stone Monument

1 Pavel 1992.
2 Of the type found in the tomb of the master builder Sennedjem at Deir el-Medina, near Thebes (19th Dynasty, *c.* 1300 BC). The Egyptian Museum, Cairo.

3 Newall 1929: 79 drew attention to the fact that 'a very large number of hammerstone chips, mostly flint, were found just below ground level around the inside face of Stones 29, 30, 1, and 2. These splinters and chips were evidently knocked off the hammerstones in reducing the height of the sarsens and cutting the tenons'.
4 Petrie 1880: 6.
5 Gowland 1902: 55. Atkinson believed that he had found a construction ramp for Stone 56 on the northwest side of the stone, implying that it had been dragged on a curiously skewed approach from the northwest towards its foundation hole. This interpretation has recently been disputed by Parker Pearson *et al.* 2007: 620–26.
6 Comprising two overlapping circles of the same radius, intersecting in such a way that the centre of each circle lies on the circumference of the other.

Conclusion: Reassessing Stonehenge

1 Abercromby 1912: 94–95.
2 The Sanctuary: Cunnington 1931; Pollard 1992; Pitts 2001B. Mount Pleasant: Wainwright 1979.
3 Pryor 2001.
4 Plutarch *Moralia* V: 30, Babbitt 1936.
5 *ibid*: 44.
6 It was Gerald Hawkins who drew attention to this reference. He was still exploring the way in which the Aubrey Holes could have been used for predicting these events, and further refining his astronomical interpretation of Stonehenge, up to his death in 2003. Hawkins 2004; obituary by Mike Pitts published in the *Guardian*, 24 July 2003.
7 Plutarch *Moralia* V: 44, Babbitt 1936.
8 *ibid*: 12.
9 Piggott 1950: 254–87.
10 O'Brien 2004.
11 Sammes 1676: 397. 'NOW to separate Truth from a Fable, and to find out an Ancient Tradition, wrapt up in ignorant and idle Tales; Why may not these Giants, so often mentioned, upon this, and other occasions, be the *Phoenicians,* as we have proved upon other occasions, and the Art of erecting these Stones, instead of the STONES themselves, brought from the farthermost parts of *Africa,* the known habitations of the *Phoenicians?*'
12 William Gough in the final edition published in 1789 refers to 'Merlin's mathematical knowledge'.
13 Piggott 1941B: 319.
14 Atkinson 1966.

Bibliography

Abercromby, J., 1912. *A Study of the Bronze Age Pottery of Great Britain and Ireland and its associated grave-goods,* Vol. 2. Oxford, Clarendon Press.

Arnold, T., 1879. *Henrici Archidiaconi Huntendunensis Historia Anglorum.* London, Longman.

Ashbee, P., 1966. 'The Fussell's Lodge long barrow excavations, 1957', *Archaeologia* 100: 1–80 .

Atkinson, R. J. C., 1953. 'The Date of Stonehenge', *Proceedings of the Prehistoric Society* 18 (for 1952): 236–37.

———, 1956. *Stonehenge.* London, Hamish Hamilton.

———, 1966. 'Moonshine on Stonehenge', *Antiquity* 40: 212–16.

———, 1976. 'The Stonehenge Stations', *Journal for the History of Astronomy* 7: 142–44.

———, 1979. *Stonehenge,* Revised Edition. Harmondsworth, Penguin Books.

Atkinson, R. J. C., S. Piggott and J. F. S. Stone, 1952. 'The excavation of two additional holes at Stonehenge, 1950, and new evidence for the date of the monument', *The Antiquaries Journal* 32: 14–20.

Babbitt, F. C., (transl.) 1936. *Plutarch, Moralia Volume V. Isis and Osiris.* The Loeb Classical Library Edition, Harvard University Press.

Baker, L., A. Sheridan and T. Cowie, 2003. 'An Early Bronze Age "dagger grave" from Rameldry Farm, near Kingskettle, Fife', *Proceedings of the Society of Antiquaries of Scotland* 133: 85–123.

Bakker, J. A., 1979. 'Lucas de Heere's Stonehenge', *Antiquity* 53: 107–11.

Barclay, E., 1895. *Stonehenge and its Earth-Works.* London, D. Nutt.

Bartlett, A. D. H. and A. E. U. David, 1982. 'Geophysical Survey of the Stonehenge Avenue', *Proceedings of the Prehistoric Society* 48: 90–93.

Bayliss, A., F. McAvoy and A. Whittle, 2007. 'The World Recreated: Redating Silbury Hill in its Monumental Landscape', *Antiquity* 81: 26–53.

Bell, M., P. J. Fowler and S. W. Hillson (eds), 1996. *The experimental earthwork project 1960–92.* York, Council for British Archaeology Report 100.

Bewley, R. H., S. P. Crutchley and C. A. Shell, 2005. 'New Light on an Ancient Landscape: Lidar Survey in the Stonehenge World Heritage Site', *Antiquity* 79: 636–47.

Bolton, E., 1624. *Nero Caesar, or Monarchie depraued An historicall worke. Dedicated, with leaue, to the Duke of Buckingham, Lord Admirall. By the translator of Lucius Florus.* London.

Boorde, A., 1555. *The fyrst boke of the introduction of knowledge.* London.

Bowen, H. C. and I. F. Smith, 1977. 'Sarsen Stones in Wessex: the Society's First Investigation in the Evolution of the Landscape Project', *The Antiquaries Journal* 57: 185–96.

Britton, J., 1847. *The Natural History of Wiltshire by John Aubrey.* Wiltshire Topographical Society.

Bronk Ramsey, C. and A. Bayliss, 2000. 'Dating Stonh.nge', in K. Lockyer, T. J. T. Sly and V. Mihăilescu-Bîrliba (eds) *CAA96: Computer Applications and Quantitative Methods in Archaeology,* 29–39. Oxford, British Archaeological Reports.

Broome, J. H., 1869. 'Reasons for Concluding that an Astronomical Date may be Assigned to the Temple at Stonehenge', *The Astronomical Register* 7: 202–4.

Broome, J. H., 1870. 'The Astronomy of, and Druidical Worship at Stonehenge', *The Astronomical Register* 8: Appendix to Part No. 85: 1–4.

Budd, P., 2000. 'Meet the Metal Makers', *British Archaeology* 56: 12–17.

Burgess, C., 1980. *The Age of Stonehenge.* London, J. M. Dent & Sons Ltd.

Burl, A., 1979. *Prehistoric Avebury.* New Haven and London, Yale University Press.

———, 1985. 'Geoffrey of Monmouth and the Stonehenge bluestones', *The Wiltshire Archaeological and Natural History Society* 79: 178–83.

———, 1987. *The Stonehenge People.* London, J. M. Dent.

———, 1994. 'Stonehenge: Slaughter, Sacrifice and Sunshine', *The Wiltshire Archaeological and Natural History Magazine* 87: 85–95.

———, 1999. *Great Stone Circles. Fables, Fictions, Facts.* London, Yale University Press.

———, 2000. *The Stone Circles of Britain, Ireland and Brittany.* New Haven and London, Yale University Press.

———, 2006. *Stonehenge. A New History of the World's Greatest Stone Circle.* London, Constable.

Burl, A. and N. Mortimer (eds), 2005. *Stukeley's 'Stonehenge' An Unpublished Manuscript 1721–1724.* New Haven and London, Yale University Press.

Burleigh, R., 1981. 'W.F. Libby and the development of radiocarbon dating', *Antiquity* 55: 96–98.

Burr, T. B.,1766. *The History of Tunbridge-Wells.* London.

Carruthers, W., 1990. 'Carbonised plant remains', in J. C. Richards (ed.) *The Stonehenge environs Project, English Heritage Archaeological Report 16.* London, Historic Buildings & Monuments Commission for England.

Case, H. 2004. 'Circles, squares, triangles and hexagons', in *Monuments and Material Culture. Papers in Honour of an Avebury Archaeologist: Isobel Smith,* in R. Cleal and J. Pollard (eds). Salisbury, Hobnob.

Castleden, R., 1993. *The Making of Stonehenge.* London and New York, Routledge.

Chandler, J. (ed.), 1993. *John Leland's Itinerary, Travels in Tudor England.* Stroud, Alan Sutton.

Chippindale, C., 1978. 'The enclosure of Stonehenge', *The Wiltshire Archaeological and Natural History Magazine* 70–1 (for 1975–6): 109–23.

———, 2004. *Stonehenge Complete, Revised Edition.* London and New York, Thames & Hudson.

Clarke, D. and P. Maguire, 2000. *Skara Brae. Northern Europe's best preserved prehistoric village.* Edinburgh, Historic Scotland.

Clarke, D. V., T. G. Cowie and A. Foxon, 1985. *Symbols of Power at the Time of Stonehenge.* Edinburgh National Museum of Antiquities of Scotland. London, HMSO.

Cleal, R. M. J. and M. J. Allen, 1994. 'Investigation of Tree-damaged Barrows on King Barrow Ridge and Luxembourgh Plantation, Amesbury', *The Wiltshire Archaeological and Natural History Magazine* 87: 54–84.

Cleal, R. M. J., K. E. Walker and R. Montague, 1995. *Stonehenge in its landscape; Twentieth-century excavations.* English Heritage Archaeological Report 10. London, English Heritage.

Crawford, O. G. S., 1954. 'The symbols carved on Stonehenge', *Antiquity* 28: 25–31.

Cunliffe, B., 2002. *The Extraordinary Voyage of Pytheas the Greek.* London, Penguin Books.

Cunliffe, B and C. Renfrew (eds), 1997. *Science and Stonehenge,* Proceedings of the British Academy 92. Oxford, Oxford University Press.

Cunnington, B. H., 1922. 'Blue hard stone, ye same as at Stonehenge' found in Boles [Bowles] Barrow (Heytesbury, 1)', *The Wiltshire Archaeological and Natural History Magazine* 41: 172–74.

———, 1924. 'The 'Blue Stone' from Boles Barrow', *The Wiltshire Archaeological and Natural History Magazine* 42: 431–37.

Cunnington, M. E., 1929a. *Woodhenge. A description of the site as revealed by excavations carried out there by Mr and Mrs B. H. Cunnington, 1926-7-8.* Devizes, G. Simpson & Co.

———, 1929b. 'Notes and News: Stonehenge', *Antiquity* 3: 223–26.

———, 1930. 'Stonehenge and the two-date theory', *The Antiquaries Journal* 10: 103–13.

———, 1931. 'The "Sanctuary" on Overton Hill, near Avebury', *The Wiltshire Archaeological and Natural History Magazine* 45: 300–35.

Cunnington, R. H., 1975. *From Antiquary to Archaeo-logist: A biography of William Cunnington 1754–1810.* Princes Risborough, Shire Publications Ltd.

Cunnington, W., 1869. 'Stonehenge Notes', *The Wiltshire Archaeological and Natural History Magazine* 11: 347–49.

———, 1883. 'Stonehenge Notes: The Fragments', *The Wiltshire Archaeological and Natural History Magazine* 21: 141–49.

———, 1889. 'Notes on Bowls Barrow', *The Wiltshire Archaeological and Natural History Magazine* 24: 104–25.

Daniel, G., 1959. 'Notes and News: Stonehenge Restored', *Antiquity* 33: 50–51.

———, 1981. *A Short History of Archaeology.* London, Thames & Hudson.

Darvill, T., 1997. 'Ever Increasing Circles: The Sacred Geographies of Stonehenge and its Landscape', in *Science and Stonehenge,* B. Cunliffe and C. Renfrew (eds). *Proceedings of the British Academy* 92. Oxford University Press: 167–202.

———, 2006. *Stonehenge The Biography of a Landscape.* Stroud, Tempus.

Darvill, T. and G. Wainwright, 2002. 'SPACES – exploring Neolithic landscapes in the Strumble-Preseli area of southwest Wales', *Antiquity* 76: 623–24.

———, 2003. 'Stone circles, oval settings and henges in south-west Wales and beyond', *The Antiquaries Journal* 83: 9–46.

Darwin, C., 1881. *The Formation of Vegetable Mould, through the Action of Worms; with Observations on their Habits.* London, John Murray.

David, A. and A. Payne, 1997. 'Geophysical Surveys within the Stonehenge Landscape: A Review of Past Endeavour and Future Potential', in *Science and Stonehenge,* B. Cunliffe and C. Renfrew (eds). *Proceedings of the British Academy* 92. Oxford University Press: 73–113.

Davis, J. B. and J. Thurnam, 1865. *Crania Britannica: Delineations and descriptions of the skulls of the aboriginal inhabitants of the British Isles, with notices of their other remains,* 2 vols. London.

Drower, M., 1985. *Flinders Petrie. A Life in Archaeology.* London, Victor Gollancz.

Duke, Rev. E., 1846. *The Druidical Temples of the County of Wilts.* London, John Russell Smith.

Easton, J., 1800. *A Description of Stonehenge on Salisbury Plain; extracted from the Works of the most eminent Authors: with some Modern Observations on that Stupendous Structure: to which is added An Account of the Fall of Three Stones, Jan. 3, 1797.* Salisbury.

Eiseley, L. C., 1962. *Francis Bacon and the modern dilemma.* Lincoln, University of Nebraska Press.

Evans, J. G., 1984. 'Stonehenge: The Environment in the Late Neolithic and Early Bronze Age and a

Beaker-age Burial', *The Wiltshire Archaeological and Natural History Magazine* 78: 7–30.

Exon, S., V. Gaffney, A. Woodward and R. Yorston, 2000. *Stonehenge Landscapes: Journeys Through Real-and-Imagined Worlds.* Oxford, Archaeopress.

Ferguson, J., 1872. *Rude Stone Monuments in All Countries: Their Age and Uses.* London, John Murray.

Field, D., 2005. 'Some observations on perception, consolidation and change in a land of stones', in *The Avebury landscape: Aspects of the Field Archaeology of the Marlborough Downs,* G. Brown, D. Field and D. McOmish (eds). Oxford, Oxbow Books: 87–94.

Fitzpatrick, A. P., 2002. '"The Amesbury Archer": a well-furnished Early Bronze Age burial in southern England', *Antiquity* 76, No. 293: 629–30.

——, 2003. 'The Amesbury Archer', *Current Archaeology* 184: 146–52.

——, 2004a: 'The Boscombe Bowmen: Builders of Stonehenge?' *Current Archaeology* 193: 10–16.

——, 2004b. 'A Sacred Circle on Boscombe Down', *Current Archaeology* 195: 106–7.

——, 2004c. 'Was Stonehenge really built by Welshmen?' *British Archaeology* 78: 14–15.

Fowles, J., (ed.), 1981. *Monumenta Britannica or A Miscellany of British Antiquities (Parts One and Two) by John Aubrey.* Boston and Toronto, Little, Brown and Company.

Free, D. W., 1948. 'Sarsen Stones and their Origin', *The Wiltshire Archaeological and Natural History Magazine* 52: 338–44.

Gibson, A., 1998. *Stonehenge and Timber Circles.* Stroud, Tempus.

Giles, J. A., 1848. *Six Old English Chronicles.* London, Henry G. Bohn.

Goskar, T. A., 2003. 'The Stonehenge Laser Show', *British Archaeology* 73: 8–13.

Gowland, W., 1902. 'Recent excavations at Stonehenge', *Archaeologia* 58: 37–105.

Green, C. P., 1997. 'The Provenance of Rocks used in the Construction of Stonehenge', in *Science and Stonehenge,* B. Cunliffe and C. Renfrew (eds). *Proceedings of the British Academy* 92, Oxford University Press: 257–70.

Grinsell, L. V., 1975. *Legendary History and Folklore of Stonehenge.* West Country Folklore No. 9. St. Peter Port, Guernsey, The Toucan Press.

Harding, J., 2003. *Henge Monuments of the British Isles.* Stroud, Tempus.

Harding, P., 1988. 'The chalk plaque pit, Amesbury', *Proceedings of the Prehistoric Society* 54: 320–27.

Harris, V. and K. Goto (eds), 2003. *William Gowland: The Father of Japanese Archaeology.* Tokyo, Asahi Shinbunsha and London, The British Museum Press.

Harrison, W. J., 1902. 'Bibliography of the Great Stone Monuments of Wiltshire – Stonehenge and Avebury: with other references', *The Wiltshire Archaeological and Natural History Magazine* 32: 1–169.

Hawkins, G. S. (in collaboration with J. B.White), 1966. *Stonehenge Decoded.* London, Souvenir Press Ltd.

——, 1971. *Photogrammetric Survey of Stonehenge and Callanish.* NGS, Washington D.C., National Geographic Society Research Reports 1965.

——, 2004. 'Stonehenge Computer', *British Archaeology* 74: 20–21.

Hawley, W., 1921. 'Stonehenge: Interim Report on the exploration', *The Antiquaries Journal* 1: 19–41.

——, 1922. 'Second Report on the Excavations at Stonehenge', *The Antiquaries Journal* 2: 36–52.

——, 1923. 'Third Report on the Excavations at Stonehenge', *The Antiquaries Journal* 3: 13–20 .

——, 1924. 'Fourth Report on the Excavations at Stonehenge', *The Antiquaries Journal* 4: 30–39.

——, 1925. 'Report on the Excavations at Stonehenge during the season of 1923', *The Antiquaries Journal* 5: 21–50.

——, 1926. 'Report on the Excavations at Stonehenge during the Season of 1924', *The Antiquaries Journal* 6: 1–25.

——, 1928. 'Report on the Excavations at Stonehenge during 1925 and 1926', *The Antiquaries Journal* 8: 149–76.

Haycock, D. B., 2002. *William Stukeley. Science, Religion and Archaeology in Eighteenth-Century England.* Woodbridge, The Boydell Press.

Healy, F., 1997. 'Site 3, Flagstones', in *Excavations along the route of the Dorchester By-pass, Dorset, 1986–8,* R. J. C. Smith, F. Healy, M. J. Allen, E. L. Morris, I. Barnes and P. J. Woodward (eds). Wessex Archaeology Report No. 11. Salisbury, Trust for Wessex Archaeology: 27–47.

Hearne, T., 1710 . *The Itinerary of John Leland the Antiquary.* Oxford (9 volumes).

Heavey, J. F., 1977. 'The Heele Stone', *Folklore* 88: 238–39.

Heck, C., 2007. 'A new medieval view of Stonehenge', *British Archaeology* 92: 10–15.

Henshilwood, C. S., 2006. 'Modern Humans and Symbolic Behavior: Evidence from Blombos Cave, South Africa', in *Origins,* G. Blundell (ed.). Cape Town, Double Storey: 78–83.

Henshilwood, C. S., F. d'Errico, R. Yates, Z. Jacobs, C. Tribolo, G. A. T. Duller, N. Mercier, J. C. Sealy, H. Valladas, I. Watts and A. G. Wintle, 2002. 'Emergence of Modern Human Behavior: Middle Stone Age Engravings from South Africa', *Science* 295: 1278–80 .

Hoare, R. C., 1812. *The Ancient History of South Wiltshire.* London, William Miller.

——, 1829. *Tumuli Wiltunenses; a Guide to the Barrows on the Plains of Stonehenge.* Shaftesbury, J. Rutter.

Howard, H., 1982. 'A petrological study of the rock specimens from excavations at Stonehenge

1979–1980', in M. W. Pitts, 'On the road to Stonehenge: Report on Investigations beside the A344 in 1968, 1979 and 1980', *Proceedings of the Prehistoric Society* 48: 104–24.

Hutton, J., 1788. 'Theory of the Earth; or an Investigation of the Laws observable in the Composition, Dissolution, and Restoration of Land upon the Globe', *Transactions of the Royal Society of Edinburgh* 1: 209–304.

Ixer, R. A. and P. Turner, 2006. 'A detailed re-examination of the petrology of the Altar Stone and other non-sarsen sandstones from Stonehenge as a guide to their provenance', *The Wiltshire Archaeological and Natural History Magazine* 99: 1–9.

Jacobs, Z., G. A. T. Duller, A. G. Wintle and C. S. Henshilwood, 2006. 'Extending the chronology of deposits at Blombos Cave, South Africa, back to 140 ka using optical dating of single and multiple grains of quartz', *Journal of Human Evolution* 51: 255–73.

James, H., 1867. *Plans and Photographs of Stonehenge and of Turusachan in the Island of Lewis with notes relating to the Druids and sketches of cromlechs in Ireland*. Southampton, Ordnance Survey.

Johnson, W., 1908. *Folk-memory or the continuity of British archaeology*. Oxford, Clarendon Press.

Jones, I., 1655. *The most notable Antiquity of Great Britain vulgarly called Stone-heng on Salisbury Plain. Restored by Inigo Jones Esquire, Architect Generall to the late King*. Edited by John Webb. London.

Judd, J. W., 1902. 'Note on the Nature and Origin of the Rock-fragments found in the Excavations made at Stonehenge by Mr. Gowland in 1901', *Archaeologia* 58: 106–18.

Judd, W. A., 1893. *Stonehenge: Its Probable Origin, Age, and Uses*. Maddington.

Kellaway, G. A., 1971. 'Glaciation and the stones of Stonehenge', *Nature* 232: 30–35.

Kendrick, T. and C. Hawkes, 1932. *Archaeology in England and Wales 1914–31*. London, Methuen.

King, N. E., 1968. 'The Kennet Valley Sarsen Industry', *The Wiltshire Archaeological and Natural History Magazine* 63: 83–93.

Kinnes, I. A., I. H. Longworth, I. M McIntyre, S. P. Needham, and W. A. Oddy, 1988. 'Bush Barrow gold', *Antiquity* 62: 24–39.

Lambarde, W. 1730. *Dictionarium Angliae topographicum & historicum. An alphabetical description of the chief places in England and Wales: with an account of the most memorable events which have distinguish'd them by William Lambarde*. London, Fletcher Gyles.

Lawlor, R., 1982. *Sacred Geometry Philosophy and Practice,* Reprinted 2001. London and New York, Thames & Hudson.

Legg, R., 1986. *Stonehenge Antiquaries*. Sherborne, Dorset Publishing Company.

Libby, W. F., 1952. *Radiocarbon dating*. University of Chicago Press.

Lockyer, J. N. and F. C. Penrose, 1902. 'An Attempt to Ascertain the Date of the Original Construction of Stonehenge from Its Orientation', *Proceedings of the Royal Society of London* 69: 137–47.

Lockyer, J. N., 1906. *Stonehenge and other British stone monuments astronomically considered*. London.

Long, W., 1876. 'Stonehenge and its Barrows', *The Wiltshire Archaeological and Natural History Magazine* 16: 1–244.

Loomis, L. H., 1930. 'Geoffrey of Monmouth and Stonehenge', *Proceedings of the Modern Language Association* 45: 400–15.

Lubbock, J., 1865. *Prehistoric Times*. London, Williams and Norgate.

Lukis, Rev. W. C., 1882. *The Family Memoirs of the Rev. William Stukeley, M.D. and the Antiquarian and Other Correspondence of William Stukeley, Roger & Samuel Gale etc*. Vol. I. The Publications of The Surtees Society Vol. 73. Durham.

———, 1885. *The Family Memoirs of the Rev. William Stukeley, M.D. and the Antiquarian and Other Correspondence of William Stukeley, Roger & Samuel Gale etc*. Vol. III. The Publications of The Surtees Society Vol. 80. Durham.

Maclagan, C., 1875. *The Hillforts, Stone Circles, and Other Structural Remains of Ancient Scotland*. Edinburgh, Edmonston & Douglas.

Mallgrave, H. F., 2005 *Modern Architectural Theory: A Historical Survey 1673–1968*. Cambridge University Press.

Masey, P. E., 1867. 'Mortise and tenon', *Notes and Queries* 3rd Series 11: 82–83.

Maskelyne, N. S., 1878. 'Stonehenge: the Petrology of its Stones', *The Wiltshire Archaeological and Natural History Magazine* 17: 147–60 .

McOrnish, D., 2003. 'Cursus: solving a 6,000-year-old puzzle', *British Archaeology* 69.

Meaden, T., 1997. *Stonehenge The Secret of the Solstice*. London, Souvenir Press.

Mowl, T., and B. Earnshaw, 1988. *John Wood Architect of Obsession*. Somerset, Millstream Books.

Neave, E. W. J., 1943. 'The Epsom Spring', *Isis* 34: 210–11.

Newall, R. S., 1929. 'Stonehenge', *Antiquity* 3: 75–88.

———, 1952. 'Stonehenge stone no. 66', *The Antiquaries Journal* 32: 65–7.

———, 1953. 'Stonehenge', *Man* 53: 144.

———, 1956. 'Stonehenge: a review', *Antiquity* 30: 137–41.

———, 1959. *Stonehenge Wiltshire*. Ministry of Public Building and Works Official Guide-book, London, HMSO.

———, 1966. 'Megaliths once near Stonehenge',

The Wiltshire Archaeological and Natural History Magazine 61: 93.

Newham, C. A., 1972. *The Astronomical Significance of Stonehenge.* Shirenewton, Gwent, Moon Publications.

North, J. D., 1996. *Stonehenge: Neolithic Man and the Cosmos.* London, Harper Collins.

O'Brien, W., 2004. *Ross Island: Mining, Metal and Society in Early Ireland.* Galway, Department of Archaeology, National University of Ireland.

O'Kelly, M. J., 1982. *Newgrange: Archaeology Art and Legend.* London, Thames & Hudson.

Oswald, A., C. Dyer, and M. Barber, 2001. *The Creation of Monuments: Neolithic Causewayed Enclosures in the British Isles.* Swindon, English Heritage.

Palmer, R., 1976. 'Interrupted Ditch Enclosures in Britain: the use of Aerial Photography for Comparative Studies', *Proceedings of the Prehistoric Society* 42: 161–86.

Parker Pearson, M., J. Pollard, C. Richards, J. Thomas, C. Tilley, K. Welham and U. Albarella, 2006. 'Materializing Stonehenge: The Stonehenge Riverside Project and New Discoveries', *Journal of Material Culture* 11: 227–61.

Parker Pearson, M., R. Cleal, P. Marshall, S. Needham, J. Pollard, J. Richards, C. Ruggles, A. Sheridan, J. Thomas, C. Tilley, K. Welham, A. Chamberlain, C. Chenery, J. Evans, C. Knüsel, N. Linford, L. Martin, J. Montgomery, A. Payne, and M. Richards, 2007. 'The age of Stonehenge', *Antiquity* 81: 617–39.

Pavel, P., 1992. 'Raising the Stonehenge lintels in Czechoslovakia', *Antiquity* 66: 389–91.

Petrie, W. M. F., 1877 *Inductive Metrology; or, the Recovery of Ancient Measures from the Monuments.* London, H. Saunders.

———, 1880. *Stonehenge: Plans, Descriptions, and Theories.* London, Edward Stanford.

Piggott, S., 1936. 'A potsherd from the Stonehenge ditch', *Antiquity* 10: 221–22.

———, 1938. 'The Early Bronze Age in Wessex', *Proceedings of the Prehistoric Society* 4: 52–106.

———, 1941a. 'The Sources of Geoffrey of Monmouth I. The 'Pre-Roman' King-List', *Antiquity* 15: 269–86.

———, 1941b. 'The Sources of Geoffrey of Monmouth II. The Stonehenge Story', *Antiquity* 15: 305–19.

———, 1950. *Prehistoric India to 1000 BC.* Harmondsworth, Middlesex, Penguin Books.

———, 1951. 'Stonehenge Reviewed', in *Aspects of Archaeology in Britain and Beyond. Essays presented to O. G. S. Crawford,* ed. W. F. Grimes. London, H. W. Edwards: 274–92.

———, 1985. *William Stukeley: An Eighteenth-*

Century Antiquary (Revised Edition). London and New York, Thames & Hudson.

———, 1993. 'John Thurnam and British prehistory', *The Wiltshire Archaeological & Natural History Magazine* 86: 1–7.

Pitts, M., 1982. 'On the Road to Stonehenge: Report on Investigations beside the A344 in 1968, 1979 and 1980', *Proceedings of the Prehistoric Society* 48: 75–132.

———, 2001a. *Hengeworld.* London, Arrow Books.

———, 2001b. 'Excavating the Sanctuary: New Investigations on Overton Hill, Avebury', *The Wiltshire Archaeological and Natural History Magazine* 58: 1–23.

Pollard, J., 1992. 'The sanctuary, Overton Hill, Wiltshire: A Re-examination', *Proceedings of the Prehistoric Society* 58: 213–26.

Pryor, F., 2001. *Seahenge. New Discoveries in Prehistoric Britain.* London, HarperCollins.

Ramsay, A. C., 1858. 'Geology of Wiltshire. Sheet 34', *Memoirs of the Geological Survey*, London.

Rastell, J., *c.* 1530. *The pastyme of people: the cronycles of dyuers realmys and most specyally of the realm of Englond.* London, Cheapside.

RCHME, 1979. *Stonehenge and its Environs: Monuments and Land Use.* Edinburgh, Royal Commission on Historical Monuments England University Press.

Read, H. C., 1922. 'Obituary. William Gowland FRS, FSA. Born 1842. Died June 10th, 1922', *Man* 22 (September): 137–38.

Repcheck, J., 2003. *The man who found time: James Hutton and the discovery of the earth's antiquity.* London, Simon & Schuster.

Richards, J. C., 1990. *The Stonehenge Environs Project.* English Heritage Archaeological Report No. 16. London, English Heritage.

———, 2004. *Stonehenge A History in Photographs.* London, English Heritage.

———, 2007. *Stonehenge: The Story So Far.* Swindon, English Heritage.

Richards, J. C. and M. Whitby, 1997. 'The Engineering of Stonehenge', in *Science and Stonehenge,* B. Cunliffe and C. Renfrew (eds). *Proceedings of the British Academy* 92, Oxford University Press: 231–56.

Roaf, M., 1990. *Cultural Atlas of Mesopotamia and the Ancient Near East.* New York, Facts on File, Inc.

Roseman, C. H., 1994. *Pytheas of Massalia: On the Ocean.* Chicago, Ares.

Ruggles, C., 1997. 'Astronomy and Stonehenge', in *Science and Stonehenge,* B. Cunliffe and C. Renfrew (eds). *Proceedings of the British Academy* 92, Oxford University Press: 203–29.

———, 1999. *Astronomy in Prehistoric Britain and Ireland.* New Haven and London, Yale University Press.

Sammes, A., 1676. *Britannia Antiqua Illustrata.* London.

Scourse, J. D., 1997. 'Transport of the Stonehenge Bluestones: Testing the Glacial Hypothesis', in *Science and Stonehenge*, by B. Cunliffe and C. Renfrew (eds). *Proceedings of the British Academy* 92: 271–314.

Shell, C. A. and P. Robinson, 1988. 'The recent reconstruction of the Bush Barrow lozenge plate', *Antiquity* 62: 248–58.

Smith, I. F., 1965. *Windmill Hill and Avebury. Excavations by Alexander Keiller 1925–1939.* Oxford, Clarendon Press.

Smith, J., 1771. *Choir Gaur; The Grand Orrery of The Ancient Druids commonly called Stonehenge on Salisbury Plain.* Salisbury.

Smith, L. T., 1964. *The itinerary of John Leland in or about the years 1535–1543.* London, Centaur Press.

Spence, C., A. Frost, T. Mowl and H. Batho, 2004. *Obsession. John Wood and the Creation of the Georgian Bath Exhibition Catalogue (7 September 2004–6 February 2005).* Bath, The Building of Bath Museum.

Stevens, F., 1927. *Stonehenge Today & Yesterday,* Revised Edition. London, HMSO.

Stone, E. H., 1924. *The Stones of Stonehenge.* London, Robert Scott.

Stone, J. F. S., 1939. 'An Early Bronze Age grave in Fargo Plantation near Stonehenge', *The Wiltshire Archaeological and Natural History Magazine* 48: 357–70.

———, 1948. 'The Stonehenge Cursus and its affinities', *The Archaeological Journal* 104 (for 1947): 7–19.

Stukeley, W., 1740. *Stonehenge A Temple Restor'd to the British Druids.* London.

———, 1743. *Abury: A Temple Restored to British Druids.* London.

Taylor, J. J., 1980. *Bronze Age Goldwork of the British Isles.* Cambridge University Press.

Thatcher, A. R., 1976. 'The Station Stones at Stonehenge', *Antiquity* 50: 144–46.

Thom, A., 1967. *Megalithic Sites in Britain.* Oxford, Clarendon Press.

———, 1971. *Megalithic Lunar Observatories.* Oxford, Clarendon Press.

Thom, A., A. S. Thom and A. S. Thom, 1974. 'Stonehenge', *Journal of the History of Astronomy* 5: 71–90.

Thom, A. and A. S. Thom, 1978. *Megalithic Remains in Britain and Brittany.* Oxford, Clarendon Press.

Thom, A. S., J. M. D. Ker and T. R. Burrows, 1988. 'The Bush Barrow Gold Lozenge: is it a Solar and Lunar Calendar for Stonehenge?' *Antiquity* 62: 492–502.

Thomas, H. H. 1923. 'The Source of the Stones of Stonehenge', *The Antiquaries Journal* 3: 239–60.

Thorpe, L., 1969. 'Geoffrey of Monmouth', *The History of the Kings of Britain.* London, The Folio Society.

Thorpe, R. S., O. Williams-Thorpe, D. Graham Jenkins and J. S. Watson, 1991. 'The Geological Sources and Transport of the Bluestones of Stonehenge, Wiltshire, UK', *Proceedings of the Prehistoric Society* 57: 103–57.

Thurnam, J., 1869. 'Long barrows', *Archaeologia* 42: 161–244.

———, 1871. 'Round barrows', *Archaeologia* 43: 285–544.

Vatcher, F. de M., 1969. 'Two Incised Chalk Plaques near Stonehenge Bottom', *Antiquity* 43: 310–11.

Wainwright, G., and I. H. Longworth, 1971. *Durrington Walls: Excavations 1966–1968.* Society of Antiquaries Research Report 29: London.

Wainwright, G., 1979. *Mount Pleasant, Dorset: Excavations 1970–1971.* Report of the Research Committee of the Society of Antiquaries No. 37: London.

———, 1990. *The Henge Monuments. Ceremony and Society in Prehistoric Britain.* London and New York. Thames & Hudson.

Warne, C., 1872. *Ancient Dorset.* Bournemouth.

Webb, J., 1665. *A vindication of Stone-Heng restored in which the orders and rules of architecture observed by the ancient Romans are discussed ….* London, R. Davenport for Tho. Bassett.

———, 1725. *The Most Notable Antiquity Of Great Britain, on Salisbury Plain, Restored … To which are added, The Chorea Gigantum, Or Stone-Heng Restored to the Danes, By Doctor Walter Charlton And Mr Webb's Vindication of Stone-Heng Restored.* James Bettenham, London.

Wheatley, H. B. and E. W. Ashbee, 1879. *The Particular Description of England 1855 with views of some of the chief towns and armorial bearings of nobles and bishops by William Smith.* London, edited from the original ms. in the British Museum with an intro by H. B. Wheatley FSA and E. W. Ashbee FSA.

Whittle, A., A. Barclay, A. Bayliss, L. McFadyen, R. Schulting and M. Wysocki, 2007. 'Building for the dead: events, processes and changing world views from the thirty-eighth to the thirty-fourth centuries cal. BC in southern England.' *Cambridge Archaeological Journal* 17: 123–47.

Williams-Thorpe, O., M. C. Jones, P. J. Potts and P. C. Webb, 2006. 'Preseli dolerite bluestones: axe-heads, Stonehenge monoliths, and outcrop sources', *Oxford Journal of Archaeology* 25: 29–46.

Wilson, D., 1851. *The Archaeology and Prehistoric Annals of Scotland.* London, Macmillan.

Wood, J., 1747. *Choir Gaure, Vulgarly called Stonehenge, on Salisbury Plain.* Oxford.

Woodward, P. J., 1988. 'Pictures of the Neolithic: Discoveries from the Flagstones House Excavations, Dorchester, Dorset', *Antiquity* 62: 266–74.

Sources of Illustrations

Frontispiece Alexander Johnson. 1 Anthony Johnson. 2, 3 Adam Stanford. 4–6 Anthony Johnson (6: the conventional phases are also indicated, after Atkinson 1979 and revised by Cleal *et al.* 1995). 7 West Air Photography, Weston-super-Mare. 8 English Heritage. 9 Steve and Karen Alexander. 10 Anthony Johnson, after M. Parker Pearson. 11, 12 Anthony Johnson. 13 Wessex Archaeology. 14 British Library, London. 15 Master and Fellows of Corpus Christi, Cambridge. 16 Bibliothèque Municipale de Douai. 17 National Portrait Gallery, London. 18 British Library, London. 19 From William Camden *Britannia*, 1789. 20, 21 From Inigo Jones *The most notable Antiquity of Great Britain vulgarly called Stone-heng on Salisbury Plain. Restored by Inigo Jones Esquire, Architect Generall to the late King*, 1655. 22 From John Webb's *A vindication of Stone-Heng restored in which the orders and rules of architecture observed by the ancient Romans are discussed: together with the customs and manners of several nations of the world in matters of building of greatest antiquity: as also, an historical narration of the most memorable actions of the Danes in England*, 1725. 23 National Portrait Gallery, London. 24 From J. Britton *Memoir of John Aubrey*, 1845. 25 From John Aubrey *Monumenta Britannica or A Miscellany of British Antiquities*. 26 From William Camden *Britannia*, 1600 and 1695. 27 Salisbury and South Wiltshire Museum. 28 Bodleian Library, Oxford. 29–31 From William Stukeley *Stonehenge: A Temple Restor'd to the British Druids*, 1740. 32–34 From John Wood's *Choir Gaure, Vulgarly called Stonehenge, on Salisbury Plain*, 1747. 35 From Sir Richard Colt Hoare *The Ancient History of South Wiltshire*, 1812. 36 From Colonel Sir Henry James *Plans and Photographs of Stonehenge*, 1867. 37 *Flinders Petrie*, 1886. 38 From Colonel Sir Henry James *Plans and Photographs of Stonehenge and of Turusachan in the Island of Lewis with notes relating to the Druids and sketches of cromlechs in Ireland*, 1865. 39 From Flinders Petrie *Inductive Metrology; or, the Recovery of Ancient Measures from the Monuments*, 1877. 40 Wiltshire Archaeological and Natural History Society. 41 Society of Antiquaries, London. 42 Anthony Johnson. 43, 44 English Heritage. 45 l Bath Preservation Trust and Bath Museum, c Wiltshire Archaeological and Natural History Society, r The National Trust, London. 46 Trustees of Sir John Soane's Museum, London. 47–49 Anthony Johnson. 50 Society of Antiquaries, London. 51, 52 Anthony Johnson. 53 English Heritage. 54 Society of Antiquaries, London. 55–57 Anthony Johnson. 58 Society of Antiquaries, London. 59 Sean Johnson. 60 From John Webb's *A vindication of Stone-Heng restored*, 2nd edition, 1725. 61 From Edgar Barclay *Stonehenge and its Earth-Works*, 1895. 62 Salisbury and South Wiltshire Museum. 63, 64 Anthony Johnson. 65 From William Stukeley *Abury: A Temple Restored to British Druids*, 1743. 66–68 Anthony Johnson. 69 English Heritage. 70 Alexander Johnson. 71, 72 Sean Johnson. 73 Austin Underwood. 74 Anthony Johnson. 75 Department of Prehistoric Archaeology, University of Edinburgh. 76, 77 Anthony Johnson. 78, 79 English Heritage. 80 Anthony Johnson. 81 Alexander Johnson. 82 Anthony Johnson. 83 Alexander Johnson. 84 Sean Johnson. 85, 86 English Heritage. 87 J. F. S. Stone. 88–91 Anthony Johnson. 92 English Heritage. 93, 94 Anthony Johnson (94 after Cleal *et al.* 1995). 95 From William Stukeley *Stonehenge: A Temple Restor'd to the British Druids*, 1740. 96–100 Anthony Johnson. 101, 102 Dr David Clarke, National Museums Scotland, Edinburgh. 103 Centre for Development Studies, University of Bergen. 104 Salisbury and South Wiltshire Museum. 105–117 Anthony Johnson. 118 Adam Stanford. 119–128 Anthony Johnson. 129 Oxford Archaeotechnics. 130, 131 Chris Honeywell. 132, 133 Anthony Johnson. 134 James Mitchell. 135 Michael Walter/Press Association. 136 Adam Stanford. 137–139 Anthony Johnson (137 based on the data presented in the English Heritage publication *Stonehenge in its Landscape* (Cleal *et al.* 1995) in conjunction with more recent reviews of the integrity of specific contexts by Bronk Ramsay and Bayliss 2000, Bayliss *et al.* 2007 and Parker Pearson *et al.* 2007). **Endpapers** Richard L. Dixon.

Index